SpringerWienNewYork

Growth, Trade, and Economic Institutions

Edited by
Tapio Palokangas
Bjarne S. Jensen
Dieter Bös †
Giacomo Corneo
Reino Hjerppe
Juha Honkatukia

Journal of Economics
Supplement 10

SpringerWienNewYork

Univ.-Prof. Dr. Tapio Palokangas
Department of Economics, University of Helsinki, Finland

Univ.-Prof. Dr. Bjarne S. Jensen
Department of Economics, Copenhagen Business School, Denmark

Univ.-Prof. Dr. Dr. Dieter Bös †

Univ.-Prof. Dr. Dr. Giacomo Corneo
Department of Economics, Free University of Berlin, Germany

General Director Dr. Reino Hjerppe
Dr. Juha Honkatukia
VATT, Helsinki, Finland

SpringerWienNewYork is part of
Springer Science + Business Media
springeronline.com

Typesetting: Camera-ready by authors
Printing: G. Grasl Ges.m.b.H., 2540 Bad Vöslau, Austria

Printed on acid-free and chlorine-free bleached paper
SPIN: 10920107

With 11 Figures

Library of Congress Control Number: 2004117221

ISSN 0084-537X
ISBN 3-211-00793-8 SpringerWienNewYork

Preface

The seven papers in this supplement issue were originally presented at the eighth conference of *Dynamics, Economic Growth, and International Trade (DEGIT)* in Helsinki, Finland, May 30-31, 2003.

The DEGIT VIII conference was organized jointly by

Copenhagen Business School (CBS), Department of Economics

University of Helsinki, Department of Economics

Government Institute for Economic Research (VATT)

Financial support from VATT and the Central Bank of Denmark is gratefully acknowledged.

This conference is a sequel to seven previous conferences with the same theme held in Denmark (1996), Hong Kong (1997), Taiwan (1998), Tilburg (1999), Rome (2000), Vienna (2001), and Cologne (2002). This series of conferences is a forum for economists working in the field of growth and trade theory. For previous DEGIT publications, see *Review of International Economics* 7(3), 1999, *Review of Development Economics* 5(2), 2001, and *German Economic Review* 4(1), 2003.

It is our sad duty to report that the sixth member of our Editorial Board, Dieter Bös, the Managing Editor of the *Journal of Economics*, died in Bonn, June 20, 2004.

January 2005   Tapio Palokangas and Bjarne S. Jensen
                                              (Special editors)

Contents

J. Econ. (2005) Suppl. 10: 1-16

Journal of Economics
Zeitschrift für Nationalökonomie

Printed in Austria

International Trade and Agglomeration: An Alternative Framework

Ronald W. Jones and Henryk Kierzkowski

Received September 1, 2003; Revised version received August 16, 2004
© Springer-Verlag 2005

The New Economic Geography, as expounded by Krugman and others, highlights the importance of greater extent of agglomeration as incomes grow in the world economy. In this paper we suggest an alternative framework in which, as incomes grow, greater degrees of economic fragmentation and dis-agglomeration are encouraged. In both approaches increasing returns to scale are crucial, but in ours these are found in service sectors that allow separate production blocks to be coordinated instead of being found within separate production blocks.

Keywords: agglomeration, fragmentation, service links, production blocks

JEL classification: D20, F12, R30

1 Introduction

In the vast array of fields in economics, international trade and economic geography should be neighbors sharing similar interests and pre-occupied with a strongly overlapping range of issues. Alas, one could say that the scientific telescopes of each specialization had been trained for a long time in different directions. This state of isolation could not last and either an international trade economist would discover that commerce, within or across countries, involves geography; or a geographer would have observed that trade is one of the best examples of spatial displacement.

In the event, Paul Krugman was the first to seize the connection in a 1991 *Journal of Political Economy* paper and has been running with the main idea ever since.[1] Other trade economists soon saw a new opening

---

[1] In the economics literature concern over spatial aspects was expressed earlier by Stephen Enke (1951) and Paul Samuelson (1952). Samuelson remarked,

and a way of enriching their discipline. Having "discovered" geography, international trade economists had no hesitation telling economic geographers how their field really *should* be structured and developed.

As in the case of the "new" trade theory, the breakthrough in the "new" economic geography has come from the application of increasing returns to scale, especially in the context of monopolistic competition utilizing the functional form made famous by Avinash Dixit and Joseph Stiglitz (1977).

Increasing returns to scale could not alone do the trick of re-orienting the field of economic geography; in addition to increased realism, transportation costs have been called in to give the new models an increased complexity in order to generate interesting results. There is no doubt that the tools and the analytical machinery developed in the course of the new trade revolution have proved very popular. However, it seems pertinent to ask what purpose is served by applying them to geography. A convincing answer would be that the traditional economic geography framework and the tools it employed were not capable of explaining the existence of some important stylized facts.

Recall that the existence of intra-industry trade and the alleged inability of the traditional international economics models to explain this trade, ushered in the "new" trade revolution almost two decades ago. Was there, more recently, a corresponding stylized fact related to economic geography that escaped explanation until the increasing-returns-to-scale artillery was brought in? The question of the agglomeration of economic activities or its opposite could be thought of as requiring proper modeling and explanation. It is not obvious, however, that there is some overwhelming empirical evidence demonstrating clear trends regarding agglomeration (or dis-agglomeration) on a country, regional or global basis. The desire to understand the mechanisms driving these

---

"Spatial problems have been so neglected in economic theory that the field is of interest for its own sake." (p. 284).

In 1976 a symposium was held in Stockholm, and the Foreward to the publication of the Proceedings (see Bertil Ohlin, Per-Ove Hesselborn and Per Magnus Wijkman, eds, 1977) commented,

"A special aim of the symposium was to bring about an exchange of ideas between economists and economic geographers interested in trade and movements of the factors of production."

The "new" economic geography has expanded in leaps and bounds. Even reviews of the existing work have become numerous. Among most comprehensive surveys are: Neary (2001), Martin and Sunley (1996), Sunley (2001), Sheppard (2001) and Urban (2001).

processes may provide sufficient justification for an interest in this subject.[2]

There exists evidence showing that the global economy does *not* consist of a single core or even a limited number of centers and peripheries. Instead, the world economy becomes an increasingly, even though not evenly distributed, complex industrial structure spanning not only individual continents but the entire globe. International production networks have emerged in a manifold of industries and products: sports footwear, mobile phones, cars, clothing, computers, and furniture to name only a few. While there obviously are agglomeration forces operating in some areas, dispersion of economic activities is also a fact of life. One of the consequences of dis-agglomeration manifests itself in a rapid expansion of international trade in parts and components.

The recent empirical study by Francis Ng and Alexander Yeats (2001) shows this new phenomenon for East Asia. Between 1984 and 1996 East Asian imports and exports of manufactured components grew annually between 2 and 3 times as fast as imports and exports of traditional production. It is highly probable that the trade in parts and components also trumped intra-industry trade. The *maquiladora* phenomenon also shows that dis-agglomeration of production takes place in the U.S. - Mexico context.[3] Further north, Canada and the United States had undertaken sharing of production many years ago, especially in the automobile industry. More recently, India has emerged as a powerful attractor for a range of intermediate activities in manufacturing and services. Europe is certainly moving in the same direction.[4]

All in all, it has been estimated by Yeats (2001) that recently about 30 percent of global manufactured goods trade takes the form of trade in parts and components. Corresponding numbers for the 1950s and 60s do not exist, but they surely must have been very small indeed. It follows that growth of intra-industry trade must have been outpaced by a new type of trade associated with dis-agglomeration.

---

[2] One of the critics of the new economic geography models based on the Dixit-Stiglitz approach takes Masahisa Fujita, Paul Krugman, and Anthony Venables, the authors of The Spatial Economy (1999), to task:

> "While such formal modeling may increase the credibility and popularity of the ideas with the economists, it provides no evidence as to their actual empirical significance and their initial assumptions appear mainly to be made on the basis of modeling convenience rather than with any regard to empirical relevance." [Sunley (2001), p. 136.]

[3] Interesting work on the phenomenon of outsourcing in the Mexican context is found in Robert Feenstra and Gordon Hanson, 1996.

[4] Interestingly enough, the grand project of a supersonic passenger plane, Concord, conceived primarily by the French and British back in the 1960s could have been one of early examples of dispersion of production across Europe.

The phenomenon of international production networks and trade in parts and components reinforces the importance of transportation costs stressed in the new economic geography. But what kind of transportation costs - producers-to-consumers or producers-to-producers? Surely it must be the latter in a world where production of a pair of jeans can be broken down into 24 stages and allocated among Pakistan, Mainland China, Hong Kong and Malaysia with more than a dozen border crossings being executed before the final product is shipped off to consumers.[5] Are producers-to-consumers transportation costs so important as to neglect producers-to-producers transportation costs? It would seem likely that the industrial landscape generated by our theoretical models looks different depending upon which transport links are brought to the fore of the analysis.

As Peter Neary (2001) has recently commented in discussing the appearance of *The Spatial Economy* (1999) by Masahisa Fujita, Paul Krugman, and Anthony Venables, "*New economic geography has come of age.*" While recognizing its important and numerous contributions, we should advance other explanations of phenomena arising in the common grounds shared by two neighbors - economic geography and international trade.

2 Two Alternative Scenarios

In suggesting an alternative framework for examining whether economic growth is accompanied by a greater degree of agglomeration or, instead, by a spread of productive activity or dis-agglomeration, we alter somewhat the focus provided in the recent work of Krugman and others

---

[5] The Economist of December 27th 2002 reports on a rapid growth of logistic companies operating on a global scale.

> "So what exactly can smart logistics do for companies? One example is TPG's contract with Ford to service its Toronto factory. This plant produces 1,500 Windstar minivans a day. To keep it running virtually round the clock, TPG has to organize 800 deliveries a day from 300 different part makers. Its software must be tied into Ford's computerised production system. Loads have to arrive at 12 different points along the assembly lines without ever being more than 10 minutes late."

But TPG is a traditional freight company. The new type of logistics company, such as Exel, does much more. It is like the chef of an orchestra. The Economist continues:

> "One of Exel's biggest contracts is with Ford, for which it organizes supplies for seven factories around Europe. Exel also works for Volkswagen in its operations in Spain and Mexico. The factory in Puebla, Mexico, turns out 1,400 new Beetles a day. And Exel helps with Nokia's logistics as well, especially in China and South-East Asia."

in order to provide a benchmark comparison. We leave out of account the question of costs involved in having produced final goods reach the consumer and, instead, enquire about the possibility of breaking an integrated production process into separate *fragments* that could be located in other areas or other countries. In asking about links among producers instead of between final producers and consumers we also dispense with the need for utilizing the Dixit-Stiglitz utility function to express taste patterns for consumers facing an array of differentiated final goods. This function has provided yeoman service in "new trade theory", growth, and political economy in supplying a foundation at the micro level for Chamberlinian monopolistic competition with firms operating in the range in which increasing returns to scale are still found. Increasing returns are essential in our alternative scenario, but they are assumed to take place in what we call *service link* activities such as communication and co-ordination services that are required to establish a functioning network among fragments of *production blocks* that are located in different geographical locations (Ronald Jones and Henryk Kierzkowski, 1990, 2001a). These service activities include (but are not limited to) transportation services, the ones that play such a crucial role in the "new economic geography", albeit assumed there to be of the constant-cost variety. Herein lies a crucial distinction with our alternative: Increasing returns are assumed to reside in service link activities (including transportation) instead of on the factory floor (within production blocks). In section 4 we suggest what empirical work has to say about the nature of service links.

In each of the two alternative scenarios we now present we compare the costs of producing a final commodity when an integrated production location (or firm, **IF**) is used as opposed to having the production process split into two fragments located in different regions or countries, perhaps produced by two different firms. If such a split occurs, costs of production (neglecting transport costs or other coordinating service link activities) are lowered since it is possible to select locations such that factor prices and/or factor productivities are for each fragment more suited to factor proportions in that fragment. Regions in which labor is relatively inexpensive are used for the more labor-intensive fragment. For example, Nike, in making sports apparel, does the design work in the United States but outsources almost all the actual production activity to firms in Asia. Likewise, the Swedish furniture firm, Ikea, early on sent its actual production activity to Poland and used its Swedish labor force to design the individual pieces. In both Fig. 1 and Fig. 2 (pages 6 and 7) final output, **Y**, is shown on the horizontal axis and a pair of total production cost loci are drawn, labeled **IF** when all activity takes place in a single location with one firm, and **OF** (outsourced fragments) when the costs in the two separate fragments

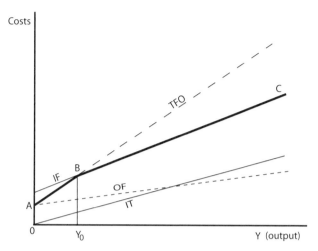

Fig. 1. Agglomeration. IF: Integrated Firm. OF: Outsourced Fragments (Production). IT: "Iceberg" Transportation. TFO: Total Fragmented Operation. ABC: Minimum Cost Schedule.

are added up (production costs only). These two fragments provide the appropriate balance of necessary output for any value of **Y**.

If production is split between two fragments located in different areas, these fragments must be brought together and coordinated, thus incurring extra costs of transportation, communication, and obtaining knowledge of where best to locate the fragments. These service link costs tend to be higher if fragments are located in different countries than if they are merely placed in different regions of a single country. Where Fig. 1 and Fig. 2 differ is in the kind of activity in which increasing returns are found. Fig. 1 characterizes our version of the assumptions made in the Fujita, Krugman and Venables model, in which increasing returns are found *within* production blocks. The simple way of modeling such increasing returns is to combine fixed costs (along the vertical axis) with constant marginal costs (shown by the slope of the total cost curve), leading to the rising **IF** and **OF** loci in Fig. 1. (Note that with two regions from which to chose, the costs of production along **OF** are everywhere lower than along the **IF**-locus if production is positive). Following their treatment we assume that the entire costs of linking the two fragments together is in the form of transport costs between fragments where the so-called *iceberg* model of such costs is used. (The iceberg analogy was introduced by Paul Samuelson in his 1954 *Economic Journal* discussion of the international transfer problem

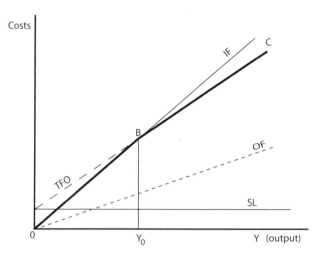

Fig. 2. Dis-Agglomeration. IF: Integrated Firm. OF: Outsourced Fragments (Production). SL: Service Link Costs. TFO: Total Fragmented Operation. OBC: Minimum Cost Schedule.

when transport costs exist.[6]) In that scenario, a unit of output exported from one locale will arrive at a different locale diminished in size, much as part of an iceberg would melt if transported from one region to another. The crucial aspect to notice is that this makes transportation a constant-returns-to-scale activity - doubling the output transferred between locations will double the loss eaten up in transport. There is no doubt that such an assumption is useful in avoiding separate activities whereby factors of production are combined to produce the services of transportation. However, it introduces a form of service link in Fig. 1 not matched in Fig. 2's alternative. The **TFO** (total fragmented operation) costs are found by adding the **OF** locus to the ray from the origin representing transportation costs.

In the alternative portrayed in Fig. 2, constant returns to scale are assumed both for the integrated production block (**IF**) and for the costs (production only) of the combined activities for the separate production blocks (**OF**), which are lower because each fragment is located in an area in which there is a better match among factor prices, technology, and factor proportions. Service link costs are required in order to co-ordinate the outputs of the separate fragments, and we make the

---

[6] As a matter of fact, Michael Rauscher has pointed out to us that the grand master of economic geography, Johann Heinrich von Thunen, 130 years previously, described how a horse that transports wheat from the country side to a city market eats a fraction of it en route.

extreme assumption that all such costs are constant regardless of the scale of activity. Thus the **TFO** cost schedule is a shifted-up version of the **OF** locus.

In each diagram the cost of the best mode of production is shown by a broken heavy line, with the break appearing at output level Y_0. Do larger scales of output encourage or discourage agglomeration? The contrast between the two scenarios is striking. In Fig. 1, the characterized version of the Fujita, Krugman and Venables model with iceberg transportation costs, disaggregated output in two locales is appropriate for small levels of output, up to Y_0. Up to this point the costs of connecting the two fragments by incurring transport costs are outweighed by the benefits of lower marginal costs in each fragment, but for higher levels of output it pays to combine all output in an integrated production block subject to increasing returns to scale and thus to obviate the need to pay for transportation. By contrast, in Fig. 2 it is a large scale of output (greater than Y_0) that encourages **dis**-agglomeration. With increasing returns found in the service link activities (including the costs of transportation), it pays to outsource the originally vertically-integrated production process into two fragments in different locales especially well-suited to their factor proportions.

In Section 4 we shall dwell more extensively on the nature of the costs of service links, including transportation. There is general agreement that there have been significant technological improvements that have brought about a lowering in the costs of service links. This is especially true of the costs of communication, which now have almost reached the vanishing point. It also holds, to a lesser extent, with the general costs of obtaining information and, as well, costs of transportation between producing regions. The consequences of such downward shifts in these costs in the two alternative settings are profound. In Fig. 1, a lowering of the iceberg transportation costs causes the (**TFO**) schedule of costs of total fragmented operation to rotate in a clockwise direction from the initial point on the vertical axis. As a result, the change-over point of output, Y_0, moves to the *right*. In Fig. 2, a technologically-inspired reduction in the costs of service links shifts the **TFO** schedule downwards, causing the change-over level of output, Y_0, to move to the *left*. The result: In *both* cases the range of outputs in which dis-agglomeration is the preferred mode of production increases. In Fig. 1 as output expands the consolidation of production in one location is delayed, whereas in Fig. 2 the desirability of fragmented production occurs at an earlier stage of growth.

One of the widely-recognized asymmetries on the international scene is the greater ease of moving commodities and middle products (including physical capital) among countries than it is to move labor. The large international migrations of labor witnessed at the end of the 19th century and beginning of the 20th century seem now a thing of the past, although some migration, both legal and illegal, still takes place. This asymmetry provides the basis for the doctrine of comparative advantage and suggests limits on the degree of international agglomeration that can be expected. Whereas within a country relatively mobile labor can aid and abet a process of agglomeration into a few urban nodes, on a global scale we have witnessed a greater degree of outsourcing of fragments of the production process in a manner reflecting both the Ricardian and Heckscher-Ohlin rationale for the nature of trade. Such dis-agglomeration among countries is encouraged by the increasing returns to scale found in many service link activities as world incomes rise, by the significant improvements in technology in the service area, as well as by a general lowering of regulatory barriers to international trade. With labor relatively immobile between countries, the doctrine of comparative advantage guarantees that no country will empty out as a consequence of the forces of agglomeration.

3 Fragmentation May Encourage Agglomeration and Growth

In the preceding section we have suggested that greater levels of output in an industry tend to encourage a fragmentation of a vertically-integrated production process, with outsourcing reaching even beyond a nation's borders. Suppose such a process is taking place not only in a single sector but also in many industries world-wide. Then it is possible to argue that fragmentation may provide a stimulus to subsequent *agglomeration* at a global level!

The argument for such a possibility rests in part on what we have termed the "*horizontal aspects of vertical fragmentation*" (see Jones and Kierzkowski, 2001b). Suppose that in a number of industrial sectors economic growth, technical progress, increasing returns in connecting service-link activities, and deregulation efforts have all conspired to promote a fragmentation, both locally and internationally, of production processes. We assume that some of these fragments more closely resemble each other in an inter-industry comparison than do the original integrated activities. This encourages further technical progress serving to make such fragments even more uniform and useful in a number of different sectors of the economy. (Consider the spread in the use of computer chips from computers to a wide range of uses ranging from toasters to automobiles). Furthermore, the overall techniques of production (or factor proportions) of such fragments may be rather similar. All this serves to encourage an agglomeration of a new industry producing such fragments for a wide array of sectors both locally and internationally.

The time-honored arguments about labor with certain skills being attracted to a center where a variety of productive activities require such skills seem appropriate in this setting. Alfred Marshall (1890) was an early exponent of the kind of externalities that may emerge when fragments of different industries share somewhat similar factor proportions and types of labor skills are located in the same region. In his words,

> "The mysteries of trade become no mystery; but are as it were in the air. Good work is rightly appreciated, invention and improvements in machinery, in processes and general organization of businesses have their merits promptly discussed: if one man starts a new idea, it is taken up by others and combined with suggestions of their own; and thus it becomes the source of further new ideas."

This Marshallian view has been picked up by other geographers. Thus,

> "Economists since Alfred Marshall have argued that cities facilitate the flow of ideas. However, most urban research focuses on the role that the density plays in reducing transportation costs between suppliers and customers (Krugman, 1991). However, Dumais et al. (1997) show that manufacturing firms in the USA since 1970 have not based their location decisions on the presence of suppliers and customers. Instead, firms locate near other firms that use the same type of workers."[7]

These ideas are consistent with a Heckscher-Ohlin basis for trade between countries based on differences in factor endowments and factor requirements in production, even without strong elements of imperfect competition. It would not be difficult formally to model externalities whereby factor productivities in one sector are positively affected by increases in activity of similar factors in other sectors closely related in their input and skill requirements.

The process of agglomeration outlined above presents an alternative to the agglomeration story told by the new economic geography. Perhaps it follows more closely what traditional economic geographers

---

[7] Edward Gleaser (2000), p. 84. Others expressed similar views. Martin and Sunley (1996) state on pages 285-6,

> "one of the most important limitations of Krugman's geographical economics is his stubborn concentration only on those externalities that can be mathematically modelled, and thus his reluctance to discuss the geographical impacts of technological and knowledge spillovers. The recent geographical literature has begun to assign key importance to technical change and technological externalities in shaping and transforming the space economy"

tell us is important. It presents a more complex world in which fragmentation of production results initially in a dispersion of economic activities. However, as a realignment of production patterns takes place within and across countries, the forces of agglomeration once again are in evidence. The addition of these externalities allows the forces of fragmentation and subsequent agglomeration to become engines of growth.[8]

As fragmentation and technical progress take place, the locales in which such pressures for agglomeration occur may change over time. An example of this was provided years ago in Ray Vernon's discussion of the product cycle (1966). At early stages of production a search is under way for the best techniques of producing a new product. In the face of uncertainty, the location of production is guided largely by the existence of labor (and perhaps capital) of a number of different skills. This leads (so Vernon argued) to a locale in an advanced country such as the United States. Eventually things settle down, and a technology requiring relatively heavy use of less skilled labor is formulated. As a consequence, the industry moves to a less developed country in which such labor is relatively inexpensive.

There is another route whereby fragmentation may eventually lead to a greater degree of agglomeration. The international fragmentation of production blocks is only made possible by the use of connecting service links, and it is in these service activities that we have argued that strong increasing returns are found. Just as in the arguments put forth by Krugman and others that increasing returns foster agglomeration, such agglomeration might be expected within the service sector. Indeed, this seems to be the case in activities such as financial services and insurance. Deregulation should certainly be given much of the credit for allowing more open trade in services, and one of the by-products of international fragmentation and its role in dis-agglomeration is the tendency for activities that provide service links themselves to agglomerate. This is consistent with the observed concentration of many service activities in advanced countries and international outsourcing of production blocks to less developed areas.

4 Increasing Returns and Technology in Service Link Activity

Where are increasing returns to be found? The crude assumptions that we have made is that they are found exclusively in the service link activities that facilitate a coordination of fragmented production blocks as opposed to constant returns to scale within such blocks. We need

---

[8] For somewhat similar views see the discussion of "clusters" as providing externalities and influences on productivity growth in Michael Porter (2000).

not rely on such a stringent dichotomy. Instead, we would argue that
the kind of economic activities that are most often associated with
increasing returns are ones in which economic information is gathered,
where financial aids to trade are obtained, where shipments are insured,
where communication between locations far apart are required, and
even where transportation activities are involved.[9]

Although some service activities are found within production blocks,
it seems difficult to find strong evidence of increasing returns in actual
production. In a relatively recent estimate of production functions in
the United States, Susanto Basu and John Fernald (1997) have come
to the following conclusion:

> "A typical (roughly) two-digit industry in the United States ap-
> pears to have constant or slightly decreasing returns to scale"
> (p. 249)

and furthermore

> "most plants and engineering studies find essentially constant
> returns to scale." (p. 263).

The evidence from Canadian manufacturing industries provides some
support for the opposite view that there are increasing returns to be
found in production.[10] Technological progress in service link activities,
including transportation, has been an impressive feature of the past few
decades. For example, one can hardly discuss global production without making reference to telecommunications. It is generally accepted
that launching telecommunications services involves high fixed costs.
By contrast, the marginal cost is miniscule. In a bygone era telephone
operators struggled to make speedy connections. Today a user dials a
number practically anywhere in the world and is put through immediately. Long-distance transmission of text or images has also become
much less costly. Sending production plans from England to Singapore
became significantly easier two decades ago with the introduction of
Fax technology and DHL. Today it is possible to transmit text and
images in living color instantaneously and almost costlessly.

---

[9] Alfred Marshall (1890) has this to say about transportation:

"A ship's carrying power varies as the cube of her dimensions, while
the resistance offered by the water increases only a little faster than
the square of her dimensions; so that a large ship requires less coal
in proportion to its tonnage than a small one. It also requires less
labour, especially that of navigation. In short, the small ship has no
chance of competing with the large ship between ports which large
ships can easily enter, and between which the traffic is sufficient to
enable them to fill up quickly."

[10] Michael Benarroch (1997), p. 1084.

5 Concluding Remarks

Both "old" and "new" geographers have cited many reasons why economic activity is not spread uniformly within a country or, indeed, among countries. Despite the standard economic doctrine of diminishing returns, many reasons can be cited for a "bunching up" of productive activities and residences. Individuals desire to consume services and products difficult to obtain in thinly settled communities (theatre, variety in shopping malls, proximity to friends and relatives, etc.) and externalities are provided by the co-existence in one locale of productive activities requiring inputs of labor of similar skills.

In the "new" economic geography, exemplified by the recent book by Fujita, Krugman and Venables, increasing returns in production and transportation costs of the Samuelsonian "iceberg" variety between consumers and producers are important ingredients in the analysis of agglomeration. In their models, consumer behavior is explicitly modeled with the aid of the Dixit-Stiglitz utility function allowing a love of variety among commodities of the same general type, leading to a Chamberlinian form of monopolistic competition. At the outset of our paper we have taken liberties with this setting, concentrating instead on the costs of connecting fragments of a production process that can be outsourced, perhaps to other countries, and leaving final consumers aside. The crucial issue is where are the increasing returns found - on the factory floor (i.e. within the production unit) or among the services required to link disparate fragments of the process.

If increasing returns are found within each production block, which is our transformation of the Fujita, Krugman and Venables model to consider the outsourcing phenomenon, we argued that if transportation services are required to link two blocks, and if these services exhibit constant returns to scale (as in the iceberg model), larger scales of output will indeed tend to cause production fragments that are initially separated spatially, to agglomerate. However, we also provided an alternative scenario that leads to opposite conclusions, one based on the model we presented initially in 1990. A production process consists of a number of production blocks that can be fragmented and located in different geographic regions of the same country, or can be outsourced to a variety of countries. The incentive to do so is provided by the different skills or factor combinations required in various fragments and the variety of factor prices and/or factor skills available in different regions or countries. Fragmentation allows a better "fit" for each production block. But extra costs are involved - those of transportation, but also of finance, co-ordination, communication, etc, and we argue that it is in these service link activities that strong degrees of increasing returns and decreasing costs are to be found. To take extreme examples we assumed that production blocks exhibit constant returns to scale, while service link activities are purely of the fixed cost variety, independent of scales of output. This difference in the location of the increasing returns activity is sufficient to lead to the result that eventually as output expands productive activity exhibits dis-agglomeration - a dispersal of productive activity to locations in which Ricardian and/or Heckscher-Ohlin differences among countries provide a better fit for the separate fragments as the scale of production expands.

Recent decades have witnessed profound productivity improvements in service links, whether of the transportation variety or in other service activities. The changes in communication costs have probably been the most significant in lowering the service costs required to co-ordinate spatially separated production fragments. We have argued that such changes have encouraged dis-agglomeration *both* in the modified Fujita, Krugman and Venables scenario as well as in our model of international fragmentation.

A melding of the two strands of argument concerning agglomeration was suggested in that international fragmentation of economic activity, promoted by larger scales of output and technological progress reducing the costs of service links, may lead to a subsequent agglomeration of fragments from different industries, fragments that nonetheless require similar relative quantities and qualities of productive inputs. This can eventuate in a re-alignment of the location of production, with encouragement for further technological progress and externalities that serve, as well, to promote economic growth.

Finally, we should note that in this, and our previous papers, we have remained relatively silent on such questions as: Will fragmentation take place within the firm or at arms-length in market transactions? Will large firms, possibly multinationals, dominate the process of international fragmentation while small firms are pushed away? These are legitimate and difficult issues, and our silence reflects a lack of comparative advantage.[11]

Acknowledgements

The authors wish to thank seminar participants in Helsinki and Osaka for valuable comments, as well as two anonymous referees. Bjarne Jensen has been very helpful in the revision of the manuscript.

---

[11] For an informed view, consider Henry Wan, Jr. (2001). He uses the concepts of closed and open networks in discussing relations between subcontractors and assemblers. He argues persuasively, with many examples from Japan, Hong Kong, Korea and Taiwan, that no unique arrangement should be expected to emerge. Which particular organizational structure is appropriate and most efficient to carry out fragmentation depends on the nature of an industry, the existence of information externalities, the speed of response to global transformation by individual firms and the economy as a whole.

References

Arndt, S, and Kierzkowski, H (eds.) (2001): *Fragmentation: New Production and Trade Patterns in the World Economy*. Oxford: Oxford University Press.

Basu, S., and Fernald. J. (1997): "Returns to Scale in U.S. Production: Estimates and Implications." *Journal of Political Economy* 105: 249-283.

Bennarroch, M. (1997): "Returns to Scale in Canadian Manufacturing: An Interprovincial Comparison." *Canadian Journal of Economics* 30: 1083-1103.

Cheng, L., and Kierzkowski, H. (eds.) (2002): *Globalization of Trade and Production in South-East Asia*. New York: Kluwer Academic Press.

Dixit, A. and Stiglitz, J. (1977): "Monopolistic Competition and Optimum Product Diversity." *American Economic Review* 67: 297-308.

Dumais, G,., Ellison, G., and Glaeser, E. (1997): "Geographic Concentration as a Dynamic Process." *NBER Working Paper 6270*.

Enke, S. (1951): "Equilibrium among Spatially Separated Markets: Solution by Electric Analogue." *Econometrica* 19: 40-47.

Feenstra, R., and Hanson, G. (1997): "Foreign Direct Investment and Relative Wages: Evidence from Mexico's Maquiladoras." *Journal of International Economics* 42: 371-94.

Fujita, M., Krugman, P., and Venables, A. (1999): *The Spatial Economy: Cities, Regions and International Trade*. Cambridge (Mass.): MIT Press.

Glaeser, E.L. (2000): "The New Economics of Urban and Regional Growth." In *The Oxford Handbook of Economic Geography*, edited by G.L. Clark et. al. Oxford: Oxford University Press.

Jones, R.W., and Kierzkowski, H. (1990): "The Role of Services in Production and International Trade: A Theoretical Framework." In *The Political Economy of International Trade*, edited by R.W. Jones and Anne Krueger, ch. 3. Oxford: Blackwells.

Jones, R.W., and Kierzkowski, H. (2001a): "A Framework for Fragmentation." In *Fragmentation: New Production and Trade Patterns in the World Economy*, edited by S. Arndt and H. Kierzkowski. Oxford: Oxford University Press.

Jones, R.W., and Kierzkowski, H. (2001b), "Horizontal Aspects of Vertical Fragmentation." in *Globalization of Trade and Production in South-East Asia*, edited by L. Cheng and H. Kierzkowski. New York: Kluwer Academic Press.

Krugman, P. (1991): "Increasing Returns and Economic Geography." *Journal of Political Economy* 99: 483-99.

Marshall, A. (1890): *Principles of Economics*. Book Four: The Agents of Production: Land, Labour, and Capital and Organization, Chapter 11, "Industrial Organization Continued. Production on a Large Scale" available on the Internet at: http://www.marxists.org/reference/subject /economics/marshall/bk4ch11.htm.

Martin, R., and Sunley, P. (1996): "Paul Krugman's Geographical Economics and its Implications for Regional Development Theory: A Critical Assessment." *Economic Geography* 72: 259 - 292.

Neary, J.P. (2001): "Of Hype and Hyperbolas: Introducing the New Economic Geography." *Journal of Economic Literature* 39: 536-561.

Ng, F., and Yeats, A. (2001): "Production Sharing in East Asia: Who Does What for Whom and Why?" In *Globalization of Trade and Production in South-East Asia,* edited by L. Cheng and H. Kierzkowski. New York: Kluwer Academic Press.

Ohlin, B., Hesselborn, P.O., and Wijkman, P.M. (eds.) (1977): *The International Allocation of Economic Activity.* The Nobel Foundation.

Porter, M.E. (2000): "Locations, Clusters, and Company Strategy." In *The Oxford Handbook of Economic Geography,* edited by G.L. Clark et. al. Oxford: Oxford University Press.

Samuelson, P.A. (1952): "Spatial Price Equilibrium and Linear Programming." *American Economic Review* 42: 283-303.

Samuelson, P.A. (1954): "The Transfer Problem and Transport Costs: The Terms of Trade when Impediments are Absent." *Economic Journal* 64: 278-304.

Sheppard, E. (2001): "How Economists Think: about Geography, for Example." *Journal of Economic Geography* 1: 131-136.

Sunley, P. (2001): "What's behind the Models? " in Critical Forum. *Journal of Economic Geography* 1: 136-139.

Urban, D. (2001): "The Special Economy: One New Economic Geographer's View." *Journal of Economic Geography* 1: 146-152.

Vernon, R. (1966): "International Investment and International Trade in the Product Cycle." *Quarterly Journal of Economics* 80: 190-207.

Wan, H., Jr. (2001): "Function vs. Form in the Fragmented Industrial Structure: Three Examples from Asia Pacific Experience." In *Globalization of Trade and Production in South-East Asia,* edited by L. Cheng and H. Kierzkowski. New York: Kluwer Academic Press.

Yeats, A. (2001), "Just How Big is Global Production Sharing?" In *Fragmentation: New Production and Trade Patterns in the World Economy,* edited by S. Arndt and H. Kierzkowski. Oxford: Oxford University Press.

Addresses of authors: – Ronald W. Jones, Department of Economics, University of Rochester, Rochester, New York 14627, USA (e-mail: jonr@troi.cc.rochester.edu); – Henryk Kierzkowski, Graduate Institute of International Studies, HEI, 11A, Avenue de la Paix 1202, Geneva, Switzerland (e-mail: kierzkow@hei.unige.ch)

J. Econ. (2005) Suppl. 10: 17-56

Journal of Economics
Zeitschrift für Nationalökonomie

Printed in Austria

General Equilibrium Dynamics of Multi-Sector Growth Models

Bjarne S. Jensen and Mogens E. Larsen

Received April 15, 2003; Revised version received August 9, 2004
© Springer-Verlag 2005

This paper analyzes Walrasian general equilibrium systems and calculates the static and dynamic solutions for competitive market equilibria. The Walrasian framework encompasses the basic multi-sector growth (MSG) models with neoclassical production technologies in N sectors (industries). The endogenous behavior of all the relative prices are analyzed in detail, as are sectorial allocations of the primary factors, labor and capital. Dynamic systems of Walrasian multi-sector economies and the family of solutions (time paths) for steady-state and persistent growth per capita are parametrically characterized. The technology parameters of the capital good industry are decisive for obtaining long-run per capita growth in closed (global) economies. Brief comments are offered on the MSG literature, together with apects on the studies of industrial (structural) evolution and economic history.

Keywords: pareto effiency, walrasian equilibria, factor accumulation

JEL classification: F11, F43, O40, O41.

1 Introduction

Dynamics is concerned with calculating the motions of the widest variety of objects, and with deriving (computing) the implications (effects) of these motions. Its basic principles and logical structure have long been a model for other scientific disciplines. The domain of dynamics in physics (mechanics) have been extended tremendously on both macro- and microscopic scales, Pais (1986). In the discipline of economics, dynamics began in macroeconomics, in particular with business cycle and the basic one- and two-sector growth models. However, standard *microeconomic* (producer/consumer) theory is more naturally involved with decentralized mechanisms for resource allocation in static *multi-sector* modeling and *general equilibrium* dynamics. We may briefly refer to passages from important theoretical and empirical contributions to multi-sectoral model building.

Regarding the character of works in *applied general equilibrium analysis* (AGE-modelling), we quote Shoven & Whalley (1992, pp.1):[1]

> "The central idea underlying this work is to convert the *Walrasian general equilibrium structure* (formalized in the 1950s by Arrow, Debreu, and others) from an abstract representation of an economy into realistic models of actual economies. Numerical, empirically based general equilibrium can then be used to evaluate concrete policy options by *specifying production and demand parameters* and incorporating data reflective of real economies"

and

> "Most contemporary applied *general models* are *numerical analogs* of traditional *two-sector general equilibrium models* popularized by James Meade, Harry Johnson, Arnold Harberger, and others in the 1950s and 1960s. Earlier analytic work with these models has examined the distortionary effects of taxes, tariffs, and other policies, along with functional incidence questions."

Computation of general equilibria usually involves solving systems of nonlinear equations. Thus, according to Judd (1998, p.147, p.3):

> "The Arrow-Debreu concept of general equilibrium reduces to finding a *price vector* at which *excess demand* is zero; it is the most famous nonlinear equation problem in economics"

and

> "The *computational general equilibrium* (CGE) literature is the most mature computational literature in economics"

Much of the *numerical* (algorithmic) methodology derives from the work of Scarf et al. (1967,1973). Numerical approaches give *approximate solutions*; many papers on numerical methods offer little in the way of showing the qualitative dependence of the solutions upon critical parameter values. Obtaining analytical solutions in theorem-proof style is preferable wherever this is possible.

Our *emphasis* in this paper will be to provide a *conceptual framework* that supports *economic intuition* and offer a general and *unified analytical approach* to the mathematical procedures of obtaining the *static, comparative static* and *dynamic general equilibrium solutions* of

---

[1] In all quotations throughout this paper Italics is ours.

an N-sector economy. We extend the methodology and mathematical-economic analysis of two-sector dynamics, Jensen (2003), to the multi-sectorial dynamics of temporal *Pareto-efficient* labor and capital allocation/accumulation.

An important contributor to multi-sector generalizations of various macrodynamic models was Jorgenson (1961), who extended the input-output methods of Leontief to *dynamic input-output analysis*. In the *macro-planning* and *development* literature, our topic of multi-sector economies had another important contributor in Johansen (1959, 1974, pp.1):

> "It is a well-known fact that the *various sectors* of an economy do *not expand* in the *same proportion* in a process of economic growth. The flows of investment and new labor are not allocated proportionately to all production sectors. Existing quantities of *capital* and *labor* may be *reallocated* during the growth process. *Terms of trade* between the production sectors may *change* in a systematic way, and so on. Such considerations illustrate aspects of the economic growth process which we shall attempt to explain and analyze within the framework of a *multi-sectoral growth model*."

Regarding structural analysis and *sectorial developments*, the three categories of Colin Clark were dealing with the reallocation of the labour force over the groups of industries: *Primary* industries (agriculture, fisheries and forestry), *Secondary* industries (manufacturing, handicraft, building and construction, Mining, Electric power production), *Tertiary* industries (wholesale and retail commerce, transport, financial services and public administration), and globally observing, Clark (1951, p.365) that:

> "by careful generalization of available facts to be the most important concomitant of economic progress, namely the movement of working population from agriculture to manufacture and from manufacture to commerce and services."

Concomitant *changes* in the *composition* of *demand*, e.g., the budget share of food (*Engel's law*, 1857) is confirmed by all surveys, Houthakker (1957).

Controversies related to "convergence" and "balanced growth" models as being incompatible with *structural change* and the process of economic development are given renewed attention in both the empirical and theoretical growth literature, Pasinetti (1981), Islam (1995), Echevarria (1997), Laitner (2000), Kongsamut, Rebelo, Xie (2001), Meckl (2002). Patterns of sectorial industrial growth will here be obtained and shortly discussed.

As we consider the relationship between *resources, technology,* and *economic evolution,* we finally quote the historian, A. P. Usher (1954, p.1):

> "Economic history is concerned with the description and the analysis of the mutual transformations taking place between human societies and their environment. The *study* of *costs* and *prices* is *important,* and the *institutional structure* of organized social life demands careful *attention,* but the *basic problems* of *economic history* lie in the field of the *management* of *resources.* - The *quantitative* analysis of economic activities requires *study* of the processes and accomplishments of the *system* of *production* in *physical units* as well as in *value units.*"

This paper deals with *dynamic foundations* of MSG models for closed (global) economies. We explain well-known empirical facts by modeling in terms of *basic microeconomic principles.* Section 2 presents an analytical framework with concepts, definitions, and various micro and macro economic equivalence relations. Section 3 studies the relationships between *factor prices* and *relative commodity prices.* In section 4, we analyze and derive GDP expenditure shares from some specific parameterizations of utility functions. Section 5 uses a proper NIPA version of *Walras's law* to obtain the *Walrasian equilibrium* of the multi-sector economy, and we derive the *timeless* (static and comparative static) *competitive general equilibrium solutions* for all the variables as *distinct composite functions* of the *factor endowments.* In section 6, we analyze the *dynamic systems* and alternative *evolutions* of multi-sector *general equilibria.* Section 7 gives various asymptotic sectorial growth rates of persistently growing multi-sector economies. Our final comments are found in section 8.

2 Analytical Framework for Multi-Sector (MS) Economies

2.1 The Supply Side, Technology and Efficient Factor Allocation

Consider an economy consisting of N *industries* (sectors), and let sector 1 be a capital good industry. Sector *technologies,* $F_i(L_i, K_i)$, are described by nonnegative smooth concave homogeneous production functions with *constant returns* to scale in labor and capital, $i = 1, \cdots, N$,

$$Y_i = F_i(L_i, K_i) = L_i F_i(1, k_i) \equiv L_i f_i(k_i) \equiv L_i y_i, \, L_i \neq 0, \quad F_i(0,0) = 0, \tag{1}$$

where the function $f_i(k_i)$, is strictly concave and monotonically increasing in the capital-labor ratio $k_i \in [0, \infty[$, i.e., f_i has the properties

$$\forall k_i > 0: \quad f_i'(k_i) = \frac{df_i(k_i)}{dk_i} > 0, \quad f_i''(k_i) = \frac{d^2 f_i(k_i)}{dk_i^2} < 0, \tag{2}$$

$$\lim_{k_i \to 0} f_i'(k_i) \equiv \bar{\mathbf{b}}_i \leq \infty, \quad \lim_{k_i \to \infty} f_i'(k_i) \equiv \underline{\mathbf{b}}_i \geq 0, \quad f_i'(k_i) \in J_i \equiv \left[\underline{\mathbf{b}}_i, \bar{\mathbf{b}}_i\right]. \tag{3}$$

Let us note that if our F_i is defined and continuous on the axes, then

$$F_i(0, 1) \geq 0, \quad F_i(1, 0) \equiv f_i(0) \geq 0, \tag{4}$$

$$F_i(0, K_i) = K_i F_i(0, 1), \quad F_i(L_i, 0) = L_i F_i(1, 0) = L_i f_i(0), \tag{5}$$

where positivity in (4) says that a factor is *non-essential*. Note also,

$$\lim_{k_i \to 0} f_i'(k_i) = \frac{\partial F_i}{\partial K_i}(1, 0), \quad \lim_{k_i \to \infty} f_i'(k_i) = F_i(0, 1), \quad \frac{\partial F_i}{\partial L_i}(1, 0) = F_i(1, 0). \tag{6}$$

The *sectorial output elasticities*, $\epsilon_{L_i}, \epsilon_{K_i}, \epsilon_i$, with respect to marginal and proportional factor variation are, cf. (1),

$$\epsilon_{L_i} \equiv \frac{\partial \ln Y_i}{\partial \ln L_i} \equiv \frac{\partial Y_i}{\partial L_i} \frac{L_i}{Y_i} = \frac{MP_{L_i}}{AP_{L_i}} = 1 - \frac{k_i f_i'(k_i)}{f_i(k_i)} > 0, \quad k_i \neq 0, \tag{7}$$

$$\epsilon_{K_i} \equiv \frac{\partial \ln Y_i}{\partial \ln K_i} \equiv \frac{\partial Y_i}{\partial K_i} \frac{K_i}{Y_i} = \frac{MP_{K_i}}{AP_{K_i}} = \frac{k_i f_i'(k_i)}{f_i(k_i)} = \frac{d \ln y_i}{d \ln k_i} > 0, \tag{8}$$

$$\epsilon_i \equiv \epsilon_{L_i} + \epsilon_{K_i} = 1. \tag{9}$$

The *factor endowments*, total labor force (L) and the total capital stock (K), are inelastically supplied and are fully employed (utilized), i.e.

$$L = \sum_{i=1}^{N} L_i, \quad \sum_{i=1}^{N} L_i/L \equiv \sum_{i=1}^{N} \lambda_{L_i} = 1, \quad \lambda_{L_i} = l_i, \tag{10}$$

$$K = \sum_{i=1}^{N} K_i, \quad \sum_{i=1}^{N} K_i/K \equiv \sum_{i=1}^{N} \lambda_{K_i} \equiv 1, \tag{11}$$

$$K/L \equiv k \equiv \sum_{i=1}^{N} \lambda_{L_i} k_i \equiv \sum_{i=1}^{N} l_i k_i, \tag{12}$$

where $\lambda_{L_i}, \lambda_{K_i}$, (10-11) are the *factor allocation fractions*.
At any point of the isoquants (1), the *marginal* rates of technical *substitution* (MRS), $\omega_i(k_i)$ are, by (2), positive *monotonic* functions,

$$\omega_i = \omega_i(k_i) = \frac{MP_{L_i}}{MP_{K_i}} = \frac{f_i(k_i)}{f_i'(k_i)} - k_i = \frac{\epsilon_{L_i}}{\epsilon_{K_i}} k_i > 0 \quad \forall k_i > 0, \tag{13}$$

and the *substitution elasticities*, σ_i between labor and capital is the proportionate change in the ratio (K_i/L_i) of inputs divided by the proportionate change in the ratio (ω_i) of the marginal products of inputs, cf. (13), (7-8),

$$\sigma_i \equiv \frac{d\ln k_i}{d\ln \omega_i} \equiv \frac{dk_i}{d\omega_i}\frac{\omega_i}{k_i} = \frac{dk_i}{d\omega_i}\frac{\epsilon_{L_i}}{\epsilon_{K_i}} = \frac{d\ln AP_{L_i}}{d\ln MP_{L_i}} = \frac{d\ln AP_{K_i}}{d\ln MP_{K_i}} > 0. \quad (14)$$

The general relation between the sectorial factor output elasticities, (7-8), and the sectorial substitution elasticities, σ_i, is:

$$\frac{d\ln \epsilon_{K_i}}{d\ln k_i} \equiv \frac{d\epsilon_{K_i}}{dk_i}\frac{k_i}{\epsilon_{K_i}} = \frac{\epsilon_{L_i}(\sigma_i - 1)}{\sigma_i}, \quad \frac{d\ln \epsilon_{L_i}}{d\ln k_i} \equiv \frac{d\epsilon_{L_i}}{dk_i}\frac{k_i}{\epsilon_{L_i}} = \frac{\epsilon_{K_i}(1 - \sigma_i)}{\sigma_i}.$$
$$(15)$$

Free *factor mobility* between the multiple industries and also *efficient* factor *allocation* impose the *common* MRS condition, cf. (13),

$$\omega = \omega_i = \omega_i(k_i) \quad (i = 1, ..., N). \quad (16)$$

For the variables k_i to satisfy (16), it is, beyond (2), further required that the intersection of the sectorial range for $\omega_i(k_i)$ is not empty,

$$\omega_i(k_i) \in \Omega_i = [\underline{\omega}_i, \bar{\omega}_i] \subseteq \mathbf{R}_+, \quad \omega \in \Omega \equiv \cap \Omega_i = [\underline{\omega}, \bar{\omega}] \neq \emptyset. \quad (17)$$

2.2 Efficient Factor Allocation, Costs, and Relative Prices

All industries are assumed to operate under *perfect competition* (zero excess profit); absolute (money) input (factor) *prices* (w, r) are the same in both industries; and absolute (money) output (product, commodity) prices (P_i) represent unit cost. Thus, in each sector we have the *competitive producer equilibrium* equations,

$$w = P_i \cdot MP_{L_i}, \quad r = P_i \cdot MP_{K_i}; \quad \omega = w/r, \quad P_i \neq 0, \quad (18)$$
$$P_iY_i = wL_i + rK_i, \quad \epsilon_{L_i} = wL_i/P_iY_i, \quad \epsilon_{K_i} = rK_i/P_iY_i, \quad (19)$$
$$P_i = (w + rk_i)/y_i, \quad \widehat{P}_i = \epsilon_{L_i}\hat{w} + \epsilon_{K_i}\hat{r}, \quad (\widehat{P}_i \equiv dP_i/P_i). \quad (20)$$

Thus the relative change, $\widehat{P}_i$, is a *convex combination*, (9), of $\hat{w}$ and $\hat{r}$. Next, (18) gives any *relative commodity price* P_i/P_j as

$$p_{ij} \equiv \frac{P_i}{P_j} = \frac{MP_{K_j}}{MP_{K_i}} = \frac{f'_j(k_j)}{f'_i(k_i)} = \frac{f_j(k_j) - k_jf'_j(k_j)}{f_i(k_i) - k_if'_i(k_i)} = \frac{MP_{L_j}}{MP_{L_i}} = \frac{y_j\epsilon_{L_j}}{y_i\epsilon_{L_i}}.$$
$$(21)$$

The *connection* between relative *factor* (service) prices and relative *commodity* prices follows from (16, 18, 21),

$$p_{ij}(\omega) = \frac{P_i}{P_j}(\omega) = \frac{MP_{K_j}[k_j(\omega)]}{MP_{K_i}[k_i(\omega)]} = \frac{f_j'[k_j(\omega)]}{f_i'[k_i(\omega)]} = \left[\frac{f_i'[k_i(\omega)]}{f_j'[k_j(\omega)]}\right]^{-1}, \; \omega = \frac{w}{r}.$$ (22)

With a common wage-rental ratio, (16), in all sectors it is clear that,

$$\epsilon_{L_i}(\omega) \gtreqless \epsilon_{L_j}(\omega) \iff \epsilon_{K_j}(\omega) \gtreqless \epsilon_{K_i}(\omega) \iff k_j(\omega) \gtreqless k_i(\omega).$$ (23)

Average and marginal productivities were objects of pioneering theoretical and empirical studies by von Thünen. In Table 1 below, the factor K is non-essential, cf. (4); accordingly, the substitution elasticity is larger than one. Hence ϵ_L, (7), (15), (18), (19), is here falling with mechanization, K/L. Evidently, with $\sigma > 1$, AP_L increases more than MP_L, (14). This table may serve as a relevant and simple illustration of key sectorial productivity growth numbers.

Table 1. Von Thünen´s Productivity Calculations.

K/L	AP_L	AP_K	MP_K	MP_L	ω	$MP_K k$	ϵ_L
0	110	–	–	110	–	–	1.00
1	150	150	40	110	2.75	40	0.73
2	186	93	36	114	3.17	72	0.61
3	218.4	72.8	32.4	121.2	3.74	97.2	0.55

Source: von Thünen (1850 [1930, p. 507]); Brems (1986, p. 86).

2.3 Macro-Equivalence Relations of Supply-Demand in MS Economies

Gross domestic product (GDP), national income, Y, is the *total* of sectoral producer *revenues* [monetary value of sector outputs, (1)]

$$Y_i = L y_i l_i, \qquad Y \equiv \sum_{i=1}^{N} P_i Y_i = L \left[\sum_{i=1}^{N} P_i y_i l_i\right] \equiv Ly,$$ (24)

and is equivalent with *competition* (18) and (19) to total *factor income*,

$$Y = wL + rK = L(w + rk) = L(\omega + k)P_i f_i'[k_i] = Ly.$$ (25)

Hence the factor income *distribution shares* $\delta_K + \delta_L = 1$, become

$$\delta_K \equiv rK/Y = rk/y, \delta_L \equiv wL/Y = w/y; \delta_K = k/(\omega + k), \delta_K/\delta_L = k/\omega.$$ (26)

The "final demand" decomposition of GDP (Y) into the aggregate expenditures on investment (I) and consumption (C) is

$$I = P_1 Y_1, \quad C = \sum_{i=2}^{N} P_i Y_i, \quad Y = C + I, \tag{27}$$

and the *composition* of GDP (24) *expenditure shares*, s_i is

$$s_i = P_i Y_i / Y, \quad \sum_{i=1}^{N} s_i \equiv \sum_{i=1}^{N} P_i Y_i / Y = 1. \tag{28}$$

Budget studies and consumption (demand) theory mostly normalize the budget shares with the total expenditure ("income") constraint, C, i.e., the expenditure shares, e_i, as

$$e_i = P_i Y_i / C, \quad \sum_{i=2}^{N} e_i = 1; \quad \underline{e} = \sum_{\sigma_i < 1} e_i, \quad \bar{e} = \sum_{\sigma_i > 1} e_i, \quad \underline{e} + \bar{e} = 1. \tag{29}$$

Evidently, the connection between the GDP shares (28) and (29) is

$$s_i = (1 - s_1) e_i, \quad i = 2, ..., N. \tag{30}$$

For later purposes, we introduce the notation, cf. (29),

$$\begin{array}{lll} \sigma_1 > 1 : & \underline{s} = (1 - s_1)\underline{e}, & \bar{s} = (1 - s_1)\bar{e} + s_1, \\ \sigma_1 < 1 : & \underline{s} = (1 - s_1)\underline{e} + s_1, & \bar{s} = (1 - s_1)\bar{e}, \end{array} \quad \bar{s} + \underline{s} = 1. \tag{31}$$

Lemma 1. *The macro factor income shares δ_L, δ_K, (26), are GDP expenditure-weighted combinations of the sectorial factor income (cost) shares, ϵ_{L_i}, ϵ_{K_i},*

$$\delta_L = \sum_{i=1}^{N} s_i \epsilon_{L_i}, \quad \delta_K = \sum_{i=1}^{N} s_i \epsilon_{K_i}, \quad \delta_K + \delta_L = 1. \tag{32}$$

The factor allocation fractions (10) and (11) are obtained by

$$L_i / L = \lambda_{L_i} = l_i = s_i \epsilon_{L_i} / \delta_L, \quad K_i / K = \lambda_{K_i} = s_i \epsilon_{K_i} / \delta_K. \tag{33}$$

The total factor endowment ratio K/L satisfies the identity [cf.(12),(26),(32)]:

$$\frac{K}{L} = k = \sum_{i=1}^{N} \lambda_{L_i} k_i = \frac{\omega \delta_K}{\delta_L} = \omega \sum_{i=1}^{N} s_i \epsilon_{K_i} \Big/ \sum_{i=1}^{N} s_i \epsilon_{L_i}, \tag{34}$$

which is a convenient representation of Walras's law (identity).

Proof: By definition, we have

$$\delta_L = wL/Y = [wL_1 + wL_2 + \cdots wL_N]/Y, \tag{35}$$
$$\delta_K = rK/Y = [rK_1 + rK_2 + \cdots rK_N]/Y. \tag{36}$$

From (19) and (28), we get

$$wL_i = \epsilon_{L_i} P_i Y_i = s_i \epsilon_{L_i} Y, \qquad rK_i = \epsilon_{K_i} P_i Y_i = s_i \epsilon_{K_i} Y. \tag{37}$$

Hence, by (35), (36) and (37), we obtain (32). Next, as stated in (33),

$$\lambda_{L_i} = \frac{L_i}{L} = \frac{wL_i}{wL} = \frac{s_i \epsilon_{L_i} Y}{\delta_L Y} = \frac{s_i \epsilon_{L_i}}{\delta_L}, \tag{38}$$

$$\lambda_{K_i} = \frac{K_i}{K} = \frac{rK_i}{rK} = \frac{s_i \epsilon_{K_i} Y}{\delta_K Y} = \frac{s_i \epsilon_{K_i}}{\delta_K}. \qquad //// \tag{39}$$

3 Relative Prices in Economies with CES Technologies

The general CES forms of $F_i(L_i, K_i)$, (1), $\gamma_i > 0, 0 < a_i < 1$ and $\sigma_i > 0$ are

$$Y_i = F_i(L_i, K_i) = \gamma_i L_i^{1-a_i} K_i^{a_i} = L_i \gamma_i k_i^{a_i}, \equiv L_i f_i(k_i), \tag{40}$$

$$Y_i = F_i(L_i, K_i) = \gamma_i \left[(1-a_i) L_i^{\frac{\sigma_i-1}{\sigma_i}} + a_i K_i^{\frac{\sigma_i-1}{\sigma_i}} \right]^{\frac{\sigma_i}{\sigma_i-1}} \tag{41}$$

$$= L_i \gamma_i \left[(1-a_i) + a_i k_i^{(\sigma_i-1)/\sigma_i} \right]^{\sigma_i/(\sigma_i-1)} \equiv L_i f_i(k_i), \tag{42}$$

$$f_i'(k_i) = \gamma_i a_i k_i^{a_i-1}, \quad f_i'(k_i) = \gamma_i a_i \left[a_i + (1-a_i) k_i^{-(\sigma_i-1)/\sigma_i} \right]^{1/(\sigma_i-1)}. \tag{43}$$

By evaluating equations (40)-(43), the limits of $f_i(k_i)$ and $f_i'(k_i)$ can be written as follows $\left[\sigma_i \gtrless 1 \Rightarrow a_i^{\sigma_i/(\sigma_i-1)} \gtrless 1 \right]$:

$$\sigma_i < 1 \begin{cases} \lim_{k_i \to 0} f_i(k_i) = 0, & \lim_{k_i \to \infty} f_i(k_i) = \gamma_i (1-a_i)^{\frac{\sigma_i}{\sigma_i-1}}, \\ \lim_{k_i \to 0} f_i'(k_i) = \gamma_i a_i^{\frac{\sigma_i}{\sigma_i-1}}, & \lim_{k_i \to \infty} f_i'(k_i) = 0, \end{cases} \tag{44}$$

$$\sigma_i > 1 \begin{cases} \lim_{k_i \to 0} f_i(k_i) = \gamma_i (1-a_i)^{\frac{\sigma_i}{\sigma_i-1}}, & \lim_{k_i \to \infty} f_i(k_i) = \infty, \\ \lim_{k_i \to 0} f_i'(k_i) = \infty, & \lim_{k_i \to \infty} f_i'(k_i) = \gamma_i a_i^{\frac{\sigma_i}{\sigma_i-1}}. \end{cases} \tag{45}$$

For the CES technologies, the *monotonic* relations between marginal rates of substitution, factor proportions, and output elasticities are [cf. (41-43)]

$$\omega_i = \frac{1-a_i}{a_i} k_i^{1/\sigma_i}, \qquad k_i = \frac{1}{c_i}[\omega_i]^{\sigma_i}, \qquad c_i = \left[\frac{1-a_i}{a_i}\right]^{\sigma_i}, \tag{46}$$

$$\epsilon_{K_i} = \left[1 + \frac{1-a_i}{a_i} k_i^{\frac{1-\sigma_i}{\sigma_i}}\right]^{-1} = \frac{1}{1+c_i\omega^{1-\sigma_i}}, \qquad \epsilon_{L_i} = \frac{c_i\omega^{1-\sigma_i}}{1+c_i\omega^{1-\sigma_i}}. \tag{47}$$

With multi-sector models and CES technologies, it is apparent, cf. (46), that sectorial *factor* ratio ("intensity") *reversals* can only be avoided if and only if $\sigma_i = \sigma_j$ and $a_i \neq a_j$. Hence, with $\sigma_i \neq \sigma_j$, the *reversal* point is, $(k_i, \omega_i) = (k_j, \omega_j) = (\bar{k}, \bar{\omega})$, $[a_i = a_j = a : (\bar{k}, \bar{\omega}) = (1, \frac{1-a}{a})]$:

$$\bar{k} = \left[\frac{a_i(1-a_j)}{a_j(1-a_i)}\right]^{\frac{\sigma_i\sigma_j}{\sigma_j-\sigma_i}} = \left[\frac{c_j^{\sigma_i}}{c_i^{\sigma_j}}\right]^{\frac{1}{\sigma_j-\sigma_i}} \qquad \bar{\omega} = \left[\frac{c_j}{c_i}\right]^{\frac{1}{\sigma_j-\sigma_i}}. \tag{48}$$

3.1 The Correspondence of Product and Factor Prices with CES

The exact form of the function (22) needs particular attention. With (43) and (46), the *relative commodity* prices (comparative costs) (22) become, with $\sigma_i = 1$, $\sigma_i \neq 1$, and $\sigma_i = \sigma$, respectively,

$$p_{ij}(\omega) = \frac{f_j'[k_j(\omega)]}{f_i'[k_i(\omega)]} = \frac{\gamma_j a_j k_j(\omega)^{a_j-1}}{\gamma_i a_i k_i(\omega)^{a_i-1}} = \frac{\gamma_j a_j^{a_j}(1-a_j)^{1-a_j}}{\gamma_i a_i^{a_i}(1-a_i)^{1-a_i}} \omega^{a_j-a_i}, \tag{49}$$

$$p_{ij}(\omega) = \frac{f_j'[k_j(\omega)]}{f_i'[k_i(\omega)]} = \frac{\gamma_j a_j \left[a_j + (1-a_j)k_j(\omega)^{-(\sigma_j-i)/\sigma_j}\right]^{1/(\sigma_j-1)}}{\gamma_i a_i \left[a_i + (1-a_i)k_i(\omega)^{-(\sigma_i-1)/\sigma_i}\right]^{1/(\sigma_i-1)}} \tag{50}$$

$$= \frac{\gamma_j a_j^{\sigma_j/(\sigma_j-1)} \left[1 + c_j\omega^{1-\sigma_j}\right]^{1/(\sigma_j-1)}}{\gamma_i a_i^{\sigma_i/(\sigma_i-1)} \left[1 + c_i\omega^{1-\sigma_i}\right]^{1/(\sigma_i-1)}}, \tag{51}$$

$$p_{ij}(\omega) = \frac{f_j'[k_j(\omega)]}{f_i'[k_i(\omega)]} = \frac{\gamma_j}{\gamma_i} \left[\left(\frac{a_j}{a_i}\right)^{\sigma} \frac{1+c_j\omega^{1-\sigma}}{1+c_i\omega^{1-\sigma}}\right]^{1/(\sigma-1)}, \qquad c_i = \left[\frac{1-a_i}{a_i}\right]^{\sigma}. \tag{52}$$

The elasticity of the functions (22), (49), (50), (51) and (52) are generally interlinked by the composite rule:

$$E[p_{ij}, \omega] = E[MP_{K_j}, k_j] E(k_j, \omega) - E[MP_{K_i}, k_i] E(k_i, \omega) \tag{53}$$

$$= (-\epsilon_{L_j}/\sigma_j)\sigma_j - (-\epsilon_{L_i}/\sigma_i)\sigma_i = \epsilon_{L_i} - \epsilon_{L_j} = \epsilon_{K_j} - \epsilon_{K_i}. \tag{54}$$

Evidently, $p_{ij}(\omega)$ is always *inelastic*, as (54) is numerically less than unity; but this is not directly seen from the explicit CES expressions (49), 51) and (52).

The Stolper-Samuelson theorem and the "magnification effects" of price changes [cf. Jones (1965)] are implications of the elasticity between the factor and commodity prices (*FPCP elasticity*) (53)-(54), which can be rewritten as

$$\left(\hat{P}_i - \hat{P}_j\right)/\left(\hat{w} - \hat{r}\right) = \epsilon_{L_i} - \epsilon_{L_j} = \epsilon_{K_j} - \epsilon_{K_i}. \tag{55}$$

Since $\hat{P}_i$ and $\hat{P}_j$ both lie between $\hat{w}$ and $\hat{r}$, cf. (20), then

$$\left|\left(\hat{P}_i - \hat{P}_j\right)/\left(\hat{w} - \hat{r}\right)\right| < 1. \tag{56}$$

Combining (54, 55), (56), with (23), we immediately obtain the following *inequalities* ("magnification relations"):

$$k_i(\omega) < k_j(\omega) : \begin{cases} \hat{P}_i > \hat{P}_j : \hat{w} > \hat{P}_i > \hat{P}_j > \hat{r}, \\ \hat{P}_j > \hat{P}_i : \hat{r} > \hat{P}_j > \hat{P}_i > \hat{w}, \end{cases} \tag{57}$$

$$k_i(\omega) > k_j(\omega) : \begin{cases} \hat{P}_i > \hat{P}_j : \hat{r} > \hat{P}_i > \hat{P}_j > \hat{w}, \\ \hat{P}_j > \hat{P}_i : \hat{w} > \hat{P}_j > \hat{P}_i > \hat{r}. \end{cases} \tag{58}$$

Since the CES marginal rate of substitution ω_i in (46) always has the limit values zero and infinity, we need, for precise geometry and intuition, to know the *limits* of the *relative prices* $p_{ij}(\omega)$, (51), for ω going to zero and infinity. To this end, let

$$p_{ij}^* \equiv \frac{\gamma_j}{\gamma_i} \frac{a_j^{\sigma_j/(\sigma_j-1)}}{a_i^{\sigma_i/(\sigma_i-1)}}, \qquad p_{ij}^{**} \equiv \frac{\gamma_j}{\gamma_i} \frac{(1-a_j)^{\sigma_j/(\sigma_j-1)}}{(1-a_i)^{\sigma_i/(\sigma_i-1)}}. \tag{59}$$

With $\sigma_i \neq \sigma_j$, (51), (48), any relative price has a unique *reversal* price ratio:

$$\bar{p}_{ij} = p_{ij}(\bar{\omega}) = \frac{\gamma_j a_j^{\frac{\sigma_j}{\sigma_j-1}} \left[1 + c_j \left(\frac{c_j}{c_i}\right)^{\frac{1-\sigma_j}{\sigma_j-\sigma_i}}\right]^{\frac{1}{\sigma_j-1}}}{\gamma_i a_i^{\frac{\sigma_i}{\sigma_i-1}} \left[1 + c_i \left(\frac{c_j}{c_i}\right)^{\frac{1-\sigma_i}{\sigma_j-\sigma_i}}\right]^{\frac{1}{\sigma_i-1}}}; \quad a_i = a_j, \quad \bar{p}_{ij} = \frac{\gamma_j}{\gamma_i}. \tag{60}$$

Proposition 1. *The graphs of the relative prices, $p_{ij}(\omega)$, (51) – the CES factor-price-commodity-price (FPCP) correspondence – have limits, classified by σ_i, as follows:*

$$\sigma_i < 1, \quad \sigma_j < 1 : \quad \lim_{\omega \to 0} p_{ij} = p_{ij}^*, \quad \lim_{\omega \to \infty} p_{ij} = p_{ij}^{**}, \qquad (61)$$

$$\sigma_i > 1, \quad \sigma_j > 1 : \quad \lim_{\omega \to 0} p_{ij} = p_{ij}^{**}, \quad \lim_{\omega \to \infty} p_{ij} = p_{ij}^*, \qquad (62)$$

$$\sigma_i > 1, \quad \sigma_j < 1 : \quad \lim_{\omega \to 0} p_{ij} = 0, \quad \lim_{\omega \to \infty} p_{ij} = 0, \qquad (63)$$

$$\sigma_i < 1, \quad \sigma_j > 1 : \quad \lim_{\omega \to 0} p_{ij} = \infty, \quad \lim_{\omega \to \infty} p_{ij} = \infty. \qquad (64)$$

The reversal price ratio, $\bar{p}_{ij} \equiv p_{ij}(\bar{\omega})$, (60), is always a maximum (iff $\sigma_i > \sigma_j$) or a minimum (iff $\sigma_j > \sigma_i$) [cf. Fig. 1]. For the substitution elasticities (61)-(63), the range of $p_{ij}(\omega)$, (51), is bounded. With $\gamma_i = \gamma_j$, and both substitutions elasticities, either small (61) or large (62), the range of $p_{ij}(\omega)$ becomes a narrow interval, and there will be only small differences between the values of p_{ij}^* and p_{ij}^{**}, (59), if a_i, a_j, have similar size [cf. Table 4].

Iff $\sigma_i = \sigma_j \neq 1$, the functions, $p_{ij}(\omega)$, (52), are always monotonic, bounded, and increasing between p_{ij}^* and p_{ij}^{**}, iff $a_j > a_i$. Only the CD relative prices $p_{ij}(\omega)$, (49), are monotonic and unbounded, cf. Fig. 1.

Proof: First, results (61)-(62). With $\sigma_i < 1$ and $\sigma_j < 1$, the brackets in (51) converge to one at $\omega = 0$, which establishes the limiting $p = p^*$. For large ω, the numerator and denominator in (51) are approximately proportional to ω^{-1} with coefficients equal to the numerator and the denominator of p^{**}, (59). Similar arguments as above establish (62).

Second, results (63)-(64). With $\sigma_i > 1$ and $\sigma_j < 1$, the numerator in (51) converges to a constant and the denominator converges to infinity at $\omega = 0$, which establish the limiting value of $p = 0$. For large ω, the numerator of (51) converges to zero, whereas the denominator converges to a non-zero constant. Hence the limiting value of p is zero. Similar arguments as above establish (64).   ////

The concrete values of, p_{ij}^*, p_{ij}^{**} and $\bar{p}_{ij}$ can be calculated for any size of the CES parameters; however, for a clear quantitative understanding of the relevant interval for any relative price, we examine the *quotients* [cf. (59), (60)]

$$q^* = \frac{p_{ij}^{**}}{p_{ij}^*} = \frac{[(1-a_j)/a_j]^{\frac{\sigma_j}{\sigma_j - 1}}}{[(1-a_i)/a_i]^{\frac{\sigma_i}{\sigma_i - 1}}} = \frac{c_j^{\frac{1}{\sigma_j - 1}}}{c_i^{\frac{1}{\sigma_i - 1}}} , \quad \frac{\bar{p}_{ij}}{p_{ij}^{**}} = \frac{\bar{q}}{q^*}, \qquad (65)$$

$$\bar{q} = \frac{\bar{p}_{ij}}{p_{ij}^*} = \left[1 + c_j \, (c_j/c_i)^{\frac{1-\sigma_j}{\sigma_j - \sigma_i}}\right]^{\frac{1}{\sigma_j - 1}} \Big/ \left[1 + c_i \, (c_j/c_i)^{\frac{1-\sigma_i}{\sigma_j - \sigma_i}}\right]^{\frac{1}{\sigma_i - 1}}, \qquad (66)$$

$$a_i = a_j = a : \quad \bar{q} = a^{\frac{\sigma_j - \sigma_i}{(\sigma_i - 1)(\sigma_j - 1)}}. \qquad (67)$$

If $a_j = a_i = \frac{1}{2}$, then $q^* = 1$ and $\bar{q}$ form the *interval* of *relative prices*.

Although the numerical value of q^* is sensitive to its many parameter combinations, the *dominating* influences on the *deviation* of this quotient *from* $q^* = 1$ are the *extent* to which both, a_j, a_i, *differ* from the critical value $\frac{1}{2}$, and the extent to which both, σ_i, σ_j, *differ* from the critical value 1.

Regarding the *size* of the *quotient* q^*, let δ_l and d_l be:

$$A_{ji} = \frac{(1-a_j)/a_j}{(1-a_i)/a_i}, \quad \delta_l = A_{ji}^{\frac{\sigma_l}{\sigma_l - 1}}, \quad d_l = \left[\frac{1-a_l}{a_l}\right]^{\frac{\sigma_i - \sigma_j}{(\sigma_i - 1)(\sigma_j - 1)}} \quad (l = i, j).$$

(68)

Lemma 2. *Exact decompositions of the quotient* q^*, *(65), are:*

$$q^* = \delta_j \, d_i = \delta_i \, d_j.$$

(69)

Proof: With q^* from (65) and d_l from (68), we get (after reductions)

$$q^* = A_{ji}^{\frac{\sigma_j}{\sigma_j - 1}} d_i = A_{ji}^{\frac{\sigma_i}{\sigma_i - 1}} d_j,$$

(70)

which is (69).   ////
   From (65)-(68) it follows that

$$\lim_{\sigma_i, \sigma_j \to \infty} q^* = A_{ji}, \quad \lim_{\sigma_i, \sigma_j \to 0} q^* = 1.$$

(71)

We illustrate Lemma 2 in Tables 2-4.

	Table 2		
	$a_i \geq a_j$	$a_i \leq a_j$
	$A_{ji} \geq 1$	$A_{ji} \leq 1$
$\sigma_l > 1$	$\delta_l \geq 1$	$\delta_l \leq 1$
$\sigma_l < 1$	$\delta_l \leq 1$	$\delta_l \geq 1$

	Table 3	
	$a_l \leq \frac{1}{2}$	$a_l \geq \frac{1}{2}$
$\sigma_i \leq \sigma_j$	$d_l \geq 1$	$d_l \leq 1$
$\sigma_i \geq \sigma_j$	$d_l \leq 1$	$d_l \geq 1$

Table 4. Numerical illustrations of benchmark cases ($\gamma_i = \gamma_j = 1$).

a_i	a_j	σ_i	σ_j	A_{ji}	δ_i	δ_j	d_i	d_j	q^*	p_{ij}^*	p_{ij}^{**}	$\bar{p}_{ij}$	$\bar{q}$
0.3	0.25	0.1	0.1	1.29	0.97	0.97	1.00	1.00	0.97	1.02	0.99	–	–
0.3	0.25	0.4	0.3	1.29	0.85	0.90	1.22	1.30	1.10	0.81	0.89	1.01	1.24
0.8	0.25	0.3	0.2	12.0	0.34	0.54	0.78	1.22	0.42	1.29	0.54	1.29	1.00
0.3	0.40	0.6	0.7	0.64	1.94	2.80	0.49	0.71	1.38	1.39	1.93	0.91	0.65
0.3	0.30	0.6	0.7	1.00	1.00	1.00	0.49	0.49	0.49	2.73	1.35	1.00	0.37
0.4	0.30	0.6	0.7	1.56	0.52	0.36	0.71	0.49	0.25	4.20	1.07	0.92	0.22
0.3	0.25	1.6	1.5	1.29	1.95	2.13	1.33	1.44	2.82	0.39	1.09	1.11	2.86
0.3	0.25	2.0	1.9	1.29	1.65	1.70	1.10	1.13	1.87	0.60	1.11	1.11	1.87
0.3	0.25	4.0	4.0	1.29	1.40	1.40	1.00	1.00	1.40	0.78	1.10	–	–

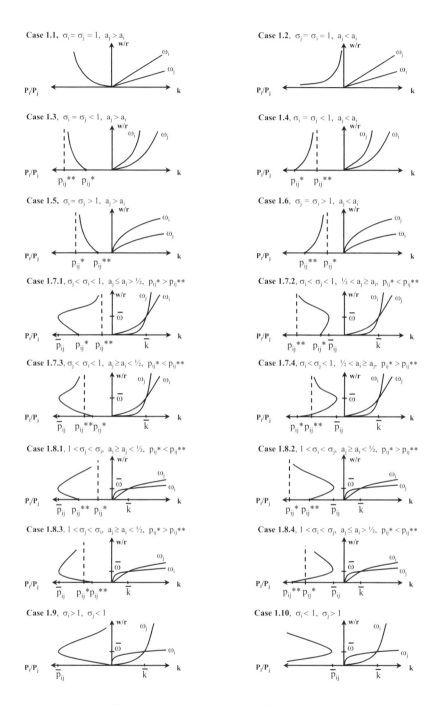

Fig. 1. FPCP correspondence $p_{ij}(\omega)$, [cf. (49), (51) and (52)].

Due to (9), the relationship between relative product (cost) prices and factor prices is not affected by factor endowments, or by any demand or any taxation/tariff system, specified in CGE models. Thus, as an *invariance*, this FPCP $p_{ij}(\omega)$, (51), is implicitly embedded in several applied CGE models (with (9) and CES technologies), and hence it can also be retrieved explicitly from (or check) presentations of the complete general equilibrium solution.

The well-known CGE calculations in Table 5 use CES parameters:

$$\gamma_i = 1.5, \ \gamma_j = 2.0, \ a_i = 0.4, \ a_j = 0.3, \ \sigma_i = 2.0, \ \sigma_j = 0.50 \qquad (72)$$

i.e., refers to Case 1.9, Fig. 1, with maximum here, $\bar{p}_{ij} = 1.35$, cf. (60).

Table 5. Computational General Equilibrium solutions,[2] and the FPCP correspondence, $p_{ij}(\omega)$, (51).

w	r	$\omega = w/r$	$p_{ij}(\omega)$	P_i	P_j	P_i/P_j
1.00	1.373	0.728	1.280	1.399	1.093	1.280
1.00	1.426	0.701	1.271	1.412	1.111	1.271
1.00	1.393	0.718	1.277	1.404	1.100	1.276
1.00	1.372	0.729	1.280	1.399	1.092	1.281
1.00	1.438	0.695	1.268	1.415	1.115	1.269

4 Preferences, Demand and Expenditure Shares of GDP

4.1 Consumption and Saving

On the demand side of the economy, the actual division of national income between saving and consumption is our first problem, posing major issues of long theoretical and empirical standing. However, attention here will only be given - as in NIPA accounting - to the accumulation of new productive capital (tangible assets), excluding intangibles such as all services, education (human capital), and portfolio & wealth evaluations ("capital gains") from entering NIPA saving accounts. Hence only the newly produced final goods of a few manufacturing, construction and building industries will enter the NIPA saving/investment share of GDP. Thus, with only one capital good ("equipment") industry, we have

$$Y = C + S, \quad s = S/Y = I/Y = P_1 Y_1/Y = s_1. \qquad (73)$$

Per capita saving/consumption, in any numeraire, are denoted by s_L/P_i, c_L/P_i,

$$s = S/Y = (S/L)/(Y/L) = s_L/y = (s_L/P_i)/(y/P_i), \quad y - s_L = c_L. \tag{74}$$

---

[2] Shoven and Whalley (1992), Tables 3.1 - 3.7.

Optimum paths for savings and consumption by a representative agent may be described in terms of the intertemporal utility functional:

$$U = \int_0^\infty u\left[\frac{c_L}{P_i}(t)\right] e^{-R[u(t)]}dt, \tag{75}$$

where $R[u(t)]$ is an *accumulated rate of time preference* by which future utility is discounted – and which summarizes the preference structure of the agent regarding the time profile of the continuous utility stream from present and future consumption, see Uzawa (1969, p. 630), (1968, p. 488). According to Uzawa (1969, p. 634), (1973, p. 58), if the *intertemporal preference* orderings are *homothetic*, then the *optimal* per capita saving (s_L/P_i) is separable and linear with respect income, (y/P_i), i.e.,

$$s_L/P_i = s_L(r, w, y) = s_L(r/P_i, w/P_i, y/P_i), \tag{76}$$
$$s_L/P_i = s_L(r/P_i, w/P_i, y/P_i) = s_L^*(r/P_i, w/P_i) \cdot (y/P_i). \tag{77}$$

Thus with (77) and (74) the overall saving rate (s) is solely determined by the "real" factor prices, and such that the saving rate (s) increases with the real rental rate and decreases in the real wages, i.e.,

$$s = s_L^*(r/P_i, w/P_i); \quad \partial s_L^*/\partial(r/P_i) > 0, \quad \partial s_L^*/\partial(w/P_i) < 0. \tag{78}$$

A further reduction in the arguments of saving function (78) may occur in a general equilibrium context with Pareto optimality [(cf. (16), (18) and (22)]

$$s = s_L^*\left[(r/P_i)(\omega), (w/P_i)(\omega)\right] = s_L^{**}(\omega), \tag{79}$$

which might allow the budget share (s) to be also formally handled by homothetic utility functions, applied to genuine consumer goods below. In the tradition of the Böhm-Bawerk & Fisherian theory of time preference, Koopmans (1960), Tinbergen (1960), Uzawa (1973, p. 59), (1968, p. 494), (1969, p. 630, 637), the *optimal* saving rate is essentially dependent on (increasing with) the *expected real rate of interest*, i_r^e, with its level being equal to the *marginal rate of time preference*, $\rho[u(t)]$, i.e., in short,

$$s = s(i_r^e), \quad (r/P_1)^e = i_r^e = \rho[u(t)]. \tag{80}$$

A serious *problem* is, however, that the saving functions (76)-(80) have not so far obtained generally accepted *functional forms*, and even less, been examined for critical values of fundamental *parameters*. Furthermore, the saving/investment share of GDP is not just a matter of optimizing consumer preferences (temporal/intertemporal). Actually, it needs to be based on joint considerations of the producer-consumer agent.

Hence, with some empirical support, we adopt a provisional assumption of mathematically treating the saving rate as a parametric ("fixed") constant:

$$s \;=\; s_1 \;=\; \text{constant (parametric variation)}. \qquad (81)$$

This assumption does not preclude seeing positive effects of relatively declining capital good prices on investment (capital stock accumulation), cf. (73). As to the observed long-run constancy of the gross private (household and business combined) saving rate, see Denison (1958, p.267), David & Scadding (1974, p.238), Tobin (1980). The constancy of the total *private saving* rate (81) may be interpreted, Tobin (1980, p.65), as an extension of the Modigliani-Miller theorem beyond *finance* to *real capital* accumulation.

4.2 Expenditure Systems and CES-Class Utility Preferences

The purpose of budget (expenditure) systems is to describe mathematically how in a certain period a given money amount of total consumption expenditures is allocated to item-specific expenditure categories. The key elements determining this budget allocation are, as usual, assumed to be consumer preferences, prices of consumer goods & services, and the given size of the total budget (expenditures). Rather than giving Marshallian demand or Hicks/Slutsky (compensated) demand functions for various preference functions, we need *explicit* analytical *expressions* of the *budget shares*, e_i (29), for here actually *solving* the static and dynamic general equilibrium systems.

We shall make use of a few benchmark specifications of preference (utility) functions - *direct*, $U(.)$, and *indirect utility*, $V(.)$ - cf. Mass-Colell et al. (1995, p. 56), Deaton & Muelbauer (1992, p. 38). Among many other references, we refer to, Silberberg & Suen (2001), Chung (1994), Wold (1952).

Introducing the notation of expenditure ("income") and price elasticities as, $\partial \ln Y_i / \partial \ln C \equiv E(Y_i, C)$, $\partial \ln Y_i / \partial \ln P_j \equiv E(Y_i, P_j)$, then demand (expenditure) systems must satisfy four basic, well-known, Frisch (1959, p.180), restrictions - which also must be met by our general equilibrium solutions:

Homogeneity: $\sum_{j=2}^{N} E(Y_i, P_j) + E(Y_i, C) = 0,$ $\qquad (82)$

Engel Aggregation : $\sum_{j=2}^{N} e_j \cdot E(Y_j, C) = 1,$ $\qquad (83)$

Cournot Aggregation : $\sum_{j=2}^{N} e_j \cdot E(Y_j, P_i) = - e_i < 0,$ $\qquad (84)$

Symmetry: $E(Y_i, P_j)/e_j + E(Y_i, C) = E(Y_j, P_i)/e_i + E(Y_j, C).$ (85)

Incidentally, note that any demand (expenditure) functions with *constant* non-unitary price and income elasticities *cannot* satisfy (83), except for a narrow range of the price and income variables involved, Wold (1952, p.106).

The CES form of the direct/indirect utility functions is the only functional form with the property of *self-duality*, i.e., the dual can be expressed exactly with same parameters; see, Samuelson (1965), Houthakker (1965).

We have [Silberberg & Suen (2001, p. 359), Chung (1994, p. 58), Shoven & Whalley (1992, p. 45, 96)]: $\alpha_i > 0$, $\sum_{i=2}^{N} \alpha_i = 1$,

$$\textbf{CES:} \quad U(Y_2, ..., Y_N) = \gamma_u \left[\sum_{i=2}^{N} \alpha_i Y_i^{\frac{\sigma_u - 1}{\sigma_u}} \right]^{\frac{\sigma_u}{\sigma_u - 1}} \tag{86}$$

$$V(P_2, \cdot, P_N, C) = \frac{1}{\gamma_u} \left[\sum_{j=2}^{N} \alpha_j^{\sigma_u} [C/P_j]^{\sigma_u - 1} \right]^{\frac{1}{\sigma_u - 1}}$$

$$= \frac{1}{\gamma_u} \left[\sum_{j=2}^{N} \alpha_j^{\sigma_u} p_{ij}^{\sigma_u - 1} \right]^{\frac{1}{\sigma_u - 1}} C/P_i, \tag{87}$$

$$e_i = \frac{P_i Y_i}{C} = \frac{\alpha_i^{\sigma_u} P_i^{1-\sigma_u}}{\sum_{j=2}^{N} \alpha_j^{\sigma_u} P_j^{1-\sigma_u}} = \left[\sum_{j=2}^{N} \left[\frac{\alpha_j}{\alpha_i} \right]^{\sigma_u} p_{ij}^{\sigma_u - 1} \right]^{-1} \tag{88}$$

$$e_i = e_i(p_{i2}, ..., p_{iN}) = \left[1 + \sum_{j=2, j \neq i}^{N} \left(\frac{\alpha_j}{\alpha_i} \right)^{\sigma_u} p_{ij}^{\sigma_u - 1} \right]^{-1} \quad (i = 2, ..., N). \tag{89}$$

Linking the relative *consumer prices* of e_i, (89), to *cost prices*, (22) and (51), we obtain

$$e_i(\omega) = \left[1 + \sum_{j=2, j \neq i}^{N} (\alpha_j/\alpha_i)^{\sigma_u} p_{ij}(\omega)^{\sigma_u - 1} \right]^{-1}, \quad i > 1, \quad 0 < e_i(\omega) < 1. \tag{90}$$

Lemma 3. *The limiting consumer expenditure shares – with CES technologies (41–43) and CES utility functions (86) – are given by*

$$\sigma_u \neq 1 : \quad \forall i \ \sigma_i < 1 : \quad \lim_{\omega \to 0} e_i(\omega) = e_i^*, \quad \lim_{\omega \to \infty} e_i(\omega) = e_i^{**}, \tag{91}$$

$$\sigma_u \neq 1 : \quad \forall i \ \sigma_i > 1 : \quad \lim_{\omega \to 0} e_i(\omega) = e_i^{**}, \quad \lim_{\omega \to \infty} e_i(\omega) = e_i^*, \tag{92}$$

where

$$e_i^* = \left[1 + \sum_{j=2,j\neq i}^{N} (\alpha_j/\alpha_i)^{\sigma_u} p_{ij}^{*\sigma_u-1}\right]^{-1} \quad i > 1, \quad \sum_{i=2}^{N} e_i^* = 1, \quad (93)$$

$$e_i^{**} = \left[1 + \sum_{j=2,j\neq i}^{N} (\alpha_j/\alpha_i)^{\sigma_u} p_{ij}^{**\sigma_u-1}\right]^{-1} \quad i > 1, \quad \sum_{i=2}^{N} e_i^{**} = 1, \quad (94)$$

and p_{ij}^*, p_{ij}^{**} are given by (59), cf. Proposition 1.
  When some of the industries have CES substitution elasticities larger and smaller than one, the limiting expenditure shares become:

$$\sigma_u < 1, \ \sigma_i > 1 > \sigma_j :$$
$$\lim_{\omega\to 0,\infty} e_i(\omega) = 0; \ \lim_{\omega\to 0} e_j(\omega) = \underline{e}_j^*, \ \lim_{\omega\to\infty} e_j(\omega) = \underline{e}_j^{**}, \quad (95)$$

$$\sigma_u > 1, \ \sigma_i > 1 > \sigma_j :$$
$$\lim_{\omega\to 0} e_i(\omega) = \bar{e}_i^{**}, \ \lim_{\omega\to\infty} e_i(\omega) = \bar{e}_i^*, \ \lim_{\omega\to 0,\infty} e_j(\omega) = 0, \quad (96)$$

where

$$\bar{e}_i^* = \left[1 + \sum_{j=2,j\neq i,\sigma_j>1} (\alpha_j/\alpha_i)^{\sigma_u} p_{ij}^{*\sigma_u-1}\right]^{-1}, \quad \bar{e}^* = \sum_{i=2}^{N} \bar{e}_i^* \leq 1, \quad (97)$$

$$\bar{e}_i^{**} = \left[1 + \sum_{j=2,j\neq i,\sigma_j>1} (\alpha_j/\alpha_i)^{\sigma_u} p_{ij}^{**\sigma_u-1}\right]^{-1}, \quad \bar{e}^{**} = \sum_{i=2}^{N} \bar{e}_i^{**} \leq 1, \quad (98)$$

$$\underline{e}_i^* = \left[1 + \sum_{j=2,j\neq i,\sigma_j<1} (\alpha_j/\alpha_i)^{\sigma_u} p_{ij}^{*\sigma_u-1}\right]^{-1}, \quad \underline{e}^* = \sum_{i=2}^{N} \underline{e}_i^* \leq 1, \quad (99)$$

$$\underline{e}_i^{**} = \left[1 + \sum_{j=2,j\neq i,\sigma_j<1} (\alpha_j/\alpha_i)^{\sigma_u} p_{ij}^{**\sigma_u-1}\right]^{-1}, \quad \underline{e}^{**} = \sum_{i=2}^{N} \underline{e}_i^{**} \leq 1, \quad (100)$$

$$\bar{e}^* + \underline{e}^* = 1, \quad \bar{e}^{**} + \underline{e}^{**} = 1. \quad (101)$$

Proof: The limiting shares (91)-(94) follow from (90), (61) and (62). The limiting shares (95)-(100) follow from (90) and (63) and (64). ////

4.3 Homothetic and Non-Homothetic Consumer Preferences

The main deficiency of many conventional and in fact any homothetic direct utility function is that all the consumer goods have an "income (C)" elasticity of one. Hence, the class of indirect utility functions attracts more attention. A *flexible* expenditure system satisfying (83) was first proposed by Leser (1941), and it was related to the indirect addilog by Houthakker (1960). We define **Indirect Addilog Utility** as follows [cf. Silberberg & Suen (2001, p. 360), Chung (1994, p. 42)]:

$$\alpha_i > 0, \quad \sum_{i=2}^{N} \alpha_i = 1, \quad 0 < \beta_i < 1,$$

$$V(P_2, \cdots, P_N, C) = \gamma_v \sum_{i=2}^{N} \alpha_i \, (C/P_i)^{\beta_i} = \gamma_v \sum_{j=2}^{N} \alpha_j p_{ij}^{\beta_j} \, (C/P_i)^{\beta_j} ,$$

$$\tag{102}$$

$$e_i = \frac{\alpha_i \beta_i (C/P_i)^{\beta_i}}{\displaystyle\sum_{j=2}^{N} \alpha_j \beta_j (C/P_j)^{\beta_j}} = \left[\sum_{j=2}^{N} \frac{\alpha_j \beta_j}{\alpha_i \beta_i} \frac{P_i^{\beta_i}}{P_j^{\beta_j}} C^{\beta_j - \beta_i} \right]^{-1}$$

$$= \left[\sum_{j=2}^{N} \frac{\alpha_j \beta_j}{\alpha_i \beta_i} p_{ij}^{\beta_j} \left(\frac{C}{P_i} \right)^{\beta_j - \beta_i} \right]^{-1} \tag{103}$$

$$\forall j \; \beta_j = \beta : \; e_i(\omega) = \left[1 + \sum_{j=2, j \neq i}^{N} [\alpha_j / \alpha_i] \, p_{ij}(\omega)^{\beta} \right]^{-1} \tag{104}$$

$$e_i(\omega, L, K) = \left\{ 1 + \sum_{j=2, j \neq i}^{N} \frac{\alpha_j \beta_j}{\alpha_i \beta_i} p_{ij}(\omega)^{\beta_j} \left[\frac{C}{P_i}(\omega, L, K) \right]^{\beta_j - \beta_i} \right\}^{-1} \tag{105}$$

The budget system (104), with $\beta = \sigma_u - 1 > 0$, is seen to be a subsystem of the homothetic CES system (90) already characterized in Lemma 3.

With $\beta_i \neq \beta_j$ the non-homothetic indirect addilog utility function has budget shares (105) with terms $C/P_i = (1 - s)Y/P_i$, cf. (73), where Y/P_i is well-defined in terms of ω, L, K, see (25). With the positivity restrictions above on α_i, β_i, the budget shares (104-105), always satisfies $0 < e_i < 1$.

Without imposing positivity restrictions on all β_i, but just *assuming*

$$\alpha_i^\star > 0, \quad \sum_{i=2}^{N} \alpha_i^\star = 1, \quad \beta_i < 1, \tag{106}$$

the Houthakker (addilog) expenditure system (105) is *generalized* to:

$$e_i(\omega, L, K) = \left\{ 1 + \sum_{j=2, j \neq i}^{N} (\alpha_j^\star / \alpha_i^\star) p_{ij}(\omega)^{\beta_j} \left[\frac{C}{P_i}(\omega, L, K) \right]^{\beta_j - \beta_i} \right\}^{-1}$$

$$\tag{107}$$

Still, (106-107) satisfies $0 < e_i(\omega, L, K) < 1$. The *indirect* utility function of this generalized budget system is *unknown* (and may never be given in closed form). But the empirical application of (107), e.g., Somermeyer (1972), Jensen (1980), works reasonably well; its *Engel curve patterns* allows negative, zero, and positive "income elasticities" (the upper bound may be greater than two), and collectively, the condition (83) is satisfied by (107).

Finally, we consider the **Translog Indirect Utility:**

$$\alpha_j > 0, \quad \sum_{j=2}^{N} \alpha_j = 1, \quad \beta_{ij} = \beta_{ji},$$

$$\ln V(P_2, \cdots, P_N, C) = \ln \alpha_0 + \sum_{j=2}^{N} \alpha_j \ln \frac{C}{P_j} + \frac{1}{2} \sum_{i=2}^{N} \sum_{j=2}^{N} \beta_{ij} \ln \frac{C}{P_i} \ln \frac{C}{P_j},$$

$$(108)$$

$$e_i = \frac{P_i Y_i}{C} = \frac{\alpha_i + \sum_{j=2}^{N} \beta_{ij} \ln(C/P_j)}{1 + \sum_{k=2}^{N} \sum_{j=2}^{N} \beta_{kj} \ln(C/P_j)}, \qquad (109)$$

$$e_i = \frac{\alpha_i + \sum_{j=2}^{N} \beta_{ij} \ln(C/P_j)}{\alpha_i + \sum_{j=2}^{N} \beta_{ij} \ln(C/P_j) + \sum_{i \neq k=2}^{N} \left[\alpha_k + \sum_{j=2}^{N} \beta_{kj} \ln(C/P_j) \right]}. \qquad (110)$$

This *translog* indirect utility function, Christensen, Jorgenson, and Lau (1971, 1975), Silberberg & Suen (2001, p. 361), Chung (1994, p. 68), is one of the most widely used flexible functional forms in empirical demand analysis. It may be interpreted as a second-order local approximation to an arbitrary indirect utility function. Its budget share is here presented in a proper explicit forms for our purposes.

The usual *monotonicity* property of *preferences* is satisfied by imposing on (108) the condition below (LHS of the implication) [see Chung (1994, p. 69)]:

$$\forall k : \quad \alpha_k + \sum_{j=2}^{N} \beta_{kj} \ln(C/P_j) > 0 \; \Rightarrow \; \forall i : 0 < e_i < 1. \qquad (111)$$

This is a sufficient condition, cf. (110), for relevant shares, e_i, too (RHS of the implication). Rewriting

$$\ln(C/P_j) = \ln[C/P_i \cdot P_i/P_j] = \ln(C/P_i \cdot p_{ij}) = \ln(C/P_i) + \ln p_{ij},$$

we obtain (110) restated (dividing by its numerator) conveniently as:

$$e_i(\omega, L, K) = \left\{ 1 + \frac{\sum_{i \neq k=2}^{N} \left[\alpha_k + \sum_{j=2}^{N} \beta_{kj} \ln p_{ij} + \ln(C/P_i) \sum_{j=2}^{N} \beta_{kj} \right]}{\alpha_i + \ln(C/P_i) \sum_{j=2}^{N} \beta_{ij}} \right\}^{-1}$$

$$(112)$$

In the non-homothetic case, the terms, C/P_i, (112) are - as mentioned above for the non-homothetic addilog - well-defined in the arguments of e_i, (112).

By direct inspection of the budget share, (109), a more tractable and simpler sufficient condition than (111) for having $0 < e_i < 1$ is

$$\forall i : \; [\forall k : \;\; P_k \leq C \;\; \wedge \;\; \beta_{ik} \leq \sum_{j=2}^{N} \beta_{kj} \; \Rightarrow \; 0 < e_i < 1] \quad (113)$$

The implication (113) follows here from using $\ln(C/P_k) > 0$ and the symmetry $\beta_{ij} = \beta_{ji}$ in (109). Accordingly, (113) also applies to budget shares, (112). Requiring in, (113), that all unit prices, P_k, are less than total expenditure, C, is hardly any practical restriction at all; such luxury goods are ignored.

For the homothetic translog with the restrictions

$$\sum_{j=2}^{N} \beta_{kj} = 0 \quad (k = 2, ..., N), \quad (114)$$

the budget shares e_i become (cf. (112))

$$e_i(\omega) = \alpha_i \, [1 - \sum_{j=2}^{N} \beta_{ij} \ln p_{ij}(\omega)\,]^{-1} \quad (i = 2, ..., N). \quad (115)$$

Besides (114), we must evidently impose further parameter restrictions on β_{ij} or indirectly upon the sizes of the relative prices, p_{ij}, for having , $0 < e_i < 1$, in (115). However, we shall not pursue such restrictions, since the homothetic translog has little factual application. With translog, it is the *non-homothetic* version and its richer *Engel curve patterns* that makes it attractive/useful.

5 Walrasian General Equilibrium of Multi-Sector Economies

The *demand side* of the multisector economy is expressed by the respective GDP expenditure shares, s_i, derived from the consumer budget shares, e_i, in section 4. The *supply side* of the economy – operating under constant returns to scale and with full (10-11) and Pareto-efficient factor utilization, (16) – is always summarized by sectorial factor allocation fractions λ_{L_i}, λ_{K_i}, which in turn are determined by s_i and the sectorial cost shares ϵ_{L_i}, ϵ_{K_i}, (33).

Theorem 1. *The Walrasian equilibrium (competitive general equilibrium) states, – by market clearing prices on the commodity/factor markets and Pareto efficient endowments allocations – are, with homogeneous production functions of degree one, and with any homothetic preferences, given by :* $\forall k \in R_+, \forall \omega \in \Omega$, *(34), (28), (30), (90), (104), (115),*

$$k = \frac{\omega \delta_K(\omega)}{\delta_L(\omega)} = \omega \sum_{i=1}^{N} s_i(\omega)\epsilon_{K_i}(\omega) \left/ \sum_{i=1}^{N} s_i(\omega)\epsilon_{L_i}(\omega) = \Psi(\omega). \right. \quad (116)$$

Corollary 1. *With CES sector technologies and any homothetic utility function, the Walrasian equilibrium* $k = \Psi(\omega)$ *becomes by (116) and (47):*

$$k = \frac{\omega \sum_{i=1}^{N} s_i(\omega)(1 + c_i \omega^{1-\sigma_i})^{-1}}{1 - \sum_{i=1}^{N} s_i(\omega)(1 + c_i \omega^{1-\sigma_i})^{-1}} = \Psi(\omega). \qquad (117)$$

Theorem 2. *For sector technologies with constant returns to scale and non-homothetic utility functions, Walrasian equilibrium states are given by (34),(28), (30), (105), (107), (112) and*

$$\frac{K}{L} = \frac{\omega \delta_K(\omega, L, K)}{\delta_L(\omega, L, K)} = \frac{\omega \sum_{i=1}^{N} s_i(\omega, L, K) \epsilon_{K_i}(\omega)}{\sum_{i=1}^{N} s_i(\omega, L, K) \epsilon_{L_i}(\omega)} = \Upsilon(\omega, L, K). \qquad (118)$$

Corollary 2. *With CES sector technologies, the Walrasian equilibrium (118) changes with (47) into:*

$$K/L = \frac{\omega \sum_{i=1}^{N} s_i(\omega, L, K)(1 + c_i \omega^{1-\sigma_i})^{-1}}{1 - \sum_{i=1}^{N} s_i(\omega, L, K)(1 + c_i \omega^{1-\sigma_i})^{-1}} = \Upsilon(\omega, L, K). \qquad (119)$$

Locus expressions (118) and (119) give ω *implicitly as a function (graph) of (L,K):*

$$\omega = \Lambda(L, K). \qquad (120)$$

Proof: The theorems and corollaries are obtained by turning Walras' law (identity), (34), into the respective Walrasian equilibrium conditions, (116)-(119). Rather than relying on fixed-point methods for searching (iteration) the equilibrium prices (vector) of numerous supply and demand equations of goods and factor markets, our general equilibrium solution procedure is formulated in variables (shares), having simple economic and observable NIPA counterparts. Since relative commodity prices are endogenous variables, they are by construction properly eliminated from our "structural" general equilibrium equations. Hence we end up with a "reduced" form of just one equation (explicit or implicit) between the remaining endogenous *relative factor prices* of general equilibrium and the exogenous (given) *factor endowments*. ////

The *competitive general equilibrium* functions, $k = \Psi(\omega)$, $\omega = \Lambda(L, K)$, are crucial for inquiring into the statics, comparative statics, and dynamics of multi-sector economies, and they are called the *factor endowment-factor price* (FEFP) *correspondence*. Having obtained ω from (116), we can go back through (22), (51), (90) (47), (32), (33) and (24) to get the associated general equilibrium values of all other endogenous variables (sector outputs, allocation fractions of inputs, income shares, relative commodity prices).

Regarding the *shape* of the graph of Ψ, (117), it is evident that, if *all* substitution elasticities are *larger* than one, $\sigma_i > 1$ for $i = 2, ..., N$, then the numerator (denominator) expression in (117) will increase (decrease) [cf. ϵ_{K_i}, ϵ_{L_i} (15)], which always ensures that the Walrasian locus $\Psi(\omega)$, (117), is *monotonically* increasing. When all σ_i are *less* than one, $\sigma_i < 1$, only a detailed examination will reveal the *global* and *local* shape of the graph.

Proposition 2. *The graphs of the Walrasian equilibrium, $\Psi(\omega)$,(117), are in Fig. 1 to be located between the extreme monotonic CES, ω_i-curves, (46). For any value of the GDP shares, s_i, and for any size of the sectorial substitution elasticities, $\sigma_i, i = 1, ..., N$, the functions, $\Psi(\omega)$, have the limit properties:*

$$\lim_{\omega \to 0} \Psi(\omega) = 0, \quad \lim_{\omega \to \infty} \Psi(\omega) = \infty, \tag{121}$$

$$\lim_{\omega \to 0} \Psi(\omega)/\Psi'(\omega) = 0, \quad \lim_{\omega \to \infty} \Psi(\omega)/\Psi'(\omega) = \infty. \tag{122}$$

With (117), the elasticities, $E(k, \omega)$, of $\Psi(\omega)$ have the finite limits:

$$\forall i : \sigma_i < 1 : \lim_{\omega \to 0} E(k, \omega) = \lim_{\omega \to \infty} E(k, \omega) = \max_i \sigma_i, \tag{123}$$

$$\forall i : \sigma_i > 1 : \lim_{\omega \to 0} E(k, \omega) = \lim_{\omega \to \infty} E(k, \omega) = \min_i \sigma_i, \tag{124}$$

$$\exists i, j : \sigma_i > 1 > \sigma_j : \lim_{\omega \to 0} E(k, \omega) = \lim_{\omega \to \infty} E(k, \omega) = 1. \tag{125}$$

Proof: The limits (121)-(122) are seen immediately from (117). The limits (123)-(125) follow from the formulas (116) and (117):

$$E(k, \omega) = \Psi'(\omega)\omega/\Psi(\omega) = 1 + E(\delta_K, \omega) - E(1 - \delta_K, \omega), \tag{126}$$

$$E(\delta_{K,\omega}) = \delta'_K(\omega)\omega/\delta_K, \quad E(1 - \delta_K, \omega) = -\frac{\delta'_K(\omega)\omega}{1 - \delta_K}. \tag{127}$$

In case of *constant* s_i, the numerators of (127), $\pm \delta'_K(\omega)\omega$, go to zero for both $\omega \to 0$ and $\omega \to \infty$, as is seen by simple calculations. The denominators of (127), δ_K, $1 - \delta_K$, go to $\bar{s}$ or $\underline{s}$ for $\omega \to 0$ and $\omega \to \infty$ in accordance with Table 6. Hence in case of, $0 < \bar{s} < 1$, cf. Table 6 (rows 1,3), the last two terms of (126) go to zero - giving (125). In case of, $\bar{s} = 0, 1$, one term of (126) goes to zero, while the other goes to the dominating power, in some cases seen by use of lHospital. This proves (123)-(124).

In the case of *variable* $s_i(\omega)$, we just have to correct the proof above by adding the limits of $s'_i(\omega)\omega/s_i(\omega)$, which, however, are both zero, since the budget shares $e_i(\omega)$ have specific limits e_i^* and e_i^{**} for the respective utility functions, cf. (91)-(100), (104) and (115).   ////

6 Dynamics and Evolution of Multi-Sector Economies

In the multi-sectoral planning literature, we often read statements like that of, e.g., Johansen (1974, p. 22):

> "The *growth process* is generated by the following *factors*, all of which are considered to be *exogenously* determined : a) Total investment, b) Growth in population; working and total, c) Growth in productivity; shifts in production functions over time, d) Changes in exogenous demand; mainly government and net foreign demand."

This broad view of the exogeneity concept refers to exogeneity (separability) assumptions of rather diverse nature. Let us consider those above in reverse order.

Some "applied/planning" growth models may include a *public sector* with government expenditure and taxation assumptions/specifications, but this sector can properly be *excluded* for other theoretical/analytical purposes. Similarly, some growth models may include *international* trade and international factor mobility. Certainly, open and in particular small open economies operate differently from closed economies, but for obtaining some actual insights about economic evolution, a relevant *closed* (global) economy growth model may suffice. Next, "shifts" in production (or utility) functions refer to "*parametric*" changes. Since most economic parameters are not "natural constants" and occasionally undergo critical changes, an important object of growth models is to qualitatively understand and identify the crucial parameters involved and their critical *numerical* values. Regarding *labour endowments* (population), no attention has so far been directed to its exogenously given size. As a state variable in a dynamic model, it may still be treated, without violating the general equilibrium model above, as *evolving exogenously* with specified parameters.

On the contrary, however, the time paths of total investments and *capital endowments* cannot be *extrapolated exogenously* without *violating the general equilibrium solutions* of Theorem 1-2. A coherent general equilibrium evolution for the *capital endowments* in continuous time can only be derived from consistently integrating the *endogenous output* paths of our sector 1, i.e., the *macrodynamic* role of the capital good industry (*machinery*) in growth models of multi-industry-economies must be carefully studied.

The equations of *factor accumulation* for multi-sector growth models, with two primary factors and flexible constant return-to-scale sector technologies, are formally given by (δ : the depreciation rate of capital),

$$dL/dt \equiv \dot{L} = nL, \tag{128}$$

$$dK/dt \equiv \dot{K} = Y_1 - \delta K = Ly_1 l_1 - \delta K = L[f_1(k_1)l_1 - \delta k]. \tag{129}$$

6.1 General Equilibrium Dynamics with Homothetic Preferences

In the general equilibrium models of multi-sector economies, k_1 and l_1 in (129) are through ω, (16), (116) and (117) *uniquely* determined by the *factor* endowments *ratio* k, cf. (47). Hence, the accumulation equations (128) and (129) become *autonomous* (time invariant) *differential equations* in the state variables L and K and represent a standard *homogeneous dynamic system*,

$$\dot{L} = Ln \equiv L\mathbf{f}(k), \tag{130}$$
$$\dot{K} = L\left\{ f_1(k_1[\Psi^{-1}(k)])l_1[\Psi^{-1}(k)] - \delta k \right\} \equiv L\mathbf{g}(k), \ L \neq 0. \tag{131}$$

As $\mathbf{g}(k)$ in (131) is an intricate composite function of k, we rewrite $\mathbf{g}(k)$ in alternative forms by (129), (25) and (26):

$$\dot{K} = s_1 Y/P_1 - \delta K = Ls_1(\omega + k)f_1'(k_1) - \delta K \tag{132}$$
$$= Lk[s_1 f_1'(k_1)/\delta_K - \delta] = L\mathbf{g}(k), \quad Lk = K, \tag{133}$$

where to succinctly express and decompose the governing functions of capital accumulation (132) - the bounded variable $\delta_K(k)$ is mainly a formal auxiliary term helpful in evaluating concrete cases.

From the *governing* functions $\mathbf{g}(k)$ and $\mathbf{f}(k)$, (130)–(133), the *director* function $h(k)$ that controls $dk/dt \equiv \dot{k}$ takes the form $h(k) \equiv \mathbf{g}(k) - k\mathbf{f}(k)$,

$$\dot{k} = h(k) = k\left[\frac{s_1 f_1'[k_1[\omega(k)]]}{\delta_K[\omega(k)]} - (n + \delta) \right], \quad \omega(k) = \Psi^{-1}(k). \tag{134}$$

The dynamic system (134) in k is difficult to evaluate *quantitatively* and generally analytically intractable; e.g., if $\sigma_i \neq \sigma_j$, then, $k = \Psi(\omega)$, (116) can not be inverted (although Ψ^{-1} exists) in closed form. But $k = \Psi(\omega)$, (116), are *continuously differentiable* functions of ω, and dynamics in k can be converted into *dual autonomous dynamics* in ω:

$$\dot{\omega} = \frac{\dot{k}}{dk/d\omega} = \frac{h(k)}{dk/d\omega} = \frac{h(\Psi[\omega])}{\Psi'(\omega)} \equiv \hbar(\omega). \tag{135}$$

Hence we get (cf. (134))

$$\hbar(\omega) = \frac{\Psi(\omega)}{\Psi'(\omega)}\left[\frac{s_1 f_1'[k_1(\omega)]}{\delta_K(\omega)} - (n + \delta) \right] \tag{136}$$

$$= \frac{\omega}{E(k,\omega)}\left[\frac{s_1 f_1'[k_1(\omega)]}{\delta_K(\omega)} - (n + \delta) \right]. \tag{137}$$

With CES technologies, from (137), (32), (30), (47), (81), we have

$$\hbar(\omega) = \frac{\Psi(\omega)}{\Psi'(\omega)} \left[\frac{s_1 \gamma_1 a_1^{\frac{\sigma_1}{\sigma_1 - 1}} (1 + c_1 \omega^{1-\sigma_1})^{1/(\sigma_1 - 1)}}{\sum_{i=1}^{N} s_i(\omega)(1 + c_i \omega^{1-\sigma_i})^{-1}} - (n + \delta) \right] \quad (138)$$

with $\Psi(\omega)$ given in (117).

6.2 Existence and Uniqueness of Steady States or Persistent Growth

The complete set (family) of $k(t)$ solutions to the dynamic systems (134) is *qualitatively* described and classified by the following theorem.

Theorem 3. *The multi-sector growth models (128) have no positive, stationary $k(t)$-solution $[k(t) = 0$ is attractor$]$, iff*

$$\forall k > 0 : \bar{\mathbf{b}}_1 < ([n + \delta]/s_1)\delta_\kappa(k) \quad (139)$$

and have at least one steady state [ray path in (L, K)-space], iff [cf. (3)]

$$\exists k > 0 : ([n + \delta]/s_1)\delta_K(k) \in J_1. \quad (140)$$

The stationary capital-labor ratios $k(t) = \kappa$ for all t are obtained by

$$f_1'[k_1(\kappa)] = ([n + \delta]/s_1)\delta_K(\kappa). \quad (141)$$

With existence (140), a sufficient condition for a unique root of $h(k)$ is

$$\forall k > 0 : E(h(k)/k, k) < 0 \Leftrightarrow \forall \omega \in \Omega : E(k, \omega) \geq 1. \quad (142)$$

The time paths of the growth model solutions, $k(t)$, display persistent growth – $\lim_{t \to \infty} k(t) = \infty$ – if and only if

$$\forall k > 0 : \underline{\mathbf{b}}_1 > ([n + \delta]/s_1)\delta_\kappa(k). \quad (143)$$

Proof: The set of solutions to (134) depends entirely on the *shape* of the *director* function, $h(k)$, and the *number* of roots of $h(k)$. The existence of nonzero roots requires that $([n + \delta]/s_1)\delta_\kappa(k)$ belongs to the range of f_1' as stated in (140). If no positive root exists, we have either the case (139) with origo as attractor, or the case (143) with persistent growth.

   If a root of (141) exists, a unique attractor in the interval stated in (140) always occurs with a global negative sign of the elasticity, $E(h(k)/k, k) < 0$, which can be derived from (134); cf. (142), (123)-(125) and Jensen [1994, p. 138, p. 129], [2003, p. 73].   ////

6.3 Dynamics of MSG Models with CES Sector Technologies

Qualitative properties of the family of *Walrasian general equilibrium solutions* $k(t)$ in multi-sector growth models with CES technologies are summarized as follows:

Theorem 4. *For the multi-sector growth models (128)-(131) with CES technologies, the sufficient conditions for the existence of at least one positive steady-state solution are* [*no positive, attractive, steady state solution* κ *(141) exists with the inequalities of (144-145), RHS, reversed*]:

$$\forall i \; \sigma_i < 1: \quad \bar{\mathbf{b}}_1 = \gamma_1 a_1^{\frac{\sigma_1}{\sigma_1 - 1}} > (n + \delta)/s_1. \tag{144}$$

With only assuming $\sigma_1 < 1$, *(144) is generalized to,* $[\beta = 1 + \frac{1-s_1}{s_1}\underline{e}^*]$

$$\bar{\mathbf{b}}_1 = \gamma_1 a_1^{\frac{\sigma_1}{\sigma_1 - 1}} > \frac{(n+\delta)\underline{s}}{s_1} = \begin{cases} (n+\delta)\beta & \text{for } \sigma_u < 1, \\ n+\delta & \text{for } \sigma_u > 1. \end{cases} \tag{145}$$

If $\sigma_1 \leq 1$ *(sufficient condition), persistent growth of* $k(t)$ *is impossible. If* $\sigma_1 > 1$, *necessary and sufficient conditions for* $\lim_{t \to \infty} k(t) = \infty$ *are:*

$$\forall i \; \sigma_i > 1: \quad \underline{\mathbf{b}}_1 = \gamma_1 a_1^{\frac{\sigma_1}{\sigma_1 - 1}} > (n + \delta)/s_1. \tag{146}$$

With only assuming $\sigma_1 > 1$, *(146) is generalized to,* $[\bar{\beta} = 1 + \frac{1-s_1}{s_1}\bar{e}^*]$

$$\underline{\mathbf{b}}_1 = \gamma_1 a_1^{\frac{\sigma_1}{\sigma_1 - 1}} > \frac{(n+\delta)\bar{s}}{s_1} = \begin{cases} (n+\delta)\bar{\beta} & \text{for } \sigma_u > 1, \\ n+\delta & \text{for } \sigma_u < 1, \end{cases} \tag{147}$$

except that (147) is occasionally not sufficient for small initial values.

Proof: The proof proceeds with the dual version, $\hbar(\omega)$. The term $\Psi(\omega)/\Psi'(\omega)$ has no influence on these limit analyses, cf. Proposition 2.

Assume first that $\sigma_1 < 1$. The fraction in the large bracket (138) goes to zero for $\omega \to \infty$; hence, there are no permanent increasing solutions of $\omega(t)$. If (144)-(145) are satisfied, then this fraction passes at least once monotonically through the constant, when ω goes from zero to infinity. The difference $\underline{s}$ in the constant comes from the denominator taking values 1 or $\underline{s}$ for $\omega \to 0$, depending on the size of other σ_i. If the inequalities are reversed, then $\hbar(\omega)$ is negative. The role of $\underline{s}$ in (145) follows from (138), (31) and (91)-(101).

Second, assume $\sigma_1 > 1$: The fraction in the large bracket (138) goes to infinity for $\omega \to 0$. If and only if (146)-(147) are satisfied, then this fraction eventually remains above the constant, when ω goes from zero to infinity. The difference s_1 in the constant comes from the denominator taking values 1 or $\bar{s}$ for $\omega \to \infty$, depending on the size of other σ_i. Hence $\hbar(\omega)$ is positive for large values of k. If the inequalities are reversed, then $\hbar(\omega)$ eventually becomes negative. The necessary conditions (146) are also sufficient, as $k(k)$ is, with respectively $\sigma_i > 1$ and $\sigma_1 > 1$, monotonically decreasing, but remain above RHS values, (146). The role of $\bar{s}$ in (147) follows from (31), (138) and (91-101).   ////

Theorem 4 shows clearly that the *global existence problem* of *steady states* (κ) or *persistent* growth of $k(t)$ depends on the *size* of the key parameters: σ_i, a_1, γ_1, s_1, n, δ, $\bar{s}$. The *accumulation* parameters (s_1, $\bar{s}$, n, δ) play some roles; but the *fundamental* role of the *technology* parameters in the *capital* good industry (σ_1, γ_1, a_1) - altering the long-run $k(t)$ *solutions* of multi-sectoral general equilibrium growth models - *complies* with *observation* and *intuition*. Evidently, the strategic importance ascribed to the capital good industries by economic historians and the general public, makes good economic sense, at least for the closed (global) economy.

The single most important parameter in Theorem 4 is the *substitution elasticity* in the capital good sector, σ_1. It must clearly be larger than one for persistent growth to take place. However, the "*total productivity*" parameter γ_1 in the capital good sector affects all the stated conditions (144-147), and they can all be violated by giving γ_1 any value between 0 and ∞.

A larger TFP parameter of the capital good sector γ_1 may give a "big push", cf. Murphy et al. [1989], Parente & Prescott [1999], Prescott [1998]. But if we restrict $\gamma_1 = 1$ and if $\sigma_1 \simeq 2$, then (146) will usually be satisfied with the other parameters, in particular, with high saving rates. The key role of the *technology* in the *capital good* industry had escaped the "mainstream" literature on two- and multi-sector growth models, cf. Jensen (2003, p.75).

As to *empirical evidence*, the theoretical general equilibrium predictions of Theorem 4 tally with studies of long-run growth conducted by, Rosenberg (1963), De Long & Summers, (1991), Rebolo (1991), and Jones [1994]. In particular, high rates of *equipment* investment ("mechanization") are prime determinants for national growth performance (per capita growth).

Furthermore, the making of various equipments become eventually highly mechanized by making various engines (steam, combustion, electric) "*cheap* as well as *good*," cf. Mokyr [1990, p. 87]. This supports factor substitution and mechanization subsequently in the consumer good industries. In this way, the *capital good* (multi-purpose machinery/equipment) is a "Lever of Riches" (productivity and per capita growth) in *several sectors* with the capital good industry itself and its technology parameters being naturally of primary importance for sustaining the economic growth process - as here mathematically demonstrated in a Walrasian general equilibrium framework.

On advances in technology and economic evolution, Usher (1954, p. 10) writes:

> "It is important *not* to presume a continuous *development* of *technology* at a *constant rate*, but it is important, also, to recognize that the process of social *evolution* consists in part in the *cumulative* development of science and technology. We *need* both a *general understanding* of the process or processes, and, when records make it possible, a *documented account* of the history of *particular periods* and *particular achievements*"

and (p. 380)

> "The *technique* of *interchangeable -part manufacture* was thus established in general outline before the invention of the sewing machine or *harvesting machinery*. The new technique was a fundamental condition of the great achievements realized by inventors and manufacturers in those fields. It made it possible to place the sewing machine in the home and it generalized the use of harvesting machinery of McCormick and Deere with astonishing rapidity. American *engineering and manufacturing firms* took the lead in this general development, achieving distinctive results over an important field that was steadily enlarged decade after decade. The group of *machine tools* became more and more *automatic*, and it became possible to build highly specialized *machinery* for *manufacturing firms*. Great refinements of execution were achieved with the *simplest labor* of attendance. These highly developed machine tools are the most distinguished "iron men" of the modern *industrial world*, for they make possible that *substitution* of *machinery* for *labor* that is so happily described as effecting a "transfer of skill"."

Can *historical stages* (parametric changes) of *increasing substitution elasticities* in the industries of consumer or especially capital goods be better and more eloquently described? Multi-sectoral *dynamics* offer the same economic message about *key parameters* behind the patterns of *industrial evolution*.

6.4 General Equilibrium Dynamics with Non-Homothetic Preferences

The qualitative insight gained by Theorem 4 and the discussion above about the dynamic role of critical parameter values is not confined to economies of homothetic consumer preferences. Evidently, with non-homothetic preferences, the factor accumulation equations (128), 129), 132) and (133) still apply,

$$\dot{L} = nL, \quad \dot{K} = Y_1 - \delta K = K \left[\frac{s_1 f_1'(k_1[\omega(\Lambda[L, K])])}{\delta_K(L, K)} - \delta \right]. \quad (148)$$

Although the equations (148), cannot be reduced to a single equation in the capital-labor ratio, k, and certainly neither in the wage-rental ratio ω, (135-138), the accumulation equations, (148), still represent a well-defined *dynamic system* in the state variable, L, K, by which, without explicit solutions, the logarithmic time derivative of $k(t)$ is easily obtained, cf. (134):

$$\widehat{K} - \widehat{L} = \hat{k} = \frac{d \ln k}{dt} = \frac{\dot{k}}{k} = \frac{s_1 f_1' \left(k_1[\omega(\Lambda[L,K])]\right)}{\delta_K(L,K)} - (n+\delta). \quad (149)$$

Thus the *qualitative* question of steady state or persistent growth of $k(t)$ from (148) similarly depends, cf. (143), on the condition

$$\mathbf{b}_1 > \left([n+\delta]/s_1\right) \delta_K(L,K) \text{ for all } L \text{ and } K. \quad (150)$$

The conditions of (147) still applies, but here with $\bar{s}$ dependent of (L, K), cf. (105), (107), (112).

Although there are obviously *quantitatively* great differences for economies with *non-homothetic* preferences (income elasticities different from one, Engels law), it is seen from (149)-(150) that the *critical role of the capital good industry and its *substitution elasticity* carry over from Theorem 4.

7 Persistent Growth and Asymptotic Growth Rates

To complement the persistent growth solutions of the *state* variable $k(t)$ or $\omega(t)$ with *disaggregate* information about the general equilibrium *evolution* for *sectorial* and other endogenous per capita variables, we characterize the respective time paths by their asymptotic growth rates $[\hat{\omega}(t) \equiv \dot{\omega}/\omega(t), \text{ etc.}]$:

Theorem 5. *With (146)-(147), the long-run growth rates of $k(t)$ and $\omega(t)$ in Walrasian multi-sector growth models (128) with CES technologies are:*

$$\forall i \, \sigma_i > 1 : \lim_{t \to \infty} \hat{\omega} = \frac{s_1 \mathbf{b}_1 - (n+\delta)}{\min\{\sigma_i\}}; \quad \lim_{t \to \infty} \hat{k} = s_1 \mathbf{b}_1 - (n+\delta). (151)$$

With only assuming $\sigma_1 > 1$, (151) is generalized to, $[\bar{\beta} = 1 + \frac{1-s_1}{s_1}\bar{e}^*]$

$$\lim_{t \to \infty} \hat{\omega} = \lim_{t \to \infty} \hat{k} = \frac{s_1 \mathbf{b}_1}{\bar{s}} - (n+\delta) = \begin{cases} \mathbf{b}_1/\bar{\beta} - (n+\delta) & \text{for } \sigma_u > 1, \\ \mathbf{b}_1 - (n+\delta) & \text{for } \sigma_u < 1. \end{cases}$$
$$(152)$$

With (151), the long-run sectorial and per capita growth rates are

$$\lim_{t \to \infty} \hat{k}_i = \lim_{t \to \infty} \hat{y}_i = \lim_{t \to \infty} \widehat{(w/P_i)} = \lim_{t \to \infty} \widehat{(y/P_i)}, \quad (153)$$

where

$$\forall i : \sigma_i > 1 : \lim_{t \to \infty} \hat{k}_i = \frac{\sigma_i}{\min\{\sigma_j\}}[s_1\underline{\mathbf{b}}_1 - (n+\delta)]. \qquad (154)$$

With (152), the long-run sectorial and per capita growth rates are

$$\lim_{t \to \infty} \hat{k}_i = \sigma_i \lim_{t \to \infty} \hat{k} = \begin{cases} \sigma_i\left[\underline{\mathbf{b}}_1/\bar{\beta} - (n+\delta)\right] & \text{for } \sigma_u > 1, \\ \sigma_i\left[\underline{\mathbf{b}}_1 - (n+\delta)\right] & \text{for } \sigma_u < 1. \end{cases} \qquad (155)$$

If only the capital good sector has a substitution elasticity, $\sigma_1 > 1$, then

$$\hat{k} \to \underline{\mathbf{b}}_1 - (n+\delta), \quad \hat{k}_1 \to \sigma_1[\underline{\mathbf{b}}_1 - (n+\delta)], \quad \hat{k}_i \to \sigma_i[\underline{\mathbf{b}}_1 - (n+\delta)], \quad (156)$$
$$\lim_{t \to \infty} \hat{k}_1 = \lim_{t \to \infty} \hat{y}_1 = \lim_{t \to \infty} \widehat{(w/P_1)} = \lim_{t \to \infty} \widehat{(y/P_1)}, \qquad (157)$$

whereas the output of all other sectors will ultimately stagnate,

$$\lim_{t \to \infty} \hat{y}_i = 0 \quad \text{and} \quad \lim_{t \to \infty} y_i = \gamma_i(1 - a_i)^{\frac{\sigma_i}{\sigma_i - 1}} \text{ for } i \neq 1. \qquad (158)$$

Proof: Theorem 5 follows from Theorem 3, (146), combined with (135), (137) and (124), and using (45)-(47), (24) and (16). Thus, by (137):

$$\lim_{t \to \infty} \hat{\omega} = \left[\lim_{\omega \to \infty} E(k,\omega)\right]^{-1}[s_1\underline{\mathbf{b}}_1/\bar{s} - (n+\delta)] \qquad (159)$$

The FEFP correspondence $k = \Psi(\omega)$ next gives

$$\hat{k} = E(k,\omega)\hat{\omega}; \quad \hat{k}_i = \sigma_i\hat{\omega}, \quad \hat{y}_i = \epsilon_{k_i}\hat{k}_i \qquad (160)$$

which holds generally with CES. These relations and limits establish the relevant asymptotic growth rates in Theorem 5. ////

As Theorem 5 supplements Theorem 3 and Proposition 2, only a few remarks are needed. The asymptotic growth rates of $\hat{k}$, (151) and (152) correspond, respectively, to those implied by (146) and (147). Evidently, with more industries to be highly mechanized ($\sigma_i > 1$) and hence larger $\bar{s}$, the slower will be the overall accumulation rate, $\hat{k}$. The same applies to the sectorial $\hat{k}_i$, (154)-(155); but for $\hat{k}_i$, what also matters is the elasticity of Ψ and its own σ_i, cf. (160).

If *maximum* growth of per *capita consumption* is the goal, then the *ranking* with, all $\sigma_j > \sigma_1 > 1$, is preferred – which contributes to mechanizing and maintaining the growth rate of all consumer goods and thereby increases the welfare per capita in any numeraire (sectorial) good, (153). The other extreme is capital accumulation for its own sake (156)-(158); capital accumulation, causing increasing wage-rental rates, makes it impossible to avoid increasing sectorial (k_i) anywhere, even though diminishing returns (with $\sigma_i < 1$) eventually terminate increases in sectorial labor productivity.

Thus, even with *homothetic* preferences and only *price elasticities* involved on the demand side, diverse patterns of industrial growth may emerge with different CES technologies on the supply side of a multi-sector economy.

8 Final Comments

The opinion of Ricardo (1965, p.263-69) on capital goods (machinery) was the following:

> "Ever since I first turned my attention to questions of political economy, I have been of opinion that such an application of machinery to any branch of production as should have the effect of saving labour was a general good, accompanied only with that portion of inconvenience which in most cases attends the removal of capital and labour from one employment to another. -These were my opinions, and they continue unaltered, as far as regards the landlord and the capitalist; but I am convinced that the substitution of machinery for human labour is often very injurious to the interests of the class of laborers.
> - The statements which I have made will not, I hope, lead to the inference that machinery should not be encouraged. To elucidate the principle, I have been supposing that improved machinery is suddenly discovered and extensively used; but the truth is that these discoveries are gradual, and rather operate in determining the employment of the capital which is saved and accumulated than in diverting capital from its actual employment".

His contemporary von Thünen [1850 (1930, p.499)] had similar opinion:

> "Während man in Europa den gedrückten Zustand der arbeitenden Klasse so haüfig der zunehmenden Anwendung von Maschinen zuschreibt, wird in dem gesellschaftlichen Zustand, den wir hier vor Augen haben, die Lage der Arbeiter immer blühender und glänzender, je ausgedehnter beim Anwachsen des Kapitals die Anwendung von Maschinen wird".

Both issues - factor *reallocations* and capital *accumulation* combined with the GDP *growth per capita* of *multi-sector* economies - are still with us and will continue to be so, in Europe and globally. In such historical and future human circumstances, it may help (as in natural sciences) - our spirit, knowledge, daily problems and nerves – being able to basically understand the logic and to formally describe the economic laws of motion (change). Mathematical models of general equilibrium dynamics for growing economies serve such purposes, as attempted in this paper.

A still widely held didactic view is the following [Myrdal (1973, p. 182)]:

> "The emergence and triumph, about a hundred years ago, of the theory of marginal utility and its embodiment in the static equilibrium conception marked an end to the interest the classical

authors, and, of course, Marx, had shown in the long-term problems of growth and development. The focus was put on problems about static efficiency and static allocation of resources, relative to given consumer preferences as expressed by aggregate demand."

As quotations above show, we do not disparage insights of classical economic writings; but some of their modes of analysis have little in common with neoclassical or modern equilibrium methodology. The significance of any *equilibrium* ("static") analysis is that it provides a *solution principle* for the economic variables that are involved with the interrelated commodity and factor markets. Moreover, "static efficiency" in allocation is not a rather trivial matter, economically or mathematically. In fact, allocative (Pareto) *efficiency* implemented by a common marginal rate of substitution (MRS), $\omega = w/r$, gave us the *basic* economic *variable* to reduce the dimension of the solution space for multi-sector economies. The FPCP correspondence, $p_{ij}(\omega)$, consistently linked the interrelated goods and factor markets. Total factor endowments and the parameters of production and utility functions ultimately determined the set (locus) of Walrasian (general) equilibria. In general equilibrium *dynamics*, we similarly solve for *equilibrium time paths*. As was seen in section 6, the dynamic system could certainly never be solved without first having obtained the Walrasian equilibrium solutions, $k = \Psi(\omega)$, or, $\omega = \Lambda(L, K)$. In economics, as in physics (mechanics), there was never any progress in dynamics before the basic problems of static were resolved. No economic growth models or any "magnificent dynamics" (in mathematical sense) were ever analyzed in the classical period.

We have come a long way and hopefully reached a higher vantage point, which offer a better view and overall understanding of the roads passed. In closing, let us observe that the dynamics of growing economies is now a worldwide field of study; extensions of this paper on both the demand/consumer and supply/producer side of MSG models should be straightforward.

Appendix

The *comparative static analysis* of exogenous factor endowment, (L, K), variations for *Walrasian equilibria* with CES sector technologies is helpful for the economic understanding of the sectorial allocation implications of critical parameter values. As benchmarks, the asymptotic factor allocations of multi–sector general equilibrium economies with various GDP income shares, δ_K and sectorial factor allocations, λ_{K_i}, λ_{L_i}, are calculated as follows:

Lemma A1. *For the CES multi-sector competitive general equilibrium economy, limits of factor allocation fractions and factor income shares - for a demand side with constant e_i, ($\sigma_u = 1$), (86), (89) - are:*

Table 6

	$k \to 0$			$k \to \infty$		
$1 > \sigma_i \neq \sigma_{max}$	$l_i \to 0$	$\lambda_{K_i} \to \frac{s_i}{\underline{s}}$	$\delta_K \to \underline{s}$	$l_i \to \frac{s_i}{\underline{s}}$	$\lambda_{K_i} \to 0$	$\delta_K \to \bar{s}$
$1 > \sigma_i = \sigma_{max}$	$l_i \to 1$	$\lambda_{K_i} \to s_i$	$\delta_K \to 1$	$l_i \to s_i$	$\lambda_{K_i} \to 1$	$\delta_K \to 0$
$1 < \sigma_i \neq \sigma_{min}$	$l_i \to \frac{s_i}{\bar{s}}$	$\lambda_{K_i} \to 0$	$\delta_K \to \underline{s}$	$l_i \to 0$	$\lambda_{K_i} \to \frac{s_i}{\bar{s}}$	$\delta_K \to \bar{s}$
$1 < \sigma_i = \sigma_{min}$	$l_i \to s_i$	$\lambda_{K_i} \to 1$	$\delta_K \to 0$	$l_i \to 1$	$\lambda_{K_i} \to s_i$	$\delta_K \to 1$

where $\underline{s}$ and $\bar{s}$ are given by (31).

If all the technologies have the same σ_i, then the limits above become:

Table 7

	$k \to 0$			$k \to \infty$		
$\sigma_i = \sigma < 1$	$l_i \to \bar{l}_i$	$\lambda_{K_i} \to s_i$	$\delta_K \to 1$	$l_i \to s_i$	$\lambda_{K_i} \to \overline{\lambda}_{K_i}$	$\delta_K \to 0$
$\sigma_i = \sigma > 1$	$l_i \to s_i$	$\lambda_{K_i} \to \overline{\lambda}_{K_i}$	$\delta_K \to 0$	$l_i \to \bar{l}_i$	$\lambda_{K_i} \to s_i$	$\delta_K \to 1$

where $\bar{l}_i \equiv s_i c_i / \sum s_j c_j$ and $\overline{\lambda}_{K_i} \equiv (s_i/c_i)/\sum s_j/c_j$.

Proof: From Lemma 1, (31), (32), (47), we get,

$$\delta_K = \sum_{\sigma_i < 1} \frac{s_i}{1 + c_i \omega^{1-\sigma_i}} + \sum_{\sigma_i > 1} \frac{s_i}{1 + c_i \omega^{1-\sigma_i}}$$

For $\omega \to \infty$, the first sum goes to 0, and the second goes to $\bar{s}$.
For $\omega \to 0$, the second sum goes to zero, and the first goes to $\underline{s}$.
From (47), we get $\epsilon_{K_i} \to 0$ for $\omega \to \infty$ and $\sigma_i < 1$, and for $\omega \to 0$ and $\sigma_i > 1$. Furthermore, we get $\epsilon_{K_i} \to 1$ for $\omega \to \infty$ and $\sigma_i > 1$, and for

$\omega \to 0$ and $\sigma_i < 1$. Together with (39), we get the limits for λ_{K_i}, and together with (38), we get the limits for l_i. ////

Lemma A2. *In the case of the CES, (88), and the indirect Addilog utility functions, (103), with the GDP shares, $s_i(\omega)$, (29), depending on ω, the same conclusions (Tables 6 and 7) hold with limits, $\bar{e}_i^*$, $\underline{e}_i^{**}$, $\bar{e}$, $\underline{e}$, given by (97)-(101) that effects $\underline{s}$ and $\bar{s}$ from (31).*

Acknowledgements

For valuable comments on earlier drafts, we are indebted to two anonymous referees, to participants at the: DEGIT VIII conference, Helsinki, May 2003; Seminars: WiSo,University of Rostock, October 2003; WIF/ ETH, Zürich, December 2003; School of Mathematical Sciences, Peking University, December 2003; School of Management and Engineering, Nanjing University, December 2003; SIPEB, Aoyama Gakuin University, Tokyo, March 2004; RIEB, Kobe University, March 2004; IEAS, Academia Sinica, Taiwan, March 2004; Dept.of Econ., National University of Singapore, March 2004; School of Economics and Management, Lund University, April 2004.

References

Aghion, P., and Howitt, P. (1998): *Endogenous Growth Theory.* Cambridge, Mass.: MIT Press.

Arrow, K.J., and Debreu, G. (1954): "Existence of an Equilibrium for a Competitive Economy." *Econometrica* 22: 265-90.

Arrow, K.J., Chenery, H.B., Minhas, B.S., and Solow, R.M. (1961): "Capital-Labour Substitution and Economic Efficiency." *Review of Economics and Statistics* 43: 225-50.

Brems, H. (1986): *Pioneering Economic Theory, 1630-1980.* Baltimore: The Johns Hopkins University Press.

Chenery, H.B. (1960): "Patterns of Industrial Growth." *American Economic Review* 50: 624-654.

Christensen, L.R., Jorgensen, D.W., and Lau, L.J. (1971): "Conjugate Duality and the Transcendental Logarithmic Production Function." *Econometrica* 39: 255-256.

Christensen, L. R., Jorgensen, D. W., and Lau, L.J. (1975): "Transcendental Logarithmic Utility Function." *American Economic Review* 65: 367-383.

Chung, J. W. (1994): *Utility and Production Functions.* Cambridge: Blackwell Publishers.

David, P. A., and Scadding, J. L. (1974): "Private Savings: Ultrarationality, Aggregation, and 'Denison's Law'." *Journal of Political Economy* 82: 225-249.

Deaton, A., and Muelbauer, J. (1994): *Economics and Consumer Behavior.* Cambridge: Cambridge University Press.

Debreu, G. (1959): *Theory of Value.* New York: J. Wiley.

De Long, J. B., and Summers, L. H. (1991): "Equipment Investment and Economic Growth." *Quart. J. Economics* 106: 445-502.

Denison, E. F. (1958): "A Note on Private Saving." *Review of Economics and Statistics* 40: 261-267.

Dhrymes, P. J. (1962): "A Multisectoral Model of Growth." *Quarterly Journal of Economics* 76: 264-278.

Echevarria, C. (1997): "Changes in Sectoral Composition Associated with Economic Growth." *International Economic Review* 38: 431-452.

Frisch, R. (1959): "A Complete Scheme for Computing All Direct and Cross Demand Elasticities in a Model with Many Sectors." *Econometrica* 27: 177-196.

Frisch, R. (1965): *Theory of Production.* Dordrecht, Holland: O. Reidel Publishing Company

Gravelle, H., and Rees, R. (2004): *Microeconomics 3. ed.* Prentice Hall.

Harberger, A. C. (1962): "The Incidence of the Corporation Income Tax." *Journal of Political Economy* 70: 215-240.

Houthakker, H. S. (1957): "An International Comparison of Household Expenditure Patterns, Commemorating the Centenary of Engel's law." *Econometrica* 25: 532-551.

Houthakker, H. S. (1960): "Additive Preferences." *Econometrica* 28: 244-257.

Houthakker, H. S. (1965): "A Note on Self-Dual Preferences." *Econometrica* 33: 797-801.

Inada, K. (1963): "On a Multi-Sector Model of Economic Growth: Comments and a Generalization." *Review of Economic Studies* 30: 119-27.

Islam, N. (1995): "Growth Empirics: A Panel Data Approach." *Quarterly Journal of Economics* 110: 1127-1170.

Jensen, B.S. (2003): "Walrasian General Equilibrium Allocations and Dynamics in Two-Sector Growth Models." *German Economic Review* 4: 53-87.

Jensen, B.S., Richter, M., Wang, C., and Alsholm, P.K. (2001): "Saving Rates, Trade, Technology, and Stochastic Dynamics." *Review of Development Economics* 5: 182-204.

Jensen, B.S., and Wang, C. (1999): "Basic Stochastic Dynamic Systems of Growth and Trade." *Review of International Economics* 7: 378-402.

Jensen, B.S. (1994a): *The Dynamic Systems of Basic Economic Growth Models.* Dordrecht: Kluwer Academic Publishers.

Jensen, B.S., and Larsen, M.E. (1994b): "Growth and Long-Run Stability." *Acta Applications of Mathematics* 9: 219-37; or in Jensen (1994a).

Jensen, B.S. (1980): "Expenditure System for the Danish Household Sector." *Symposium i Anvendt Statistik (1980)*. Lyngby, Denmark: NEUCC: 263-296.

Johansen, L. (1974): *A Multi-Sectorial Study of Economic Growth. 2. Ed.* Amsterdam: North-Holland.

Jones, R.W. (1965): "The Structure of Simple General Equilibrium Models." *Journal of Political Economy* 73: 557-72.

Jorgenson, D. W. (1961): "The Structure of Multi-Sector Dynamic Models." *International Economic Review* 2: 276-293.

Judd, K. L. (1998): *Numerical Methods in Economics*. Cambridge (Mass.): MIT Press, Mass.

Kongsamut, P., Rebelo, S., and Xie, D. (2001): "Beyond Balanced Growth." *Review of Economic Studies* 68: 869-882.

Koopmans, T.C. (1960): "Stationary Ordinal Utility and Impatience." *Econometrica* 28: 287-309.

Laitner, J. (2000): "Structural Change and Economic Growth." *Review of Economic Studies* 67: 545-561.

Leser, C.E.V. (1941): "Family Budget Data and Price Elasticities of Demand." *Review of Economic Studies* 9: 40-57.

Mas-Colell, A., Whinston, M.D., and Green, J.R. (1995): *Microeconomic Theory*. New York: Oxford University Press.

Meckl, J. (2002): "Structural Change and Generalized Balanced Growth." *Journal of Economics* 77: 241-266.

Mokyr, J. (1990): *The Lever of Riches: Technological Creativity and Economic Progress*. New York: Oxford University Press.

Murphy, K. M., Shleifer, A., and Vishny, R. (1989): "Industrialization and the Big Push." *Quarterly Journal of Economics* 97: 1003-1026.

Myrdal, G. (1973): *Against the Stream. Critical Essays on Economics*. New York: Pantheon Books.

Pais, A. (1986): *Inward Bound. Of Matter and Forces in the Physical World*. Oxford: Oxford University Press.

Parente, S.L., and Prescott, E.C. (1994): "Barriers to Technology Adoption and Development." *The Journal of Political Economy* 102: 298-321.

Pasinetti, L. L. (1981): *Structural change and Economic Growth*. Cambridge: Cambridge University Press.

Prescott, E. C. (1998): "A Theory of Total Factor Productivity." *International Economic Review* 39: 525-551.

Rebelo, S. (1991): "Long-Run Policy Analysis and Long-Run Growth." *Journal of Political Economy* 99: 500-21.

Ricardo, D. (1965): *The Principles of Political Economy and Taxation*. London: J. M. Dent & Sons.

Rosenberg, N. (1963): "Technological Change in the Machine Tool Industry, 1840-1910." *The Journal of Economic History* 23: 414-443.

Samuelson, P. A. (1953): "Prices of Factors and Goods in General Equilibrium." *Review of Economic Studies* 21: 1-20.

Samuelson, P. A. (1965): "Using Full Duality to Show that Simultaneously Additive Direct and Indirect Utilities Implies Unitary Price Elasticity of Demand." *Econometrica* 33: 781-796.

Scarf, H. E. (1967): "The Approximation of Fixed Points of a Continuous Mapping." *SIAM Journal of Applied Mathematics* 15: 1328-43.

Scarf, H. E., and Hansen, T. (1973): *The Computation of Economic Equilibria*. Yale: Yale University Press.

Shoven, J.B., and Whalley, J. (1984): "Applied General-Equilibrium Models of Taxation and International Trade: An Introduction and Survey." *Journal of Economic Literature* 22: 1007-1051.

Shoven, J.B., and Whalley, J. (1992): *Applying General Equilibrium*. Cambridge: Cambridge University Press.

Silberberg, E., and Suen, W. (2001): *The Structure of Economics, A Mathematical Analysis*. Singapore: McGraw-Hill.

Somermeyer, W.H., and Langhout, A. (1972): "Shapes of Engel Curves and Demand Curves: Implications of the Expenditure Allocation Model, Applied to Dutch Data." *European Economic Review* 3: 351-386.

Stiglitz, J.E., and Uzawa, H. (eds.) (1969): *Readings in the Modern Theory of Economic Growth*. Cambridge (Mass.): M.I.T. Press.

Stolper, W. F., and Samuelson, P. A. (1941): "Protection and Real Wages." *Review of Economic Studies* 9: 58-73.

Tinbergen, J. (1960): "Optimum Savings and Utiility Maximation Over Time." *Econometrica* 28: 481-489.

Tobin, J. (1980): *Asset Accumulation and Economic Activity*. Yrjö Jahnsson Lectures. Oxford: Basil Blackwell Publishers.

Usher, A. P. (1954): *A History of Mechanical Inventions*. Revised Edition. New York: Dover Publications.

Uzawa, H. (1969): "Time Preference and the Penrose Effect in a Two-Class Model of Economic Growth." *Journal of Political Economy* 77: 628-652.

Uzawa, H. (1968): "Time Preference, the Consumption Function, and Optimum Asset Holdings." in *Papers in Honour of Sir John Hicks: Value, Capital, and Growth*, edited by J.N. Wolfe, pp. 485-504. Edinburgh: University Press.

Uzawa, H. (1973): "Towards a Keynesian Model of Monetary Growth." p. 53-74, in: Mirrlees, J. A. & Stern, N. H.: *Models of Economic Growth*. London: Macmillan.

Varian, H. R. (1992): *Microeconomic Analysis*., 3. ed. New York: W. W. Norton.

von Thünen, J. H. (1960): *Der isolierte Staat in Beziehung auf Landwirtschaft und Nationalökonomie*. Hamburg, (1826); 2.ed., Band 1: Rostock, 1842, Band 2: Rostock, 1850. *Der isolierte Staat* (Band 1-2): Sammlung sozialwissenschaftlicher Meister. Waentig, H., ed. Jena (1930): Verlag Gustav Fischer, Jena. Translations: Wartenberg, C. M.: *Von Thünen's Isolated State*, Oxford, 1966. Dempsey, B. W.: *The Frontier Wage, Jesuit Studies*, Chicago, 1960.

Walras, L. (1954): *Elements of Pure Economics*. Jaff, W. (trans.) (1954): London: George Allen and Unwin.

Wan, H.Y., Jr. (1971): *Economic Growth*. New York: Harcourt Brace Jovanowich.

Wold, H. (1953): *Demand Analysis*. New York: J. Wiley and Sons.

Addresses of authors: – Bjarne S. Jensen, Department of Economics, Copenhagen Business School, Solbjerg Plads 3, 2000 Frederiksberg, Denmark (e-mail: bsj.eco@cbs.dk); – Mogens E. Larsen, Department of Mathematics, Institute for Mathematical Sciences, Universitetsparken 5, 2100 Copenhagen, Denmark (e-mail: mel@math.ku.dk)

J. Econ. (2005) Suppl. 10: 57-76

Journal of Economics
Zeitschrift für Nationalökonomie

Printed in Austria

Common Markets, Economic Growth, and Creative Destruction

Tapio Palokangas

Received April 15, 2003; Revised version received August 1, 2004
© Springer-Verlag 2005

Economic integration is examined in a multi-economy Schumpeterian growth model where economies differ in their research environment, and consequently in the productivity of R&D. It is shown that economies with more or less the same productivity of R&D integrate. In equilibrium, there can be many common markets with different growth rates as well as stagnating economies with decreasing relative income. A small economy with low incentives to save can avoid stagnation, if its R&D is so productive that a common market with a positive growth rate can accept it as a member.

Keywords: endogenous growth, convergence, economic integration

JEL classification: F15, F21, O40.

1 Introduction

It is known that different institutions are reflected in the different levels of productivity in the R&D sector. Many historically determined factors, e.g., bad working practices, a low standard of legal institutions and a high rate of criminality, decrease the productivity of R&D.[1] Because institutions change slowly, country-specific differences in the productivity of R&D may emerge for a long time. In the EU, new members will have weaker research environment than the old members. It is instructive to examine the consequences of this change.

In this study, we show that the expansion of a common market to economies with lower productivity in R&D has two opposing effects on welfare. New members increase welfare through a wider variety of products, but on the other hand they decrease the average productivity in R&D in the common market, which lowers R&D, the growth rate

---

[1] See e.g., Barro (1998).

and welfare. When these two effects are balanced, an optimal common market obtains.

In this study, we also examine how country-specific differences in the productivity of R&D affect growth and economic integration. We give one possible explanation for the following stylized facts:

1. There has been a wide dispersion in cross-country growth rates;[2]
2. many countries have had a common long-term growth rate;[3]
3. some small countries have been able to grow much faster than others; and[4]
4. some countries started to grow much faster after establishing a common market with a greater economy.[5]

Common market studies have mainly concerned two aspects of integration: (i) free trade, and (ii) the equalization of the rates of return. Walz (1998) shows that the integration of a third, technologically lagging economy into a common market of two technologically advanced economies causes a reallocation of resources which stimulates overall growth. According to Baldwin and Forslid (2000), trade liberalization stimulates growth via increased competition in the R&D and financial sectors. Peretto (2003) shows that integration slows down growth via higher fixed costs for a greater variety of goods, but speeds up growth via greater economies of scale. He argues that the latter effect tends to dominate and growth and welfare will rise. In contrast to these papers, we focus on a third aspect of economic integration, the reallocation of research activity among the member economies. From that viewpoint, common markets generate interesting development patterns. For instance, an economy, which did not undertake R&D before, may start doing so if it joins a common market.

Howitt (2000) composes a model of creative destruction with international technology spillover. He specifies institutional aspects that impinge directly on the incentive to invest and innovate as shadow subsidies (or taxes) and obtains the following results. Economies with R&D converge to parallel growth paths with different productivity levels, but the other economies stagnate. The world growth rate depends positively on the R&D subsidy rate in all economies. In Howitt (2000), the main reason for the convergence of the national growth rates is that every economy with R&D gradually adopts the same frontier technology. In this paper, we show that the growth rates of all economies belonging to the same common market converge, although the economy-specific lev-

---

[2] See e.g., Barro and Sala-i-Martin (1995).
[3] See e.g., Howitt (2000).
[4] E.g., Ventura (1997) and the East Asian Miracle.
[5] E.g., Ireland and Portugal after joining the EU.

els of productivity in R&D were exogenously given. Hence, no transfer of technology is needed to explain growth convergence.

The remainder of this paper is organized as follows. Section 2 constructs the basic model, for which section 3 presents the equilibrium properties. Section 4 examines households that save by investing in R&D firms in the same common market. Section 5 analyzes the effects of economic integration.

2 The Model

2.1 Technology

The borders of common markets impose implicit costs on both trade and investment flows. We take this property to the extreme, for simplicity, and assume that such costs are at prohibitive levels. Since there is no trade or investment between common markets, the model has the nice property that the price levels of different common markets are totally independent.

In the model, a great number J of economies exists. Any set of these economies, $\Gamma \subset \{1, ..., J\}$, can form a common market. In each economy j, there is one firm at a time which produces intermediate good j from local labor. The R&D firms located in economy $j \in \Gamma$ attempt to improve intermediate good j. They employ labor everywhere in the same common market Γ and finance their expenditure wholly by issuing shares. We assume that the level of productivity λ_j in R&D is exogenously given and differs throughout the economies $j = 1, .., J$. When λ_j is high (low), we say that research environment is good (bad) in economy j.

We assume that research firms in economy j try to make a better version of intermediate good j and employ labor everywhere in the common market to which economy j belongs. The arrival rate of innovations in the R&D process is therefore given by

$$\Lambda_j = \int_{k \in \Gamma} \lambda_k z_{jk} dk, \qquad (1)$$

where z_{jk} is the demand for labor in economy k by R&D firms located in economy j, and λ_k the (exogenously given) productivity of R&D in economy k. We denote time by τ and characterize technological change in economy j by a Poisson process q_j as follows. During a short time interval $d\tau$, there is an innovation $dq_j = 1$ with probability $\Lambda_j d\tau$, and no innovation $dq_j = 0$ with probability $1 - \Lambda_j d\tau$. In the advent of success, a R&D firm drives the old local monopoly out of the market and takes over the production of the intermediate good. R&D firms finance their investment by issuing shares. Each new generation of any intermediate good provides exactly $\varepsilon > 1$ times as many services as the product of the generation before it. We denote the serial number of technology in economy k by t_k. The level of productivity in the production of intermediate good k, $B_k(t_k)$, is determined by the currently most advanced technology t_k. The invention of a new technology raises t_k by one and the level of productivity $B_k(t_k)$ by $\varepsilon > 1$. This implies

$$B_k(t_k) = B_k(0)\varepsilon^{t_k}. \tag{2}$$

2.2 Consumption-Good Producers

The size of common market Γ is measured by

$$\theta(\Gamma) \doteq \int_{k \in \Gamma} dk \leq J. \tag{3}$$

A large number of competitive firms produces the consumption good from all intermediate goods k made in the same common market Γ through Cobb-Douglas technology with constant returns to scale,

$$C = \mu(\theta(\Gamma)) \prod_{k \in \Gamma} (B_k x_k)^{1/\theta(\Gamma)}, \quad \mu' > 0, \tag{4}$$

where C is consumption in common market Γ, x_k the demand for intermediate input k, B_k the productivity of input k and $\theta(\Gamma)$ the size of Γ. The function $\mu(\theta)$ with $\mu' > 0$ characterizes the property that a wider variety of products (i.e., a bigger θ) yields more services to the households and thereby increases welfare.[6] This is the main motivation of economic integration.

The representative consumption-good firm in common market Γ maximizes its profit

$$\Pi \doteq PC - \int_{k \in \Gamma} p_k x_k dk$$

by inputs x_k, $k \in \Gamma$, subject to technology (4), given the input prices p_k, $k \in \Gamma$, and the output price P. This yields

$$p_k = P\frac{\partial C}{\partial x_k} = \frac{PC}{\theta(\Gamma)x_k} \quad \text{for} \ k \in \Gamma. \tag{5}$$

---

[6] In other papers, the property that product variety increases welfare is commonly established through a CES production function. In this study, the replacement of the Cobb-Douglas function (4) by a CES function would excessively complicate the analysis.

2.3 Intermediate-Good Producers

All potential producers of intermediate good k take part in Bertrand competition and can produce one unit of their product from one labor unit. They maximize their profit $\pi_k \doteq p_k x_k - w_k x_k$ by output x_k, given the wage in $k \in \Gamma$, w_k. Only one firm has access to the technology for a state-of-the-art product, while another is able to manufacture the product that is one step behind on the quality ladder. Because each new generation of any intermediate good provides exactly $\varepsilon > 1$ times as many services as the product of the generation before it, to keep entrants away from the market, the incumbent firm sets its output price p_k equal to εw_k. This yields[7]

$$p_k = \varepsilon w_k, \quad \pi_k \doteq p_k x_k - w_k x_k = (1 - 1/\varepsilon) p_k x_k. \tag{6}$$

Since there is no trade or investment between common markets, we can choose a separate numeraire for each common market Γ and normalize total consumption expenditure PC at $\theta(\Gamma)$. Given $PC = \theta(\Gamma)$, (5) and (6), we obtain

$$p_k x_k = 1, \quad \pi_k = 1 - 1/\varepsilon, \quad w_k = p_k/\varepsilon = 1/(\varepsilon x_k). \tag{7}$$

2.4 Economic Growth

The average productivity of R&D in common market Γ is given by

$$\lambda(\Gamma, \{\lambda_{k \in \Gamma}\}) \doteq \frac{1}{\theta(\Gamma)} \int_{k \in \Gamma} \lambda_k \, dk, \tag{8}$$

where $\{\lambda_{k \in \Gamma}\}$ denotes the levels of productivity λ_k throughout all its members $k \in \Gamma$. Because the average growth rates are in fixed proportion ($\log \varepsilon$) to the arrival rates Λ_k,[8] we can use Λ_k as proxies of the growth rates of economies. From the production function (4) it follows that in common market Γ the level of productivity in the consumption-good sector is given by

$$B \doteq \prod_{k \in \Gamma} B_k(t_k)^{1/\theta(\Gamma)}, \tag{9}$$

and the average growth rate of consumption ($=$ the arrival rate of jumps $\varepsilon > 1$ in the level of productivity in the consumption-good sector) by

$$\Lambda \doteq \frac{1}{\theta(\Gamma)} \int_{k \in \Gamma} \Lambda_k \, dk. \tag{10}$$

---

[7] Cf. Grossman and Helpman (1991), chapter 4.
[8] For this, see Aghion and Howitt (1998), p. 59.

2.5 Endowment

We assume that there is no migration between economies. There is a fixed number κ_k of households in each economy k. Each of these κ_k households supplies $1/\kappa_j$ units of labor, which can be used either in production or in R&D. Total labor devoted to R&D in economy k is

$$z_k \doteq \int_{j \in \Gamma} z_{jk} dj, \tag{11}$$

where z_{jk} is the demand for labor in economy k by R&D firms located in economy j. Because R&D firms employ z_k units and the intermediate-good firm x_k units of labor, and households supply one labor unit in economy k, the equilibrium condition of the labor market is

$$1 = x_k + z_k \text{ for all } k. \tag{12}$$

3 Equilibrium Properties

Because labor inputs z_{jk} are perfect substitutes in the production function (1), R&D firms employ labor in the economy $k \in \Gamma$ with the lowest unit cost w_k/λ_k. In equilibrium, w_j/λ_j is then uniform for $j \in \Gamma$,

$$w_j = \lambda_j w \text{ for } j \in \Gamma, \tag{13}$$

where w is the wage per effective labor in R&D in common market Γ. Given (7), (8), (10), (11) and (12), we obtain

$$\lambda_k/\lambda_j = w_k/w_j = x_j/x_k \text{ for } j, k \in \Gamma, \quad \lambda_j x_j = \lambda_k x_k \text{ for } j, k \in \Gamma,$$

$$\Lambda \doteq \frac{1}{\theta} \int_{k \in \Gamma} \Lambda_k dk = \frac{1}{\theta} \int_{k \in \Gamma} \lambda_k z_k dk = \frac{1}{\theta} \int_{k \in \Gamma} \lambda_k (1 - x_k) dk = \lambda - \lambda_j x_j.$$

From (13) and (14) it follows that the demand for labor in production in economy k, x_k, and the wage per effective labor w are determined by

$$x_j = \frac{\lambda - \Lambda}{\lambda_j}, \quad w = \frac{w_j}{\lambda_j} = \frac{1}{\varepsilon \lambda_j x_j} = \frac{1}{\varepsilon} \frac{1}{\lambda - \Lambda} \text{ for } j \in \Gamma, \quad \lambda > \Lambda. \tag{14}$$

We assume that households can save only by investing in the shares of R&D firms. We denote household ι's investment in R&D ($= \iota$'s saving) in economy j by $S_{j\iota}$. In economy j, aggregate saving by households, $\int_\iota S_{j\iota} d\iota$, is equal to the issue of shares by R&D firms, which in turn is equal to aggregate investment $\int_{k\in\Gamma} w_k z_{jk} dk$. Given (1) and (13), this condition takes the form

$$\int_\iota S_{j\iota} d\iota = \int_{k\in\Gamma} w_k z_{jk} dk = w\int_{k\in\Gamma} \lambda_k z_{jk} dk = w\Lambda_j. \qquad (15)$$

Let $i_{j\iota}$ be household ι's true share of the profits in economy j. The sum of these throughout all households in economy j must be equal to unity:

$$\int_{\iota=1}^{\kappa_j} i_{j\iota} dj = 1. \qquad (16)$$

Household $\iota \in \{1, ..., \kappa_j\}$ in economy j supplies $1/\kappa_j$ units of labor, and receives the wage w_j and the share $i_{j\iota}$ of the total profit of the intermediate-good firm, π_j.[9] Given (13) and (7), its total income is then

$$A_{j\iota} = \frac{w_j}{\kappa_j} + i_{j\iota}\pi_j = \frac{w_j}{\kappa_j} + \left(1 - \frac{1}{\varepsilon}\right)i_{j\iota} = \lambda_j \frac{w}{\kappa_j} + \left(1 - \frac{1}{\varepsilon}\right)i_{j\iota}. \qquad (17)$$

Because income $A_{j\iota}$ is equal to savings $S_{j\iota}$ plus consumption expenditure $PC_{j\iota}$, consumption $C_{j\iota}$ is determined by

$$C_{j\iota} = \frac{A_{j\iota} - S_{j\iota}}{P} = \frac{1}{P}\left[\lambda_j \frac{w}{\kappa_j} + \left(1 - \frac{1}{\varepsilon}\right)i_{j\iota}\right] - \frac{S_{j\iota}}{P}. \qquad (18)$$

4 Households

When a household has financed a successful R&D project, it acquires a certain share of the profit the successful firm earns. We assume that it receives a share of the firm's profit which is equal to its investment relative to total investment made in the same successful project. A successful project also implies that the old firm is driven out of the market. In such a case, all shares held by a household in the old firm lose their value. Following Wälde (1999a), we assume that the change in the true profit share, $di_{j\iota}$, is a function of the increment dq_j of a Poisson process q_j and the investment share $I_{j\iota}$ of household ι out of total investment (15):

$$di_{j\iota} = (I_{j\iota} - i_{j\iota})dq \text{ for all } j \text{ and } \iota, \text{ where } I_{j\iota} = \frac{S_{j\iota}}{\int_{\iota\in\Gamma} S_{j\iota} dk} = \frac{S_{j\iota}}{w\Lambda_j}. \qquad (19)$$

---

[9] Because the consumption-good firms are subject to constant returns to scale, in equilibrium they do not yield profits.

When a household does not invest at all in the upcoming vintage (i.e., $I_{j\iota} = 0$), its share-holdings are reduced to zero (i.e., $di_{j\iota} = -i_{j\iota}$) in the case of R&D success $dq = 1$. If it invests in the upcoming vintage, then the size of the share-holdings depends on relative investment $I_{j\iota}$.

A household averts risk and maximizes utility over an infinite horizon, given random technological change. We define the utility of household $\iota \in \{1, ..., \kappa_j\}$ in economy j from an infinite stream of consumption beginning at time T as:

$$U_j(C_{j\iota}, T) = E \int_T^\infty \frac{C_{j\iota}^{1-\beta} - 1}{1 - \beta} e^{-\rho_j(\tau - T)} d\tau, \quad \rho_j > 0, \quad \beta < 1, \quad (20)$$

where τ is time, E the expectations operator, $C_{j\iota}$ consumption by household ι, ρ_j the constant rate of time preference and β the constant degree of relative risk aversion. Household ι maximizes its utility (20) subject to stochastic process (19) and the budget constraint (18) by its saving $S_{j\iota}$, taking the wages w_j and w, the consumption price P and the arrival rate of innovations Λ_j as given. We denote the value of receiving a share $i_{j\iota}$ of the profit of the producers possessing current technology t_j by $\Omega(i_{j\iota}, t_j)$, and the value of receiving a share I_j of the profit of the producers discovering the next technology $t_j + 1$ by $\Omega(I_j, t_j + 1)$. The Bellman equation for the household's program is then[10]

$$\rho_j \Omega(i_{j\iota}, t_j) = \max_{S_{j\iota} \geq 0} \{C_{j\iota}^{1-\beta}/(1-\beta) + \Lambda_j[\Omega(I_{j\iota}, t_j+1) - \Omega(i_{j\iota}, t_j)]\}, \quad (21)$$

where $C_{j\iota}$ is given by (18). This leads to the first-order condition

$$\Lambda_j \frac{\partial}{\partial S_{j\iota}}[\Omega(I_{j\iota}, t_j + 1) - \Omega(i_{j\iota}, t_j)] = -C_{j\iota}^{-\beta} \frac{\partial C_{j\iota}}{\partial S_{j\iota}} = C_{j\iota}^{-\beta}/P. \quad (22)$$

We focus entirely on the households' stationary equilibrium in which the allocation of resources is invariable across technologies, and ignore dynamics during the transitional period before the equilibrium is reached. We try the solution that consumption expenditure $PC_{j\iota}$ is a share $0 \leq c_{j\iota} \leq 1$ of income $A_{j\iota}$, and that the value function is

$$\Omega = (c_{j\iota}A_{j\iota})^{1-\beta}/[(1 - \beta)r_{j\iota}], \quad (23)$$

where the expenditure-income ratio $c_{j\iota}$ and the household's subjective interest rate $r_{j\iota}$ are independent of income $A_{j\iota}$. Inserting these solutions into (21) and (22), we obtain that in common market Γ the subjective

---

[10] Cf. Dixit and Pindyck (1994), and Wälde (1999a), (1999b).

interest rates $r_{j\iota}$ and the expenditure-income ratios $c_{j\iota}$ are uniform (Appendix A):

$$r_{j\iota} = r_j \doteq \rho_j + [1 - \varepsilon^{(1-\beta)/\theta(\Gamma)}]\Lambda_j > 0 \text{ for all } j \in \Gamma, \qquad (24)$$

$$1 - \frac{S_{j\iota}}{A_{j\iota}} = c_{j\iota} = c_j \doteq \min\left\{1, \frac{\rho_j + [1 - \varepsilon^{(1-\beta)/\theta(\Gamma)}]\Lambda_j}{(\varepsilon - 1)(\lambda - \Lambda)\varepsilon^{(1-\beta)/\theta(\Gamma)}}\right\} \text{ for all } j \in \Gamma. \qquad (25)$$

Now we can show the following:

Proposition 1. *A non-integrated economy j does not grow at all, if its households are impatient enough for $\rho_j \geq (\varepsilon - 1)\lambda_j\varepsilon^{1-\beta}$ to hold.*

Proof: Given (14), (24) and (25), economy $j \in \Gamma$ saves ($c_j < 1$) only if

$$(\varepsilon - 1)(\lambda - \Lambda)\varepsilon^{(1-\beta)/\theta(\Gamma)} > \rho_j + [1 - \varepsilon^{(1-\beta)/\theta(\Gamma)}]\Lambda_j. \qquad (26)$$

If condition (26) does not hold, then economy $j \in \Gamma$ consumes all its income, $c_j = 1$. If this economy is left alone as a separate common market, $\Gamma = \{j\}$ and $\theta = 1$, then, given (8), (1), (15) and (25), it does not save or invest in R&D, $S_{j\iota} = z_j = 0$, consequently it does not grow at all, $\Lambda = \Lambda_j = 0$, and $\lambda = \lambda_j$. Hence, inequality (26) does not hold if and only if $\rho_j \geq (\varepsilon - 1)\lambda_j\varepsilon^{1-\beta}]$ holds. This means that $\Lambda_j = 0$ for $\rho_j \geq (\varepsilon - 1)\lambda_j\varepsilon^{1-\beta}$. ////

Proposition 1 can be intuitively explained as follows (see Fig. 1 below). In the (x_j, z_j) plane, the equilibrium condition of the labor market

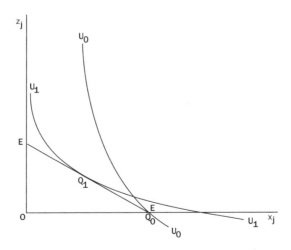

Fig. 1. Possible equilibria for an isolated economy.

(12) corresponds to the downward-sloping line EE. Because economy j must always produce the consumption good (i.e., $x_j > 0$) but need not do R&D (i.e., $z_j = 0$ is possible), preferences in economy j can be represented by indifference curves which intersect the horizontal axis but approach the vertical axis asymptotically. Depending on preferences, there can then be two cases. When the households are impatient enough (i.e., a high enough rate of time preference, ρ_j), there is a corner solution Q_0 with no investment and saving, $z_j = 0$, but otherwise there is an interior solution Q_1 with investment and saving, $z_j > 0$. The indifference curve corresponding to the equilibrium Q_0 is given by $U_0 U_0$ and that corresponding to Q_1 by $U_1 U_1$.

5 Economic Integration

Because the average growth rate of consumption in common market Γ is given by (10), we obtain our first result as follows:

Proposition 2. *The members of a common market Γ have parallel consumption growth paths. They may have different levels of productivity, but their consumption grows at the same rate (10).*

In contrast to Howitt (2000), where growth convergence results from international technology spillover, the unification of the growth rates is here caused by free movement of R&D firms in the common market.

Let Υ be the set of economies which do not save at all. Then, given (25),

$$c_j = 1 \text{ and } \Lambda_j = 0 \text{ for } j \in \Upsilon \tag{27}$$

obtains. In Appendix B, we prove

$$\Lambda\big(\Gamma, \{\rho_{k \in \Gamma - \Upsilon}\}, \{\lambda_{k \in \Gamma}\}\big) \text{ with}$$

$$0 < \frac{(\varepsilon - 1)[\theta(\Gamma) - \theta(\Gamma \cap \Upsilon)]}{\theta(\Gamma)[\varepsilon\theta(\Gamma) - (\varepsilon - 1)\theta(\Gamma \cap \Upsilon)]}$$

$$< \frac{\partial \Lambda}{\partial \lambda_j} < \frac{\partial \lambda}{\partial \lambda_j} = \frac{1}{\theta(\Gamma)}$$

$$\text{for } j \in \Gamma \cap \Upsilon \text{ and a big enough } \theta(\Gamma), \tag{28}$$

where $\{\rho_{k \in \Gamma - \Upsilon}\}$ denotes ρ_k for $k \in \Gamma - \Upsilon$ and $\{\lambda_{k \in \Gamma}\}$ λ_k for $k \in \Gamma$.

Total consumption in common market Γ is obtained by summing throughout all economies and households in Γ,

$$C \doteq \int_{j \in \Gamma} \left(\int_0^{\kappa_j} C_{j\iota} d\iota \right) dj.$$

In the stationary state, given (8), (4), (9), (14) and (28), we can define

$$\frac{C}{B} = \chi\big(\Gamma, \{\rho_{k\in\Gamma}-r\}, \{\lambda_{k\in\Gamma}\}\big) \doteq \mu(\theta(\Gamma)) \prod_{k\in\Gamma} x_k^{1/\theta(\Gamma)}$$

$$= \mu(\theta(\Gamma))\big[\lambda\big(\Gamma, \{\lambda_{k\in\Gamma}\}\big) - \Lambda\big(\Gamma, \{\rho_{k\in\Gamma}-r\}, \{\lambda_{k\in\Gamma}\}\big)\big] \prod_{k\in\Gamma} \lambda_k^{-1/\theta(\Gamma)}$$

with $\quad \dfrac{1}{\chi}\dfrac{\partial\chi}{\partial\lambda_j} = \dfrac{1}{\lambda - \Lambda}\left(\dfrac{\partial\lambda}{\partial\lambda_j} - \dfrac{\partial\Lambda}{\partial\lambda_j}\right) - \dfrac{1}{\theta(\Gamma)\lambda_j} > -\dfrac{1}{\theta(\Gamma)\lambda_j}$

for $j \in \Gamma \cap \Upsilon$ and a big enough $\theta(\Gamma)$. $\hspace{3cm}$ (29)

Given (8), (20), (28) and (29), we obtain the welfare of the representative household in common market Γ of size $\theta(\Gamma)$ as follows:

$$U = E \int_T^\infty \frac{1}{1-\beta} C^{1-\beta} e^{-\rho(\tau-T)} d\tau$$

$$= E \int_T^\infty \frac{1}{1-\beta} \chi^{1-\beta} B^{1-\beta} e^{-\rho(\tau-T)} d\tau. \hspace{2cm} (30)$$

The arrival rate of Poisson jumps in the level of consumption, B, is given by (10). Noting (28), (29) and (30), we obtain the expected value of the stream of welfare (30) subject to the Poisson process as follows:

$$\Psi(t, \rho_{k\in\Gamma}-r, \lambda_{k\in\Gamma}) \doteq \frac{\chi(\Gamma, \rho_{k\in\Gamma}-r, \lambda_{k\in\Gamma})^{1-\beta} B(t)^{1-\beta}}{(1-\beta)[\rho + (1-\varepsilon^{1-\beta})\Lambda(\Gamma, \rho_{k\in\Gamma}-r, \lambda_{k\in\Gamma})]}$$

with $\quad \dfrac{1}{\Psi}\dfrac{\partial\Psi}{\partial\lambda_j} = \dfrac{1-\beta}{\chi}\dfrac{\partial\chi}{\partial\lambda_j} + \dfrac{\varepsilon^{1-\beta}-1}{\rho + (1-\varepsilon^{1-\beta})\Lambda}\dfrac{\partial\Lambda}{\partial\lambda_j}$

$\quad > \left\{\dfrac{\beta-1}{\lambda_j} + \dfrac{(\varepsilon-1)[\theta(\Gamma) - \theta(\Gamma\cap\Upsilon)]}{\varepsilon\theta(\Gamma) - (\varepsilon-1)\theta(\Gamma\cap\Upsilon)}\dfrac{\varepsilon^{1-\beta}-1}{\rho + (1-\varepsilon^{1-\beta})\Lambda}\right\}\dfrac{1}{\theta(\Gamma)}$

for $j \in \Gamma \cap \Upsilon$ and a big enough $\theta(\Gamma)$. $\hspace{2cm}$ (31)

The social planner of common market Γ maximizes the expected welfare Ψ by choosing the members of the common market (i.e., the set Γ) among those who are willing to join in.

To simplify the analysis, we assume that a common market expands by taking new members economy by economy and that an economy can freely leave the common market whenever it wants to do so. We can then prove:

Proposition 3. *In equilibrium, there can be a number of common markets with different positive growth rates as well as a number of stagnating economies which do not grow at all.*

Proof: Let 1 be the economy which is most productive in R&D in the whole world, $\lambda_1 = \max_k \lambda_k$, and Γ_1 the frontier common market containing economy 1. We define the order of economies in Γ_1 as follows. If economy 1 forms the common market alone, $\Gamma_1 = \{1\}$, then it prefers economy 2 as the second member, and these two together economy 3 as the third member, etc. Common market Γ_1 expands, until any new member j would decrease welfare in Γ_1 or any economy j would decrease its welfare by joining in Γ_1:

$$\Psi\big(t, \Gamma_1, \{\rho_{k \in \Gamma_1 - r}\}, \{\lambda_{k \in \Gamma_1}\}\big)$$
$$> \Psi\big(t, \Gamma_1 + \{j\}, \{\rho_{k \in \Gamma_1 - r}\}, \rho_j, \{\lambda_{k \in \Gamma_1}\}, \lambda_j\big) \text{ or}$$
$$\Psi(t, \{j\}, \rho_j, \lambda_j) > \Psi\big(t, \Gamma_1 + \{j\}, \{\rho_{k \in \Gamma_1 - r}\}, \rho_j, \{\lambda_{k \in \Gamma_1}\}, \lambda_j\big)$$
$$\text{for all } j > \theta_1 \doteq \theta(\Gamma_1) = \int_{\Gamma_1} dk.$$

Let $\theta_1 + 1$ be the economy which is the most productive in R&D among those economies which are outside Γ_1, and Γ_2 the common market containing economy $\theta_1 + 1$. By the same reasoning as above, we obtain the following equilibrium condition for Γ_2:

$$\Psi\big(t, \Gamma_2, \{\rho_{k \in \Gamma_2 - r}\}, \{\lambda_{k \in \Gamma_2}\}\big)$$
$$> \Psi\big(t, \Gamma_2 + \{j\}, \{\rho_{k \in \Gamma_2 - r}\}, \rho_j, \{\lambda_{k \in \Gamma_2}\}, \lambda_j\big) \text{ or}$$
$$\Psi(t, \{j\}, \rho_j, \lambda_j) > \Psi\big(t, \Gamma_2 + \{j\}, \{\rho_{k \in \Gamma_2 - r}\}, \rho_j, \{\lambda_{k \in \Gamma_2}\}, \lambda_j\big)$$
$$\text{for all } j > \theta_2 \doteq \theta(\Gamma_2) = \int_{\Gamma_2} dk.$$

Hence, by induction, we obtain a (finite) sequence $\{\Gamma_i\}$ of common markets. Outside sets $\{\Gamma_i\}$, there are only economies which do not grow at all.   ////

Proposition 3 can be intuitively explained as follows (see Fig. 2, page 69). Given (29), there is a negative relationship $E_0 E_0$ between C and Λ: the more resources are devoted to R&D (i.e., the higher Λ), the less common market Γ can consume (i.e., the lower C). The utility function (31) can be represented by a family of indifference curves which approach the vertical axis asymptotically but may intersect the horizontal axis. Let the original equilibrium be Q_0 and the corresponding indifference curve be $U_0 U_0$. The adoption of a new member in common market Γ has two effects. First, with a wider variety of products, the productivity of the consumption-good sector increases and the resource constraint shifts to the right $E_0 E_0 \rightarrow E_0 E_1$.[11] Second, if the new member has a lower level of productivity in R&D than the remainder of

---

[11] If there is no consumption, $C = 0$, then these two curves coincide at point E_0.

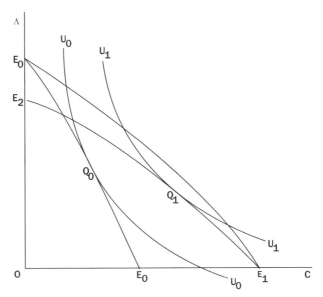

Fig. 2. The expansion of a common market.

common market Γ, then the arrival rate of innovations, Λ, falls. This shifts the resource constraint to the left $E_0 E_1 \rightarrow E_2 E_1$.[12] As long as the former effect is stronger, the new equilibrium Q_1 is above $U_0 U_0$ and welfare in common market Γ increases $U_0 U_0 \rightarrow U_1 U_1$ with the new member.[13] Each new member is less and less productive in R&D, which means that the shift $E_0 E_1 \rightarrow E_2 E_1$ increases with the number of members. When there are enough members in common market Γ, the new equilibrium is is below $U_0 U_0$ and no more applicants will be accepted. This shows that the optimal size of common market Γ can be finite. Consequently, there can be many common markets which grow at different rates. Some economies can form common markets alone which do not grow at all.

Our last result is the following:

Proposition 4. *(Windows of opportunity) Consider economy $j \in \Upsilon$ which has insufficient saving incentives (i.e., with a too high ρ_j) to grow if left alone. This economy can grow if the productivity of its R&D, λ_j, is so high that it can join a large common market with a positive growth rate.*

---

[12] If there is no R&D, $\Lambda = 0$, then these two curves coincide at point E_1.

[13] If the new member has a higher level of productivity in R&D than the remainder of common market Γ, then the arrival rate of innovations, Λ, rises, and the resource constraint shifts further to the right. In this case, the applicant is accepted as a member right away.

Proof: Given proposition 1 and (27), inequality $\rho_j \geq (\varepsilon - 1)\lambda_j \varepsilon^{1-\beta}$ holds for economy $j \in \Upsilon$. We assume that economy j has an incentive to join in Γ, i.e., its welfare is higher as a member of Γ than alone:

$$\Psi(t, \{j\}, \rho_j, \lambda_j) \leq \Psi(t, \Gamma + \{j\}, \{\rho_{k \in \Gamma} - r\}, \rho_j, \{\lambda_{k \in \Gamma}\}, \lambda_j).$$

Common market Γ accepts economy j as a member, if

$$\Psi(t, \Gamma, \{\rho_{k \in \Gamma} - r\}, \{\lambda_{k \in \Gamma}\}) \leq \Psi(t, \Gamma + \{j\}, \{\rho_{k \in \Gamma} - r\}, \rho_j, \{\lambda_{k \in \Gamma}\}, \lambda_j). \tag{32}$$

Now assume that common market Γ is large enough (i.e., $\theta(\Gamma)$ is big enough). Given (31), we then obtain $\partial \Psi / \partial \lambda_j > 0$ for

$$\lambda_j > (1 - \beta)\left(\frac{\rho}{\varepsilon^{1-\beta} - 1} - \Lambda\right)\frac{\varepsilon\theta(\Gamma) - (\varepsilon - 1)\theta(\Gamma \cap \Upsilon)}{(\varepsilon - 1)[\theta(\Gamma) - \theta(\Gamma \cap \Upsilon)]}.$$

From this and (32) it follows that if economy λ_j is large enough, then common market Γ accepts it as a member. Combining the two inequalities, we conclude that when common market Γ is large enough and the productivity of R&D in economy j, λ_j, is within the range

$$(1 - \beta)\left(\frac{\rho}{\varepsilon^{1-\beta} - 1} - \Lambda\right)\frac{\varepsilon\theta(\Gamma) - (\varepsilon - 1)\theta(\Gamma \cap \Upsilon)}{(\varepsilon - 1)[\theta(\Gamma) - \theta(\Gamma \cap \Upsilon)]} < \lambda_j \leq \frac{\rho_j}{(\varepsilon - 1)\varepsilon^{1-\beta}},$$

then economy j does not save and grow at all if left alone, but starts growing if it joins Γ.   ////

   Proposition 4 can be explained as follows (see Fig. 3, page 71). Let $U_0 U_0$ be the indifference curve for the representative household, $E_0 E_0$ the resource constraint, Q_0 the equilibrium in economy j which alone forms a common market but which does not grow at all,[14] and $U_1 U_1$ the indifference curve for the representative household in common market Γ as regards to the use of labor in economy j. On the other hand, let $U_1 U_1$ be the indifference curve for the representative household, $E_1 E_1$ the resource constraint, and Q_1 the equilibrium in common market Γ. If economy j is very small relative to common market Γ, then the preferences $U_1 U_1$, the resource constraint $E_1 E_1$ and the equilibrium Q_1 will not significantly change with the membership of economy j. If Q_1 is above $U_0 U_0$, economy j applies the membership of Γ and it is accepted as a member if its productivity in R&D is high enough. Because Q_1 is above the horizontal axis and (in line with proposition 2)) all members of Γ grow at a positive rate, the membership of Γ starts investment and technological change in economy j.

---

[14] Curve $E_0 E_0$ is a line, because it corresponds to equation (12) in the case the economy is isolated.

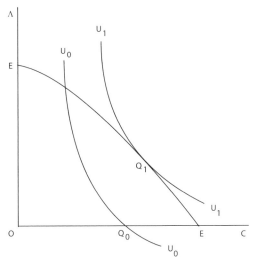

Fig. 3. Windows of opportunity.

6 Conclusions

This paper examines a multi-economy world where growth is generated by creative destruction as follows. Consumption is produced from intermediate goods. An R&D firm that creats the latest technology of an intermediate good through a successful R&D project crowds the other firms with older technologies out of the market so that they lose their value. The firms finance their R&D by selling shares, and households save only by buying these shares. Any set of economies can form a common market in which intermediate goods are freely traded and R&D firms can freely operate. We examine the effects of the establishment and expansion of a common market on growth and social welfare. The main findings can be summarized as follows.

Common markets that do more R&D, produce more innovations and grow faster. The expansion of a common market has two effects. New members increase welfare through a wider variety of products. On the other hand, if the new members have a lower productivity of R&D or a lower savings rate than the old members of the common market, technological change will be slower and the level of welfare lower for the old members. When these advantages and disadvantages of economic integration are balanced, the common market is of optimal size.

Economies integrate only if the productivity of R&D does not differ too much for them. After integration they grow at the same rate, but at different levels of productivity. The integration of two common markets

increases the growth rate of the one whose R&D is less productive
and decreases that of the other whose R&D is more productive. If the
productivity of R&D differs too much for them, then the one with the
less productive R&D declines the integration. For it, the welfare loss of
a lower growth rate outweighs the welfare benefit of a wider variety of
products.

Because economies with roughly the same productivity of R&D integrate, there can be a number of common markets with different growth
rates. Some economies stagnate, because their incentives to save are too
weak (e.g., households are too impatient) for R&D and growth. Such an
economy can, however, escape from stagnation if it is productive enough
in R&D to join a large common market with persistent growth. It can
then grow even without domestic saving, because its R&D projects will
be wholly financed by the savings of the other member economies.

Appendix

A. The Behavior of a Household

We denote variables depending on technology t_j by superscript t_j.
Since, given (17), household ι's income $A_{j\iota}^{t_j}$ depends on $i_{j\iota}^{t_j}$, we note
$A_{j\iota}^{t_j}(i_{j\iota}^{t_j})$. On the assumption that c_j is invariable across technologies,
we obtain

$$P^{t_j}C_{j\iota}^{t_j} = c_j A_{j\iota}^{t_j}(i_{j\iota}^{t_j}), \quad S_{j\iota}^{t_j} = (1-c_j)A_{j\iota}^{t_j}(i_{j\iota}^{t_j}) = (1/c_j-1)P^{t_j}C_{j\iota}^{t_j}. \quad (A.1)$$

Household ι's share in the next producer $t_j + 1$ is determined by its
investment under technology t_j, $i_{j\iota}^{t_j+1} = I_{j\iota}^{t_j}$. Given (23), the value functions are

$$\Omega(i_{j\iota}^{t_j}, t_j) = \frac{(C_{j\iota}^{t_j})^{1-\beta}}{(1-\beta)r_j} = \frac{[c_j A_{j\iota}^{t_j}(i_{j\iota}^{t_j})/P^{t_j}]^{1-\beta}}{(1-\beta)r_j},$$

$$\Omega(I_{j\iota}^{t_j}, t_j + 1) = \frac{(C_{j\iota}^{t_j+1})^{1-\beta}}{(1-\beta)r_j} = \frac{[c_j A_{j\iota}^{t_j+1}(I_{j\iota}^{t_j})/P^{t_j+1}]^{1-\beta}}{(1-\beta)r_j}. \quad (A.2)$$

Given this and (17), we obtain

$$\partial\Omega(i_{j\iota}^{t_j}, t_j)/\partial S_{j\iota}^{t_j} = 0. \quad (A.3)$$

From (1), (8), (19), (17) and (A.2) it follows that

$$\frac{\partial I_{j\iota}^{t_j}}{\partial S_j^{t_j}} = \frac{1}{w^{t_j}\Lambda_j^{t_j}}, \quad \frac{\partial[A_{j\iota}^{t_j+1}(I_{j\iota}^{t_j})]}{\partial I_{j\iota}^{t_j}} = \frac{\partial[A_{j\iota}^{t_j+1}(i_{j\iota}^{t_j+1})]}{\partial i_{j\iota}^{t_j+1}} = 1 - \frac{1}{\varepsilon},$$

$$\frac{\partial \Omega(I_{j\iota}^{t_j}, t_j+1)}{\partial S_j^{t_j}} = (1-\beta)\frac{\Omega(I_{j\iota}^{t_j}, t_j+1)}{A_{j\iota}^{t_j+1}} \frac{\partial A_{j\iota}^{t_j+1}}{\partial I_j^{t_j}} \frac{\partial I_j^{t_j}}{\partial S_j^{t_j}}$$

$$= \left(1 - \frac{1}{\varepsilon}\right)(1-\beta)\frac{\Omega(I_{j\iota}^{t_j}, t_j+1)}{A_{j\iota}^{t_j+1} w^{t_j}\Lambda_j^{t_j}}. \tag{A.4}$$

We focus on a stationary equilibrium in which the allocation of labor in (12) is invariable across technologies, $z_j^{t_j} = z_j$ and $x_j^{t_j} = x_j$. Given this, (1), (7), (17) and (A. 1), wages, income, expenditure and the arrival of innovations are also invariable across technologies, $w^{t_j} = w$, $A_{j\iota}^{t_j} = A_{j\iota}$, $P^{t_j}C_{j\iota}^{t_j} = P^{t_j+1}C_{j\iota}^{t_j+1}$ and $\Lambda_j^{t_j} = \Lambda_j$. Because in a stationary state consumption $C_{j\iota}^{t_j}$ and the level of productivity in the consumption-good sector, B^{t_j}, grow at the same rate, given (9) and (A.2), we obtain

$$P^{t_j}/P^{t_j+1} = C_{j\iota}^{t_j+1}/C_{j\iota}^{t_j} = B^{t_j+1}/B^{t_j} = [B_j(t_j+1)/B_j(t_j)]^{1/\theta(\Gamma)}$$
$$= \varepsilon^{1/\theta(\Gamma)},$$
$$\Omega(I_{j\iota}^{t_j}, t_j+1)/\Omega(i_{j\iota}^{t_j}, t) = (C_{j\iota}^{t_j+1}/C_{j\iota}^{t_j})^{1-\beta} = \varepsilon^{(1-\beta)/\theta(\Gamma)}. \tag{A.5}$$

Inserting these results, (A. 1) and (A.2) into equation (21), we obtain

$$0 = (\rho_j + \Lambda_j)\Omega(i_{j\iota}^{t_j}, t) - (C_{j\iota}^{t_j})^{1-\beta}/(1-\beta) - \Lambda_j\Omega(I_{j\iota}^{t_j}, t_j+1)$$
$$= \left\{\rho_j - r_j + [1 - \varepsilon^{(1-\beta)/\theta(\Gamma)}]\Lambda_j\right\}\Omega(i_{j\iota}^{t_j}, t).$$

This leads to (24).

Inserting (14), (24) and (A. 1)-(A.5) into (22) and noting (7) yield

$$0 = \Lambda_j\left[\frac{\partial\Omega(I_{j\iota}^{t_j}, t_j+1)}{\partial S_j^{t_j}} - \frac{\partial\Omega(i_{j\iota}^{t_j}, t)}{\partial S_j^{t_j}}\right] - \frac{(C_{j\iota}^{t_j})^{-\beta}}{P^{t_j}}$$

$$= (1 - 1/\varepsilon)(1-\beta)\Omega(I_{j\iota}^{t_j}, t_j+1)/(A_{j\iota}w) - (C_{j\iota}^{t_j})^{-\beta}/P^{t_j}$$

$$= (\varepsilon - 1)(\lambda - \Lambda)(1-\beta)\Omega(I_{j\iota}^{t_j}, t_j+1)/A_{j\iota} - (C_{j\iota}^{t_j})^{-\beta}/P^{t_j}$$

$$= \left[(\varepsilon - 1)(\lambda - \Lambda)(1-\beta)\frac{P^{t_j}\Omega(I_{j\iota}^{t_j}, t_j+1)}{A_{j\iota}(C_{j\iota}^{t_j})^{-\beta}} - 1\right]\frac{(C_{j\iota}^{t_j})^{-\beta}}{P^{t_j}}$$

$$= \left[(\varepsilon - 1)(\lambda - \Lambda)(1-\beta)\varepsilon^{(1-\beta)/\theta(\Gamma)}\frac{P^{t_j}\Omega(i_{j\iota}^{t_j}, t)}{A_{j\iota}(C_{j\iota}^{t_j})^{-\beta}} - 1\right]\frac{(C_{j\iota}^{t_j})^{-\beta}}{P^{t_j}}$$

$$= \left[(\varepsilon-1)(\lambda-\Lambda)\varepsilon^{(1-\beta)/\theta(\Gamma)}\frac{P^{t_j}C_{j\iota}^{t_j}}{A_{j\iota}r_j}-1\right]\frac{(C_{j\iota}^{t_j})^{-\beta}}{P^{t_j}}$$

$$= \left[(\varepsilon-1)(\lambda-\Lambda)\varepsilon^{(1-\beta)/\theta(\Gamma)}\frac{c_j}{r_j}-1\right]\frac{(C_{j\iota}^{t_j})^{-\beta}}{P^{t_j}}$$

$$= \left\{\frac{(\varepsilon-1)(\lambda-\Lambda)\varepsilon^{(1-\beta)/\theta(\Gamma)}c_j}{\rho_j+[1-\varepsilon^{(1-\beta)/\theta(\Gamma)}]\Lambda_j}-1\right\}\frac{(C_{j\iota}^{t_j})^{-\beta}}{P^{t_j}}.$$

This, (24) and $c_j < 1$ yield (25), the expenditure-income ratio.

B. The Function (28)

Given (3), (8), (10), (15), (16), (14), (17), (25) and (27), we obtain

$$\Lambda_j = \frac{1}{w}\int_\iota S_{j\iota}d\iota = (1-c_j)A_j/w = (1-c_j)[\lambda_j + (1-1/\varepsilon)/w]$$

$$= (1-c_j)\{\lambda_j + (\varepsilon-1)[\lambda(\Gamma,\{\lambda_{k\in\Gamma}\})-\Lambda]\} \text{ for } j\in\Gamma-\Upsilon, \quad (A.6)$$

$$c_j = \frac{\rho_j+[1-\varepsilon^{(1-\beta)/\theta(\Gamma)}]\Lambda_j}{(\varepsilon-1)[\lambda(\Gamma,\{\lambda_{k\in\Gamma}\})-\Lambda]\varepsilon^{(1-\beta)/\theta(\Gamma)}} \text{ for } j\in\Gamma-\Upsilon, \quad (A.7)$$

$$\Lambda \doteq \frac{1}{\theta(\Gamma)}\int_{k\in\Gamma}\Lambda_k dk = \frac{1}{\theta(\Gamma)}\int_{k\in\Gamma-\Upsilon}\Lambda_k dk$$

$$= \frac{1}{\theta(\Gamma)}\int_{k\in\Gamma-\Upsilon}(1-c_k)[\lambda_k+(\varepsilon-1)(\lambda-\Lambda)]dk$$

$$= \frac{1}{\theta(\Gamma)}\int_{k\in\Gamma-\Upsilon}(1-c_k)\lambda_k dk + (\varepsilon-1)\frac{\lambda-\Lambda}{\theta(\Gamma)}\int_{k\in\Gamma-\Upsilon}(1-c_k)dk$$

$$= \frac{1}{\theta(\Gamma)}\int_{k\in\Gamma-\Upsilon}\lambda_k dk - \frac{1}{\theta(\Gamma)}\int_{k\in\Gamma-\Upsilon}c_k\lambda_k dk$$

$$+(\varepsilon-1)(\lambda-\Lambda)\left[\frac{1}{\theta(\Gamma)}\int_{k\in\Gamma-\Upsilon}dk - \frac{1}{\theta(\Gamma)}\int_{k\in\Gamma-\Upsilon}c_k dk\right]$$

$$= \frac{1}{\theta(\Gamma)}\int_{k\in\Gamma}\lambda_k dk - \frac{1}{\theta(\Gamma)}\int_{k\in\Gamma\cap\Upsilon}\lambda_k dk - \frac{1}{\theta(\Gamma)}\int_{k\in\Gamma-\Upsilon}c_k\lambda_k dk$$

$$+(\varepsilon-1)(\lambda-\Lambda)$$

$$\left[\frac{1}{\theta(\Gamma)}\int_{k\in\Gamma}dk - \frac{1}{\theta(\Gamma)}\int_{k\in\Gamma\cap\Upsilon}dk - \frac{1}{\theta(\Gamma)}\int_{k\in\Gamma-\Upsilon}c_k dk\right]$$

$$= \lambda(\Gamma,\{\lambda_{k\in\Gamma}\}) - \frac{1}{\theta(\Gamma)}\int_{k\in\Gamma\cap\Upsilon}\lambda_k dk - \frac{1}{\theta(\Gamma)}\int_{k\in\Gamma-\Upsilon}c_k\lambda_k dk$$

$$+(\varepsilon-1)[\lambda(\Gamma,\{\lambda_{k\in\Gamma}\})-\Lambda]$$

$$\left[1-\frac{\theta(\Gamma\cap\Upsilon)}{\theta(\Gamma)} - \frac{1}{\theta(\Gamma)}\int_{k\in\Gamma-\Upsilon}c_k dk\right]. \quad (A.8)$$

In the system (A.6), (A.7) and (A.8), there are $2\theta(\Gamma) - 2\theta(\Upsilon) + 1$ equations, $2\theta(\Gamma) - 2\theta(\Upsilon) + 1$ endogenous variables, Λ_j for $j \in \Gamma - \Upsilon$, c_j for $j \in \Gamma - \Upsilon$, and Λ, and exogenous variables ρ_j for $j \in \Gamma$ and λ_j for $j \in \Gamma - \Upsilon$. This system defines the function Λ in (28). Letting $\theta(\Gamma) \to \infty$ for (A.7) and (A.8), we obtain

$$\varepsilon^{(1-\beta)/\theta(\Gamma)} \to 1, \quad c_j = \rho_j/[(\varepsilon - 1)(\lambda - \Lambda)]$$

and

$$
\begin{aligned}
0 = \lambda - \Lambda &- \frac{1}{\theta(\Gamma)} \int_{k \in \Gamma \cap \Upsilon} \lambda_k dk - \frac{1}{\theta(\Gamma)} \int_{k \in \Gamma - \Upsilon} c_k \lambda_k dk \\
&+ (\varepsilon - 1)(\lambda - \Lambda)\left[1 - \frac{\theta(\Gamma \cap \Upsilon)}{\theta(\Gamma)} - \frac{1}{\theta(\Gamma)} \int_{k \in \Gamma - \Upsilon} c_k dk \right] \\
= &- \frac{1}{\theta(\Gamma)} \int_{k \in \Gamma \cap \Upsilon} \lambda_k dk - \frac{1}{(\varepsilon - 1)(\lambda - \Lambda)\theta(\Gamma)} \int_{k \in \Gamma - \Upsilon} \rho_k \lambda_k dk \\
&+ (\lambda - \Lambda)\left[\varepsilon - (\varepsilon - 1)\frac{\theta(\Gamma \cap \Upsilon)}{\theta(\Gamma)} \right] - \frac{1}{\theta(\Gamma)} \int_{k \in \Gamma - \Upsilon} \rho_k dk. \quad (A.9)
\end{aligned}
$$

From (3) and (8) it follows that $\partial \lambda / \partial \lambda_j = 1/\theta(\Gamma)$ and $\theta(\Gamma \cap \Upsilon) < \theta(\Gamma)$. Noting these results and $\varepsilon > 1$, and differentiating the equation (A.9) with respect to λ_j for $j \in \Gamma \cap \Upsilon$, we obtain

$$
\begin{aligned}
\frac{1}{\theta(\Gamma)} &= \left\{ \underbrace{\frac{1}{(\varepsilon - 1)(\lambda - \Lambda)^2 \theta(\Gamma)}}_{+} \underbrace{\int_{k \in \Gamma - \Upsilon} \rho_k \lambda_k dk}_{+} \right. \\
&\quad + \underbrace{\left[\varepsilon - (\varepsilon - 1)\frac{\theta(\Gamma \cap \Upsilon)}{\theta(\Gamma)} \right]}_{+} \Bigg\} \underbrace{\left[\frac{\partial \lambda}{\partial \lambda_j} - \frac{\partial \Lambda}{\partial \lambda_j} \right]}_{+} \\
&> \left[\varepsilon - (\varepsilon - 1)\frac{\theta(\Gamma \cap \Upsilon)}{\theta(\Gamma)} \right]\left[\frac{\partial \lambda}{\partial \lambda_j} - \frac{\partial \Lambda}{\partial \lambda_j} \right] \\
&= \left[\varepsilon - (\varepsilon - 1)\frac{\theta(\Gamma \cap \Upsilon)}{\theta(\Gamma)} \right]\left[\frac{1}{\theta(\Gamma)} - \frac{\partial \Lambda}{\partial \lambda_j} \right] \quad (A.10)
\end{aligned}
$$

and

$$
0 < \frac{(\varepsilon - 1)[\theta(\Gamma) - \theta(\Gamma \cap \Upsilon)]}{\theta(\Gamma)[\varepsilon\theta(\Gamma) - (\varepsilon - 1)\theta(\Gamma \cap \Upsilon)]} < \frac{\partial \Lambda}{\partial \lambda_j} < \frac{\partial \lambda}{\partial \lambda_j} = \frac{1}{\theta(\Gamma)}.
$$

Acknowledgements

The author thanks the participants in the eighth international conference on "Dynamics, Economic Growth and International Trade (DEGIT)", Helsinki, Finland, May 30-31, 2003, and two anonymous referees for useful comments. Financial support from the Yrjö Jahnsson Foundation is gratefully acknowledged. Needless to say, the author is responsible for any remaining errors.

References

Aghion, P., and Howitt, P. (1998): *Endogenous Growth Theory.* Cambridge, MA: MIT Press.

Baldwin, R.E., and Forslid, R. (2000): "Trade Liberalization and Endogenous Growth: a q-Theory Approach." *Journal of International Economics* 50: 497–517.

Barro, R.J. (1998): *Determinants of Economic Growth.* Cambridge, MA: MIT Press.

Barro, R.J., and Sala-i-Martin, X. (1994): *Economic Growth.* New York: McGraw-Hill.

Dixit, A., and Pindyck, K. (1994): *Investment under Uncertainty.* Princeton: Princeton University Press.

Grossman, G., and Helpman, E. (1991): *Innovation and Growth.* Cambridge, MA: MIT Press.

Howitt, P. (2000): "Endogenous Growth and Cross Country Differences." *American Economic Review* 90: 829–846.

Peretto, P.F. (2003): "Endogenous Market Structure and the Growth and Welfare Effects of Economic Integration." *Journal of International Economics* 60: 177–201.

Ventura, J. (1997): "Growth and Interdependence." *The Quarterly Journal of Economics* 112: 57–84.

Walz, U. (1998): "Does an Enlargement of a Common Market Stimulate Growth and Convergence." *Journal of International Economics* 45: 297–321.

Wälde, K. (1999a): "A Model of Creative Destruction with Undiversifiable Risk and Optimizing Households." *The Economic Journal* 109: C156–C171.

Wälde, K. (1999b): "Optimal Saving under Poisson Uncertainty." *Journal of Economic Theory* 87: 194–217.

Address of author: – Tapio Palokangas, Department of Economics, P.O. Box 17 (Arkadiankatu 17), 00014 University of Helsinki, Finland (e-mail: tapio.palokangas@helsinki.fi)

J. Econ. (2005) Suppl. 10: 77-118

Journal of Economics
Zeitschrift für Nationalökonomie

Printed in Austria

Schumpeterian Growth and the Political Economy of Employment Protection

Wolf-Heimo Grieben

Received September 2, 2003; Revised version received June 17, 2004
© Springer-Verlag 2005

This paper analyzes the differing attitudes concerning political support for employment protection between skilled and unskilled workers in a quality-ladder growth model. Creative destruction through innovation results in "Schumpeterian unemployment" of unskilled workers. By voting on firing costs, unskilled workers consider a trade-off between the benefit of fewer unemployment spells and the cost of lower quality growth of consumer goods. Skilled workers, although not threatened by unemployment, may vote for even larger firing costs. Alleviating one labor market rigidity by increasing the matching efficiency between firms and unskilled workers aggravates another rigidity by creating political support for additional firing costs.

Keywords: Non-Scale Growth, Schumpeterian Unemployment, Firing Costs

JEL classification: J63, O33, E24, D72

1 Introduction

Employment protection is often considered to be excessive in many European countries, resulting in involuntary unemployment.[1] More specifically, firing costs are set to maintain workers in dying industries. Instead of simply advising politicians to remove these firing costs, serious economists need to understand the underlying political economics of employment protection legislation. This seems to be even more important since rigid European labor markets are often claimed to cause

---

[1] The OECD (1999, Chapt. 2) provides an extensive summary of employment protection legislation (EPL) for 27 OECD countries and analyses its effects on employment. No significant effect of the strictness of EPL on *overall* unemployment is found. However, the problem of long-term unemployment tends to be aggravated by stricter EPL because job turnover is dampened significantly.

a long-run growth slowdown in addition to creating unemployment. Therefore, this paper aims at analyzing the driving forces behind the demand for employment protection of different groups of workers within a simple and by now standard Schumpeterian endogenous growth model.

As argued in a stimulating paper by Saint-Paul (2002) within a vintage model of *exogenous* growth, incumbent workers form a majority and vote for a specific level of employment protection by considering the trade-off between the costs and benefits of it. The benefits are due to a longer job duration at a wage strictly above the alternative income set by the social security net (opportunity costs of working). The difference between the wage rate and the opportunity costs of working is a rent that exists because of the assumption of match-specific human capital - workers of a specific vintage have larger productivity than unemployed. The costs of employment protection consist of staying in a less productive firm at a wage below the level that could be paid in the leading-technology firm. Saint-Paul shows that in his model, these costs increase with the growth rate (rate of creative destruction), thereby reducing the political support for firing costs. Firing costs are set according to the single-peaked preferences of the median (employed) voter.

Our growth framework is borrowed from the seminal paper of Dinopoulos and Segerstrom (1999). They build a two-country Schumpeterian quality ladder growth model without scale effects that is used to analyze the effects of North-North trade liberalization on wage inequality. More precisely, we apply the PEG ("permanent effects on growth") version of that model, which results in a steady-state innovation and growth rate that can be influenced by public policies. The basic quality-ladder framework builds on the model of Grossman and Helpman (1991), where consumers only buy goods with the lowest quality-adjusted price.[2]

We will restrict the analysis to a closed economy, but introduce labor market frictions. This is done through the use of Şener's (2001) matching model of "Schumpeterian unemployment", where the flow into the pool of unemployed workers is determined by the endogenous innovation rate that forces technologically-backward firms to shut down and lay off their (unskilled) production workers. In that setting, jobs are created by new innovative firms, and R&D is only performed by skilled workers who do not face the risk of becoming unemployed. However, a successful match between the technology of a new quality leader and an unemployed worker only takes place after a search period of given exogenous length, which results in matching unemployment. Contrary to the model of Şener, the exit of old quality leaders overtaken by

---

[2] Other pioneering contributions to neo-Schumpeterian growth theory include most notably Segerstrom et al. (1990) and Aghion and Howitt (1992).

new innovators is costly in our model, and all workers as well as the unemployed vote on the level of firing costs. Due to the assumption of perfect unemployment insurance, unskilled employed and unemployed workers have the same preferences.

Contrary to the model of Saint-Paul (2002), we have no further need for the assumption of a productivity differential between employed and unemployed workers that creates the rent for incumbent workers, which in turn provides incentives to vote for employment protection. Here, productivities of employed and unemployed workers are identical. However, the time spent for a successful match with an unemployed worker involves costs for an incumbent firm (forgone profit during search period), which results in an unskilled wage rate strictly above the level of unemployment benefits.

The steady-state unemployment rate of unskilled workers increases in proportion to the (endogenous) innovation rate. An increase in firing costs is shown to reduce the steady-state innovation rate and to increase the proportion of unskilled workers. The latter follows from the declining unemployment rate which raises expected wage earnings of unskilled workers, thereby reducing education incentives. We also derive a critical level of the innovation rate below (above) which an increase in firing costs raises (reduces) the skilled wage rate. We assign empirically 'plausible' values to the parameters of our model and find that for most of the parameter ranges, the innovation rate will stay below this critical level. Hence in most cases, after a change in firing costs, the steady-state innovation rate and the skilled wage rate move in opposite directions.

When considering a vote for a specific level of firing costs, both worker groups take into account a trade-off between the benefit of rising per capita consumption quantity (due to a higher expected wage income) and the cost of a declining growth rate of consumer goods quality, both in terms of the individual discounted lifetime utility of a given household. Workers do not have to take into account the effects on firm profits, because we assume (as does Saint-Paul, 2002) that workers do not own firms, and profits go to a small group of capitalists whose political power can be neglected for the sake of simplicity. This will allow us to concentrate on the political conflict between skilled and unskilled workers, instead of mixing it up with a conflict between shareholders and workers. However, we will also discuss how our results are affected when accounting for workers' firm ownership.

The unique preferred level of firing costs is explicitly derived for the unskilled. It depends positively on the (exogenous) efficiency of the matching function. Since a more efficient matching technology is shown to increase the steady-state innovation and growth rate, we can conclude the following: in the case of a more flexible labor market with

a higher turnover that accelerates economic growth, unskilled workers ceteris paribus favor stricter employment protection. If this vote
turns into actual economic policy, it slows down product quality growth
but reduces unskilled unemployment. The latter raises expected lifetime earnings and thereby increases consumption quantity of any unskilled worker. Furthermore, if the innovation rate is below the critical
level, skilled workers would favor even stricter employment protection
of the unskilled workers than the unskilled themselves (because of the
positive effect on the skilled wage rate).[3] Our results shed light on the
questions of whether a high-growth or a low-growth environment tends
to create more support for policies to make the labor market more flexible, and whether cross-country growth differentials can be attributed
to differences in specific aspects of labor market flexibility.

The remainder of this paper is organized as follows: Sect. 2 presents
the building blocks of our model, which comprises household and firm
behavior as well as a description of how unemployment is created in
our model. Sect. 3 derives the unique steady-state equilibrium of our
model with endogenous growth and a positive unemployment rate of
unskilled workers. In addition, we analyze in detail the various steady-
state effects of rising firing costs. Sect. 4 derives the preferences for
firing costs of skilled and unskilled workers. Sect. 5 discusses the interaction of different aspects of labor market flexibility and the trade-off
between growth and employment protection. It is established that the
link between labor market flexibility and growth may be more complex than is usually supposed. In addition, we place our findings in the
context of important contributions of Saint-Paul (2002) and Arnold
(2002) on this topic. In Sect. 6, after discussing the results and possible
limitations, our analysis is extended in several dimensions. In particular, we cover the case of a net negative effect of firing costs on hiring,
and we discuss the case of repeated voting on firing costs. Sect. 7 provides our conclusions.

2 The Model

2.1 Household Behavior and Skill Acquisition

The household side of the model is almost identical to Dinopoulos and
Segerstrom (1999) and repeated by Şener (2001), hence we can be brief.

---

[3] If public opinion polls revealed a stronger support for strict EPL among
less-skilled than among skilled workers, this must not necessarily be viewed
as empirical evidence against our theoretical results. Actual voting behavior
may be short-sighted, or voters may lack rational expectations. Our results
refer to the case of fully rational workers as members of dynastic families with
a bequest motive who vote on the level of firing costs for an infinite horizon.

There is a continuum of households indexed by ability $\theta \in [0,1]$ with all members of household θ having the same ability level equal to θ that is common knowledge for the individual member himself and all potential employers. Furthermore, all households have the same number of members at each point in time, and the total population is growing exogenously according to $N(t) = N_0 e^{nt}$ with normalization $N_0 \equiv 1$. The optimization problem of a dynastic family with ability θ and a constant subjective time preference rate $\rho > 0$ is to maximize its discounted utility

$$Z_\theta = \int_{t=0}^{\infty} e^{-(\rho-n)s} \log z_\theta(s) ds \tag{1}$$

by choice of the allocation of labor income across consumer goods that enter the instantaneous utility function $z_\theta(s)$ at each point in time s, by the evolution of consumption expenditure over time, and by the decision whether to become skilled or not. There is a continuum of vertically differentiated goods Q, each produced at a single industry out of a continuum $\omega \in [0,1]$. We denote by $q_\theta(j,\omega,s)$ the quantity of vertically differentiated goods with j improvements of its quality (each improvement being of size $\lambda > 1$) in industry ω at time s consumed by an individual with ability θ. Since the goods produced in each industry just differ in their quality, and λ units of quality j are a perfect substitute for one unit of quality $j+1$, only goods with the lowest quality-adjusted price p are consumed. As is usual in quality-ladder growth models (see Grossman and Helpman, 1991), it follows that there is a unit-elastic demand function $q_\theta(j,\omega,s) = c(s,\theta)/p$ in each industry ω, where $c(s,\theta)$ is the consumption expenditure per capita. Thus, we can define the instantaneous utility function of each household member as

$$\log z_\theta(s) = \int_0^1 \log \left[\lambda^{j(\omega,s)} \frac{c(s,\theta)}{p} \right] d\omega. \tag{2}$$

Utility maximization is subject to an intertemporal budget constraint

$$W_\theta(t) = \int_t^{\infty} e^{ns} e^{-[R(s)-R(t)]} c(s,\theta) ds \tag{3}$$

where $W_\theta(t)$ denotes the family's discounted wage income from time t on, and $R(t) \equiv \int_0^t r(s) ds$ is the market discount factor with $\dot{R}(t) = r(t)$ denoting the instantaneous interest rate at time t. Note that we do not need to rule out savings altogether. Households can borrow and lend with each other or with the capitalists at the market interest rate. The only necessary additional assumption in (3) is that we do not allow workers to own firms (firm ownership *by the capitalists* yields revenues in this type of model because quality leaders earn monopoly profits).

Therefore, the value of firms - that will be affected by the level of firing costs - does not affect the workers' welfare.

As is usual, the steady-state interest rate is determined by the optimal saving decision of workers and capitalists (where in the capitalists' problem, the accumulation of financial assets is accounted for in the budget constraint replacing (3)). This yields the usual Keynes-Ramsey rule $\dot{c}/c = r_t - \rho$ for the optimal path of per-capita consumption expenditure of workers and capitalists. In a steady state with a constant nominal wage rate, per-capita consumption of all individuals must be constant, which implies $r_t = \rho$. We assume $\rho > n$ to have finite lifetime utility for all households.

Each individual lives for an exogenously given period of time $D > 0$. He can choose either to remain unskilled for his entire lifetime, earning the wage rate w_L regardless of his ability if employed or zero if unemployed (unemployment benefits are normalized to zero), or to spend an exogenously given period $T < D$ on education in order to become a skilled worker. This second possibility yields zero income during the period of education and an ability-dependent wage income θw_H during the period of employment of length $D - T$ without any unemployment risk. Therefore, an individual with ability θ invests in education if and only if

$$\int_0^D e^{-\rho t} w_L(s)(1-u)ds < \int_T^D e^{-\rho t}\theta w_H(s)ds \qquad (4)$$

holds.[4] Setting (4) to hold as an equality and normalizing $w_L \equiv 1$, we get the unique steady-state threshold ability level as

$$\theta_0 = \frac{(1-u)w_L}{w_H}\frac{1-e^{-\rho D}}{e^{-\rho T}-e^{-\rho D}} \equiv \frac{1-u}{w_H}\sigma, \quad \sigma > 1. \qquad (5)$$

Individuals with ability below $\theta_0 \in]0,1[$ choose to remain unskilled whereas those with ability $\theta \geq \theta_0$ invest in education.

2.2 Production and R&D

The production side of the model is a closed-economy version of Şener (2001). In any industry $\omega \in [0,1]$, the production function is simply $Q_t = (1-u)L_t = (1-u)\theta_0 N_t$, irrespective of the corresponding quality level. Hence, output equals the amount of *employed* unskilled labor,

---

[4] Writing the unskilled discounted wage income this way assumes implicitly the existence of perfect unemployment insurance - these workers only care about the *expected* lifetime income, not about length or frequency of unemployment spells in particular, and the wage income $(1-u)w_L$ is certain. This will simplify our analysis later on since it means identical policy preferences for unskilled employed and unemployed workers.

where $L_t = \theta_0 N_t$ is the unskilled labor supply as a fraction θ_0 of total population.

The R&D process specified below results in a unique quality leader in each industry who is protected by an exclusive patent on his production technology. Once another innovation (that is, an improvement of the quality of consumer goods of size $\lambda > 1$) occurs in the same industry, this patent expires and becomes common knowledge. The current quality leader in each industry reaps all profits by engaging in limit pricing: Since consumers only buy goods with the lowest quality-adjusted price, the quality leader charges the price $p = \lambda - \epsilon, \epsilon \to 0$, that drives all quality followers (who produce one-step inferior goods and can do no better than charging the unit-cost price 1) out of the market. Given a unit-elastic demand function $q = c/\lambda$, marginal production costs $w_L = 1$ and a total of N consumers, this strategy yields monopoly profits of $\pi = (\lambda - 1)cN/\lambda$. Total consumption cN/λ equals total output Q and thus total unskilled labor demand, hence it follows:

$$c = \lambda(1 - u)\theta_0. \tag{6}$$

This establishes a one-to-one relationship between per-capita consumption quantity $q = c/\lambda$ and the employed unskilled workforce.

There are sequential and stochastic R&D races in each industry $\omega \in [0, 1]$. There is free entry in R&D, and all participating firms are using the same technology in discovering the next higher quality of consumer goods. Skilled labor is the only input used to carry out R&D in any industry ω and is assumed to be perfectly mobile across industries. Any R&D firm i that hires h_i units of skilled labor in industry ω at time t is successful in discovering the next higher quality product with instantaneous probability $\eta h_i / X(\omega, t)$, where $X(\omega, t)$ is an R&D difficulty index and $\eta > 0$ is a given technology parameter. Therefore, $\eta h_i / X(\omega, t)$

"[...] is the probability that the firm will innovate by time $t + dt$ conditional on not having innovated by time t, where dt is an infinitesimal increment of time" (Segerstrom, 1998, p. 1297).

Since we assume that R&D returns are independently distributed across firms, across industries and over time, the industry-wide instantaneous probability of innovation at time t is

$$I(\omega, t) = \eta H(\omega, t) / X(\omega, t) \tag{7}$$

with $\sum_i h_i(\omega) = H(\omega)$ as the industry-wide employment of skilled labor in R&D.[5] R&D difficulty is assumed to be proportional to the size of

---

[5] This means that the arrival of innovations in each industry ω is governed by a Poisson process with arrival rate $I(\omega, t)$ which in turn depends on R&D employment in a linear way.

the market:[6]

$$X(\omega, t) = kN_t, \ k > 0. \tag{8}$$

Next, we will consider the stock market. Usually in this type of model, consumer savings are lent to firms investing in R&D. However, since we will have consumers voting on firing costs which ultimately affects unemployment, the skilled wage rate, the education decision and growth, we want to avoid considering effects on share values simultaneously. Therefore, we follow Saint-Paul (2002) in assuming that savings *in R&D funds* (however, not savings altogether) come from a small class of capitalists who do not play a significant role in the political process to be discussed later. In Sect. 6.1 we will argue that this assumption does not affect our main results qualitatively.

As is standard in quality-ladder growth models, efficiency in the stock market requires that the expected rate of return of a stock issued by a successful R&D firm must be equal to the riskless rate of return r (since capitalists can completely diversify the industry-specific risk of unsuccessful R&D expenditure by holding shares of all existing firms). Defining $\vartheta(\omega, t)$ as the expected discounted profits of a monopolist, the *no-arbitrage condition in the stock market* states

$$\frac{\pi}{\vartheta} dt + \frac{\dot{\vartheta}}{\vartheta} dt (1 - Idt) - \left(\frac{\vartheta + F}{\vartheta}\right) Idt = rdt. \tag{9}$$

The first term on the LHS is the dividend per share during the time interval dt, the second term on the LHS denotes share appreciation during this time interval (due to increasing consumption demand because of population growth). This only takes place when there is no further innovation in this industry within dt (the probability of this is given in brackets). The third term on the LHS denotes full capital loss for share owners of this particular firm when there is further innovation during dt which is often called the *"creative-destruction effect"*. In addition, this term contains the new variable $F_t \equiv BN_t, B > 0$, denoting firing costs that are indexed to the size of the economy, and that the previous quality leader has to bear in case innovation by a competitor drives him out of the market. It is assumed that F_t does not include redundancy payments to the laid-off worker. The indexing is necessary in order to

---

[6] Dinopoulos and Segerstrom (1999, p. 459) call this the "permanent-effects-on-growth" (PEG) specification, because it implies a steady-state innovation and growth rate that can permanently be affected by various economic policies. The intuition behind this specification is that the larger the market, the higher are marketing costs to introduce a new technology and the higher are the replacement costs in the case of flaws in newly invented products (Dinopoulos and Thompson, 1996, p. 399). The main purpose of rising R&D difficulty over time is to remove counterfactual scale effects from the growth model. See Jones (1995, 1999) and Segerstrom (1998) for detailed discussions of scale effects and different ways to avoid them.

prevent firing costs becoming negligible in a growing economy. Later on, we will introduce the voting of all workers on B.

All three terms on the LHS of (9) together denote expected returns per share of any firm investing in R&D during dt, and this must equal the return r of a riskless asset during the same time period given on the RHS. In the limit $dt \rightarrow 0$, we obtain

$$\vartheta(\omega, t) = \frac{\pi(t) - FI(\omega, t)}{r(t) + I(\omega, t) - \frac{\dot{\vartheta}(\omega, t)}{\vartheta(\omega, t)}}, \tag{10}$$

which gives us the appropriately discounted *"reward for innovating"* with $\pi = (\lambda - 1)cN/\lambda$. In order not to discourage innovation activity completely, firing costs have to satisfy

$$BI < \frac{\lambda - 1}{\lambda} c. \tag{11}$$

Note that (10) gives the reward for innovating only if the firm immediately starts producing after having innovated the leading technology. However, following Şener (2001), we assume a frictional labor market for unskilled workers which requires that the new quality leader searches for an exogenously given time period $y > 0$ for the appropriate unskilled worker to be matched with the new vacancy. Thus, given the interest rate r, the reward for innovating needs to be discounted by the factor e^{-yr}.

A firm i chooses its R&D intensity $I_i(\omega, t)$ by maximizing the *expected* reward for innovating (since innovation success is not certain but occurs with instantaneous probability I_i) minus costs at each point in time. Hence, it maximizes $e^{-yr}\vartheta I_i - w_H h_i$, with $I_i = \eta h_i / X$, through the optimal choice of h_i. Due to free entry into the R&D sector, these expected profits are competed away, and in equilibrium we must have the skilled wage rate defined by the *"R&D equilibrium condition"*

$$w_H = e^{-yr} \frac{\eta \vartheta}{X} = \frac{e^{-yr} \eta}{k} \frac{c(1 - 1/\lambda) - IB}{r + I - \frac{\dot{\vartheta}}{\vartheta}}, \tag{12}$$

which is valid in any industry ω by symmetry of the model.

2.3 Job Matching and Unemployment

The details of our model concerning matching and unskilled "Schumpeterian" unemployment are a slightly changed, closed-economy version of those in Şener (2001) who in turn builds on Aghion and Howitt (1994). Unskilled workers are continuously engaged in an on-the-job search, while firms can only start searching for the appropriate unskilled worker to use the new production technology after having innovated. Thus, they start producing and reaping monopoly profits with an exogenously given delay of length $y > 0$. The matching process is deterministic, and the successful matching of technology leaders with unskilled workers follows a "well-behaved" matching function $Am(V_t, L_t)$, where $A > 0$ is a constant efficiency parameter.[7] This matching function is concave, homogenous of degree one and increasing both in vacancies V_t created by innovating firms and the total unskilled workforce L_t. The aggregate job-finding rate (per efficiency unit A of the matching function) $p(\nu_t)$ measures the rate at which a worker who starts search at any day finds a new job. This rate is defined as $p(\nu_t) = m(\nu, 1) > 0 \; \forall \; \nu_t > 0$ with the vacancy rate $\nu_t = V_t/L_t$, and we assume that $p(0) = 0$ and $p(\infty) = \infty$ holds.[8] The aggregate recruiting-success rate (per efficiency unit A of the matching function) $q(\nu_t)$ measures the rate at which a firm that has just innovated successfully matches a worker with the new technology. This rate is defined as $q(\nu_t) = m(\nu_t, 1)/\nu_t > 0 \; \forall \; \nu_t > 0$, and we assume that $q(\infty) = 0$ and $q(0) = \infty$ holds. $q(\nu_t)$ and y are closely related as will be discussed in Sect. 3 below.

The aggregate rate of change in the number of vacancies V within a time interval $[t, t + dt]$ is given by

$$\dot{V}_t dt = \frac{c_{t+y} N_{t+y}}{\lambda} I_t dt + \frac{c_{t+y} N_{t+y}}{\lambda} \beta dt - Am(V_t, L_t) dt. \qquad (13)$$

The first expression on the RHS of (13) gives the flow of newly posted vacancies at time t equal to the expected unskilled labor demand at time $t + y$ that occurs with the innovation probability I_t. This term follows from the production function that assumes a one-to-one relationship between unskilled labor input and consumer goods output, and the unit-elastic consumption demand. Furthermore, it takes into account that positions can only be filled after a matching time y, when total consumption has changed. The second expression on the RHS of (13) takes into account the change of the market size within the time interval $[t+y, t+y+dt]$, that is, for the growing unskilled labor demand *after* production of the new leading-quality goods begins. In that interval, population grows at the exogenous rate $n = \beta - \delta > 0$ (with β and δ denoting the birth rate and the death rate, respectively), and positions

---

[7] In order to avoid the problem that workers may be matched while still being employed, we have to assume that (deterministic) matching time is long enough, as in Aghion and Howitt (1998, p. 126, fn. 7).

[8] The only difference to Şener (2001) is that he considers the special case $A = 1$. Here, we introduce the matching-productivity parameter A in order to have an *exogenous* parameter that allows us to perform a comparative static exercise with respect to the efficiency of the matching process (in Sect. 5.1 below).

of dying employed unskilled workers must be filled. The third expression on the RHS of (13) denotes outflow of vacancies due to successful matching during dt. Note that vacancy creation at time t is determined by additional labor demand at time $t + y$, but it is determined by the value of the matching function at time t.

Similarly, the aggregate rate of change in the unemployment level $U \equiv uL$ within a time interval $[t, t + dt]$ is given by

$$\dot{U}_t dt = \frac{c_t N_t}{\lambda} I_t dt + \beta L_t dt - \delta u_t L_t dt - Am(V_t, L_t) dt. \qquad (14)$$

The four terms on the RHS of (14) denote, respectively, layoffs by the current quality leader in any industry ω in the case of innovation by a competing firm, newly born individuals who decide not to take education before they enter the labor market, dying unemployed workers, and outflow of unemployment due to successful matching, all measured during the time interval dt.

Thus, the total unemployment level consists of Schumpeterian and demographic unemployment. Firing costs do not *directly* affect vacancy creation or unemployment flows, but they will have indirect effects via the endogenous variables I_t, c_t and u_t.

3 Steady State and Rising Firing Costs

We define the steady state of our model as the long-run equilibrium with market clearing and constant values for our variables θ_0, w_H, I, c, v and u, given the level $B = F/N$ of firing costs to be determined later by the majority-winning preferences of workers.

We begin by deriving the steady-state unemployment rate, following Şener (2001). Dividing (14) by dt, using $m(V, L) = p(\nu)L$, $L = \theta_0 N$, $U/L = u$ and (6) yields

$$\frac{\dot{U}}{U} = \frac{(1 - u)I + \beta - \delta u - Ap(\nu)}{u} = \beta - \delta = n, \qquad (15)$$

where the second equality follows from imposing the restriction of a constant steady-state unemployment rate. Equation (15) can easily be solved for

$$u = 1 - \frac{Ap(\nu^*)}{I + \beta} \qquad (16)$$

with ν^* denoting the steady-state vacancy rate.[9] This can be derived in a similar fashion from (13), using

$$\frac{\dot{V}}{V} = \beta - \delta, \; c_{t+y} = c_t = c, \; N_{t+y} = N_t e^{ny}$$

and the result in (16):

$$\nu^* = \frac{Ap(\nu^*)(e^{ny} - 1)}{n}. \tag{17}$$

The aggregate recruiting-success rate q and the matching time y are related as follows (cf. Şener, 2000, pp. 579-80):

$$Aq(\nu_t) = \frac{Am(\nu_t, 1)}{\nu_t} = \frac{Ap(\nu_t)}{\nu_t} = \frac{n}{e^{ny} - 1} \tag{17a}$$

where the first two equations follow from our definitions of $q(\nu)$ and $p(\nu)$, and the last equation follows from (17). Whereas $Aq(\nu_t)$ is a monotonically decreasing function of ν_t, $n/(e^{ny} - 1)$ is a positive constant, which defines uniquely the steady-state value ν^* as a function of exogenous parameters. In the limit $n \to 0$, we obtain $Aq(\nu_t) = 1/y$ by applying L'Hôpital's rule. This is the special case (for $A = 1$) considered in Aghion and Howitt (1994): with no population growth, the matching time y is simply the inverse of the aggregate recruiting-success rate $1/q$, which is the *instantaneous* expected matching time for a fixed pool of searching workers. With $n > 0$, however, it holds $y < 1/q$ since firms can choose from a continuously growing pool of searching workers (note that $n/(e^{ny} - 1)$ decreases in n). In Sect. 5.1 we will conduct comparative statics on A with keeping ν^* constant, so that the value of y is adjusted accordingly.

The only endogenous variable affecting (positively) the unskilled unemployment rate u in (16) is the innovation rate I: more frequent innovations reduce the expected incumbency period $1/I$ of current quality leaders in any industry ω, thereby reducing the duration of employment spells of unskilled workers and raising their unemployment rate by increased labor market turnover.[10] Note that the finding of

---

[9] Similar to Şener (2001, p. 136), we note that the additional assumption $Ap(\nu) > \beta$ is needed to rule out that "biological turnover" alone suffices to produce a positive unemployment rate.

[10] There are two reasons for why in addition to this positive "creative destruction effect" of growth on unemployment, there is no negative "capitalization effect". First, as argued by Aghion and Howitt (1998, p. 127), since the quality leader does not upgrade its own technology, the capitalized value of each innovation does not grow with higher labor productivity (in terms of consumer goods quality), hence no *additional* incentives of follower firms to create vacancies arise. Second, unlike in the model of Aghion and

an unambiguously positive long-run relationship between growth and unemployment hinges crucially on the fact that we are only considering the quality dimension of growth (increasing quality of consumer goods), while neglecting the quantity dimension. The latter could be introduced e.g. by accounting for human capital accumulation, with the level of human capital entering the production function of goods. Then, growth in the quantity dimension would raise production and hence the unskilled labor demand for any given innovation rate, thereby working toward a reduction in unemployment.

Next, we will determine the steady-state values for both I and θ_0. To this end, we solve (12) for I, use (6) to replace c, (5) to replace w_H, (16) to replace u, and use $r_t = \rho$. Proceeding in this manner, we get

$$I = \frac{\eta e^{-\rho y} Ap(\nu^*)\theta_0^2(\lambda - 1) - (\rho - n)\sigma Ap(\nu^*)k}{\sigma Ap(\nu^*)k + (\beta + I)\eta e^{-\rho y}\theta_0 B}. \tag{18}$$

In Appendix A we prove by use of the implicit function theorem that $dI/d\theta_0 > 0$ holds in (18). A second equation in the variables I and θ_0 is derived by the skilled labor market equilibrium condition. Whereas skilled labor demand equals IkN/η from (7) and (8), skilled labor supply can be derived as $(1 - \theta_0^2)\phi N/2$ with $\phi \equiv [e^{n(D-T)} - 1]/(e^{nD} - 1) < 1$ (see Dinopoulos and Segerstrom, 1999, p. 456). Putting both together, the skilled labor market clearing condition is

$$\theta_0 = \sqrt{1 - \frac{2kI}{\eta\phi}}. \tag{19}$$

Equations (18) and (19) together determine the unique steady-state combination (I, θ_0) as depicted in Fig. 1 (next page).[11] There, we also illustrate the following (formal proof is provided in Appendix B):

Proposition 1. *A rise in firing costs reduces unambiguously both the steady-state innovation rate and the proportion $1 - \theta_0$ of skilled workers.*

It will prove useful to derive the steady-state equilibrium also in (w_H, I)-space. This is done in Fig. 2 (page 91). To derive Fig. 2, we

---

Howitt (1994, p. 483; 1998, p. 135), the capitalization effect does not enter when considering forward-looking behavior of firms. This is because in (10), the instantaneous expected income from innovating is growing with the size of the market (n) which does not depend on the rate of innovation. Therefore, a higher growth and innovation rate does not reduce (actually, it increases) the net discount rate at which quality leaders capitalize their expected profits.

[11] Şener (2001, p. 138, Fig. 1) studies the steady-state effects of trade-liberalization using exactly the same graph.

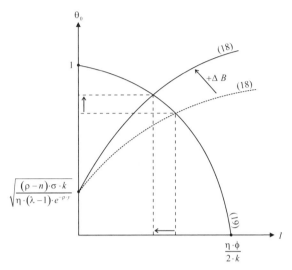

Fig. 1. Steady-state effects of rising firing costs in (I, θ_0)-space

first solve (12) for I, use (6) to substitute for c, (5) to substitute for $1 - u$, and (19) to substitute for θ_0. This yields

$$I = \frac{\frac{\eta}{\sigma}e^{-\rho y}(\lambda - 1) - (\rho - n)k}{k\left[1 + \frac{2e^{-\rho y}(\lambda - 1)}{\sigma \phi}\right] + \frac{\eta e^{-\rho y}B}{w_H}}, \tag{20}$$

which is unambiguously decreasing in B. Then, we use (5), (16) and (19) to write w_H as a function of I alone:

$$w_H = \frac{\sigma A p(\nu^*)}{(\beta + I)(1 - \frac{2kI}{\eta \phi})^{1/2}}. \tag{21}$$

In (21), w_H is decreasing in I for $I < (\theta_0^2 \eta \phi / k) - \beta$ and rising for larger I. Equations (20) and (21) together determine the unique steady-state combination (I, w_H) as depicted in Fig. 2.

Equation (20) captures the R&D equilibrium with skilled labor market clearing. Its positive slope indicates that the higher the innovation rate in equilibrium, the higher the skilled wage rate will be due to the rising demand for skilled workers. Equation (21) accounts for the equilibrium education decision of individuals, the steady-state unemployment rate and the skilled labor market clearing condition. It gives for each level of the equilibrium innovation rate (that implies an equilibrium unemployment rate via (16)) the required skilled wage rate that makes the individual with threshold ability θ_0 indifferent with respect

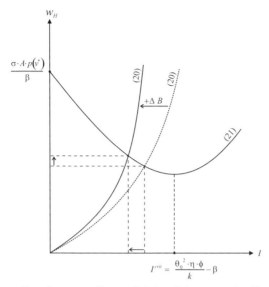

Fig. 2. Steady-state effects of rising firing costs in (I, w_H)-space

to his educational decision, given skilled labor market clearing. This curve is U-shaped. For low levels of I, on the one hand, unskilled unemployment is relatively low, hence expected unskilled wage income is relatively high, which raises the required skilled wage rate (*"education equilibrium effect"*). On the other hand, skilled labor market clearing would call for a low level of w_H (*"skilled labor demand effect"*) because demand for R&D labor is low. For low I, the *education equilibrium effect* dominates the *skilled labor demand effect*, and this is why the required w_H is high in this case. For high levels of I, unskilled unemployment is high, thus expected unskilled wage income is low. Ceteris paribus, this yields a low required w_H. However, this *education equilibrium effect* is dominated by the *skilled labor demand effect*: a high I creates a large demand for skilled workers that drives up w_H. This is why the required w_H is high for large I. For $I = (\theta_0^2 \eta \phi / k) - \beta$, both effects together imply the minimum level of w_H consistent with (5), (16) and (19). In addition to this, Fig. 2 also illustrates the following:

Proposition 2. *An increase in firing costs raises the skilled wage rate for $I < I^{crit} \equiv (\theta_0^2 \eta \phi / k) - \beta$ and reduces it for $I > I^{crit}$.*

Proposition 2 simply follows from the fact that an increase in firing costs raises unambiguously the denominator of (20), thus this curve shifts to the left in Fig. 2 without affecting the curve for (21). As drawn, the initial steady-state innovation rate is below the critical value

$$I^{crit} = (\theta_0^2 \eta \phi / k) - \beta.$$

To see whether this assumption is plausible, we assign the following benchmark simulation values to our parameters, taken from Dinopoulos and Segerstrom (1999, p. 467): a population growth rate of $n = 0.01$, a time preference rate $\rho = 0.03$ to get a 3-percent steady-state real interest rate $r = \rho$, a working life of $D = 40$ years[12], a duration of college education of $T = 4$ years[13] (implying $\sigma = 1.193$ and $\phi = 0.881$), and a 35-percent improvement in product quality through each innovation ($\lambda = 1.35$). As noted by Steger (2003, p. 4), average estimates about the monopolists' percentage markup over marginal costs $\lambda - 1$ lie in the interval $[0.1, 0.4]$, hence reasonable values for λ are in the range $[1.1, 1.4]$. In addition, we also follow Dinopoulos and Segerstrom (1999) by imposing a 2-percent steady-state utility growth rate[14] $\dot{z}/z = I \log \lambda = 0.02$, from which we get $I = 0.0666$. It remains to derive a parameter value for η/k and a value for θ_0. The latter is determined endogenously by (18) and (19). Even for a given $I = 0.0666$, this yields θ_0 as a function of $y, A, p(\nu^*)$ - all of which are unknown and not straightforward to derive - and of B which will be derived endogenously in Sect. 4 below. Therefore, we prefer to choose θ_0 from the data in order to derive a 'plausible' value for η/k.[15] The OECD (2003, Table A2.4) reports trends in educational attainment at the tertiary level from 1991 to 2001, which corresponds to $1 - \theta_0$ in our model. We take the most recent values from 2001 for the US, Germany and Italy, where the percentage of the population of 25 to 34-year-old males that have attained tertiary education equaled 36, 23 and 10, respectively. This implies that the threshold ability level

---

[12] This yields a birth rate of $\beta = ne^{nD}/(e^{nD} - 1) \approx 0.03$. See Dinopoulos and Segerstrom (1999 p. 454) for a derivation.

[13] Hence, a "skilled worker" is defined as having taken four years of college, whereas unskilled workers only have a high-school degree.

[14] As is usual in quality-ladder growth models, this steady-state growth rate is found by noting that the expected number of innovations up to time t equals $\int_0^1 j(w, s)d\omega = \int_0^s I(t)dt$. Using this in the instantaneous utility function (2) and differentiating with respect to time gives the result.

[15] Hence, our procedure is explained by help of Fig. 1 as follows: first, we impose a fixed value for the innovation rate I that follows from the assumption of a two percent steady-state utility growth rate, depending on a particular value for λ. This means that we draw a vertical line for a specific I instead of the curve for (18). The intersection of this vertical line with the curve for (19) defines θ_0, but this depends on the value for η/k. Second, we impose a value for θ_0 as suggested by the data. Given I and θ_0, a "plausible" value for η/k follows from (19), which defines the position of this curve in Fig. 1. Note that our only purpose of assigning specific values to θ_0 from the data is to derive values for η/k. In Sect. 4 below, we will use a specific value for η/k and derive both I and θ_0 *endogenously*.

for the US (Germany, Italy) is $\theta_0 = 0.64$ $(0.77, 0.90)$.[16] Given this, a value for η/k follows for given I from (7) and (8):

$$I = \eta(1 - \theta_0^2)\phi/(2k).$$

Table 1 (page 94) provides a robustness check for the comparison of I and I^{crit}.[17]

Table 1 indicates for each λ the critical threshold ability level θ_0^{crit} for which $I = I^{crit}$ holds. The table shows that our implicit assumption $I < I^{crit}$ in Fig. 2 does (not) hold in the case of the US for low (high) values of λ (the bold numbers indicate a violation of this condition; for $\lambda = 1.2912$, $I = I^{crit}$ holds for given $\theta_0 = 0.64$). For the cases of Germany ($\theta_0 = 0.77$) or Italy ($\theta_0 = 0.90$), the condition $I < I^{crit}$ is fulfilled over the whole range $\lambda \in [1.1, 1.4]$. Thus, in countries with a relatively high proportion of people who have attained tertiary education (e.g. Japan, Canada), an increase in firing costs reduces the skilled wage rate, i.e., the *skilled labor demand effect* dominates the *education equilibrium effect*. This implies that the skilled wage rate and the innovation rate move in the same direction after a change in firing costs. In countries with a relatively low proportion of people who have attained tertiary education (e.g. France, UK, Germany), the skilled wage rate and the innovation rate move in opposite direction after a change in firing costs.

In all cases, after an increase in firing costs, the declining innovation rate implies a decrease in the unskilled unemployment rate because of slower labor market turnover (see (16)), which ceteris paribus induces fewer individuals than before to invest in education since the expected unskilled wage income increases. In the case of $I < I^{crit}(I > I^{crit})$, the rise (decline) in the skilled wage rate works in the opposite (same) direction. In any case, the net effect on θ_0 is positive as depicted in Fig. 1. However, the net effect on the *aggregate* unemployment rate $u_a = \theta_0 u$ in principle is ambiguous.[18] Finally, the decline in unskilled unemployment and the rise in the proportion of unskilled workers both increase

---

[16] From Table A2.4 in OECD (2003), we derive the following threshold ability levels of other major OECD countries for males in 2001: $\theta_0 = 0.54$ in Japan, $\theta_0 = 0.55$ in Canada, $\theta_0 = 0.66$ in Sweden, $\theta_0 = 0.68$ in France, $\theta_0 = 0.70$ in the UK, and $\theta_0 = 0.74$ in the Netherlands. In 1991, the lowest values for males available in the OECD dataset were $\theta_0 = 0.70$ for Canada and $\theta_0 = 0.71$ for the US.

[17] Note from Fig. 1 that the maximum feasible innovation rate consistent with an interior steady-state equilibrium is below $I^{max} = \eta\phi/(2k)$. In Table 1, $I^{crit} > I^{max}$ holds in the case of Italy ($\theta_0 = 0.90$) for the whole range $\lambda \in [1.1, 1.4]$, and in the case of Germany ($\theta_0 = 0.77$) for all λ except $\lambda = 1.4$.

[18] Using (19) and (16), with I as given in (18) and $dI/dB < 0$ from Proposition 1, it is straightforward to derive the following condition for a rise in firing costs to *reduce* the aggregate unemployment rate: $I < \frac{1}{2-u}[\frac{\eta\phi}{k}(1 - u) - \beta u]$. Given our benchmark values (implying $I = 0.0666$) and the intermediate

Table 1. Robustness check for the comparison of I and I^{crit}

	I	η/k	I^{crit}	I^{max}
$\lambda = 1.4$:	0.0594			
$\theta_0 = 0.64$		0.2285	**0.0521**	0.1007
$\theta_0 = 0.77$		0.3314	0.1428	0.1460
$\theta_0 = 0.90$		0.7101	0.4765	0.3128
$\theta_0^{crit} = 0.6559$		0.2368	0.0594	0.1043
$\lambda = 1.35$:	0.0666			
$\theta_0 = 0.64$		0.2562	**0.0621**	0.1129
$\theta_0 = 0.77$		0.3716	0.1638	0.1637
$\theta_0 = 0.90$		0.7962	0.5379	0.3508
$\theta_0^{crit} = 0.6490$		0.2614	0.0666	0.1152
$\lambda = 1.3$:	0.0762			
$\theta_0 = 0.64$		0.2931	**0.0754**	0.1291
$\theta_0 = 0.77$		0.4251	0.1917	0.1873
$\theta_0 = 0.90$		0.9107	0.6196	0.4012
$\theta_0^{crit} = 0.6414$		0.2940	0.0762	0.1295
$\lambda = 1.25$:	0.0896			
$\theta_0 = 0.64$		0.3446	0.0940	0.1518
$\theta_0 = 0.77$		0.4998	0.2307	0.2202
$\theta_0 = 0.90$		1.0708	0.7339	0.4717
$\theta_0^{crit} = 0.6332$		0.3396	0.0896	0.1496
$\lambda = 1.2$:	0.1097			
$\theta_0 = 0.64$		0.4218	0.1219	0.1858
$\theta_0 = 0.77$		0.6117	0.2892	0.2695
$\theta_0 = 0.90$		1.3106	0.9050	0.5774
$\theta_0^{crit} = 0.6242$		0.4080	0.1097	0.1797
$\lambda = 1.15$:	0.1431			
$\theta_0 = 0.64$		0.5502	0.1682	0.2424
$\theta_0 = 0.77$		0.7979	0.3865	0.3515
$\theta_0 = 0.90$		1.7096	1.1898	0.7531
$\theta_0^{crit} = 0.6143$		0.5217	0.1431	0.2298
$\lambda = 1.10$:	0.2098			
$\theta_0 = 0.64$		0.8068	0.2608	0.3554
$\theta_0 = 0.77$		1.1701	0.5809	0.5154
$\theta_0 = 0.90$		2.5070	1.7588	1.1044
$\theta_0^{crit} = 0.6033$		0.7489	0.2098	0.3299

effective unskilled labor supply, which increases goods production and thus consumption quantity $q = c/\lambda$, see (6).

---

case of Germany with $\eta/k = 0.3716$ (derived from setting $\theta_0 = 0.77$), this condition is fulfilled for unskilled unemployment rates up to $u < 0.6676$.

4 Preferences Regarding Firing Costs

In this Section we derive the preferences regarding firing costs of skilled and unskilled workers in a once-and-for-all vote on $B = F/N$, while taking into account that with forward-looking agents, all individuals decide concurrently about their education and their vote on B. This requires three steps of procedure: First, we consider the education decision of a household by comparing the two corresponding discounted lifetime utility streams. This comparison reveals that all households with ability $\theta^i < \theta_0(I)$ $(\theta^i > \theta_0(I))$ prefer to stay unskilled (to become skilled). Second, we maximize separately the discounted (expected) lifetime utility of a skilled and an unskilled household with respect to B under the assumption of a given skill choice. Third, we show that those households who lose the ballot under majority voting (i.e., the skilled) can do no better than staying with their educational decision, even if they perfectly foresee that they would lose the ballot. The level of per-capita firing costs demanded by the majority of unskilled households will be implemented, which results unambiguously in a particular "desired" innovation rate. Depending on this innovation rate, the threshold ability level $\theta_0(I)$ adjusts according to (19).

We will restrict the analysis to a steady-state welfare comparison. This somewhat limits the scope of our analysis, because when assuming a particular starting value B_0 of per-capita firing costs, the welfare comparison should take the transitional period into account.[19] At the end of this section we argue that the implied imprecision is unlikely to change our results qualitatively. Since all individual members of a given household are identical, maximizing discounted lifetime utility of a representative household member is the same as maximizing it for the whole household. Since finitely living household members behave like

---

[19] Since the transitional dynamics are analytically intractable in this kind of model, *one* way is to rely on numerical simulations similar to, e.g., Joseph and Weitzenblum (2003). In a model of unemployment, moral hazard and precautionary savings, they simulate the transitional welfare effects of a cut of the replacement rate, financed by a tax and paid to unemployed workers. Such an analysis is beyond the scope of our paper. *Another* way out is to focus on "stationary political equilibria" as suggested by Saint-Paul (2002, pp. 687-88). This type of equilibrium has two properties: first, we start in a (unique) steady-state equilibrium for a given level of per-capita firing costs B. Second, this initial level of per-capita firing costs equals the majority-winning level, which in our case will be the level preferred by all individuals who choose to stay unskilled under these firing costs. Starting from there, a once-and-for-all vote on the level of B would affirm the current equilibrium. Saint-Paul considers this

> "[...] as the limit steady state of a repeated voting equilibrium as the frequency of voting goes to zero" (ibid, p. 687).

In Sect. 6.4 we will argue that in our particular case, the frequency of voting is irrelevant for the steady-state level of firing costs that we obtain.

a dynastic family, this maximization is done over an infinite horizon. Therefore, the particular age of the (unskilled) median voter does not matter. Due to the assumption of perfect unemployment insurance, the employment status of an unskilled voter also does not matter.

Let us consider first the voting problem of a household in case its members decide to stay unskilled under a given level of firing costs that results from majority voting. Inserting instantaneous utility (2) into total discounted utility (1), and using $p = \lambda$ and

$$\int_0^1 j(w,s)d\omega = \int_0^s I(t)dt$$

yields

$$Z(\theta^i < \theta_0) = [1/(\rho - n)][\log(1 - u) - \log \lambda + I \log \lambda/(\rho - n)] \quad (22)$$

as discounted lifetime utility of an unskilled household with ability $\theta^i < \theta_0$ for all of its members. Since workers do not own firms, the expected consumption expenditure per period of this household is simply $(1 - u)w_L = 1 - u$. Using this and (16) in (22) gives:

$$Z(\theta^i < \theta_0) = \frac{1}{\rho - n} \left\{ \log \left[\frac{Ap(\nu^*)}{\beta + I(B)} \right] - \log \lambda + \frac{I(B) \log \lambda}{\rho - n} \right\}. \quad (23)$$

Differentiating (23) with respect to B yields the f.o.c.

$$\frac{dZ(\theta^i < \theta_0)}{dB} = \frac{1}{\rho - n} \left\{ \frac{\beta + I(B)}{Ap(\nu^*)} \left[-\frac{Ap(\nu^*)dI/dB}{[\beta + I(B)]^2} \right] + \frac{dI}{dB} \frac{\log \lambda}{\rho - n} \right\} = 0,$$

from which we derive the aggregate innovation rate desired by all unskilled workers:

$$\hat{I}(\theta^i < \theta_0) = [(\rho - n)/\log \lambda] - \beta. \quad (24)$$

This is the innovation rate that optimally balances the unskilled workers' conflicting interests in rising consumption quantity versus rising growth of consumer goods quality. Any slightly faster rate of technical progress would result in a net utility loss because the marginal utility gain of faster quality growth (increase in the third term in curly brackets in (23)) would be more than offset by the marginal utility loss of lower consumption quantity (decrease in the first term in curly brackets in (23)). The argument for the case of a slightly lower rate of technical change is analogous. Using our benchmark parameter values, (24) implies $\hat{I}(\theta^i < \theta_0) = 0.0363$ which is well below the innovation rate used above $I = 0.0666$ to generate a 2-percent steady-state utility growth rate. Inserting (24) into (18) and (19) allows us to solve the model for the unique per-capita firing costs preferred by all unskilled workers:

$$\hat{B}(\theta^i < \theta_0) = Ap(\nu^*) \left\{ \frac{\rho - n}{\log \lambda} \eta \theta_0 [\hat{I}(\theta^i < \theta_0)] \left(\frac{\rho - n}{\log \lambda} - \beta \right) \right\}^{-1}$$
$$\{\eta(\lambda - 1)\theta_0 [\hat{I}(\theta^i < \theta_0)]^2 - \sigma k e^{\rho y}[(\rho - n)(1 + 1/\log \lambda) - \beta]\}, \quad (25)$$

where $\theta_0[\hat{I}(\theta^i < \theta_0)]$ denotes the threshold ability level that results after inserting (24) in (19).[20] If $\theta_0 > 0.5$ holds, (25) would also give the level of per-capita firing costs preferred by the majority of all workers.[21] Given equal participation rates of skilled and unskilled workers in a vote on B, the median voter will be unskilled, hence (25) will be realized. In Sect. 5.1 we will exploit the fact that $\hat{B}(\theta^i < \theta_0)$ is rising in the matching efficiency parameter A to analyze effects of a change in the exogenous (A) on the endogenous (B) component of labor market flexibility.

Let us now consider the voting problem of a household in case its members decide to become skilled under a given level of firing costs that results from majority voting. The discounted lifetime utility of a skilled household with ability $\theta^i \geq \theta_0$ of all its members is

$$Z(\theta^i \geq \theta_0) = [1/(\rho - n)][\log(\theta^i w_H) - \log \lambda + I \log \lambda/(\rho - n)]. \quad (26)$$

---

[20] For our benchmark parameter values and $\eta/k = 0.3716$ from the intermediate case of Germany, we derive $\theta_0[\hat{I}(\theta^i < \theta_0)] = 0.8821$. Then (25) implies a positive value of firing costs (and $\partial \hat{B}(\theta^i < \theta_0)/\partial A > 0$ which will be used later) for a matching time up to $y \leq 13.4$ years. Finally, in order to check whether the inequality (11) is fulfilled, we have to assign additional specific parameter values for $y, p(\nu^*)$ and A. A value for $p(\nu^*)$ is imposed by assigning an empirically 'plausible' value for the unskilled unemployment rate in (16). According to Reinberg and Hummel (2003, Table 1b), the average unemployment rate among West German males aged 15-64 with no finished vocational education has been 20.1% within the period 1987 to 2002. Given $\hat{I}(\theta^i < \theta_0) = 0.0363$ and imposing an unskilled unemployment rate $u = 0.2$ and $A = 1$, (16) yields $p(\nu^*) = 0.0533$. Using this and a matching time as low as $y = 0.1$ (note that $\hat{B}(\theta^i < \theta_0)$ is decreasing in y for all $\lambda \in [1.1, 1.4]$), we verify by using (6) that $\hat{B}(\theta^i < \theta_0)\hat{I}(\theta^i < \theta_0) \approx 0.0825 < c(\lambda - 1)/\lambda = (\lambda - 1)(1 - u)\theta_0 \approx 0.2467$.

[21] Since θ_0 is endogenous, we need to state the assumption $\theta_0 > 0.5$ in terms of the exogenous parameters. Inserting (24) into (19), this assumption is equivalent to $\frac{3}{8} > \frac{[(\rho-n)/\log \lambda] - \beta}{(\eta/k)\phi}$. For the whole range of parameter values for λ and η/k that is covered by Table 1, this assumption is clearly satisfied (given our benchmark parameter values for ρ, n, β and ϕ). Moreover, the empirical evidence given in OECD (2003, Table A2.4) suggests threshold ability levels between $\theta_0 = 0.54$ (Japan) and 0.90 (Italy) for males in 2001.

The expected consumption expenditure per period of this household is simply $\theta^i w_H$. Using this and (21) for the skilled wage rate in (26) gives

$$Z(\theta^i \geq \theta_0) =$$
$$\frac{1}{\rho - n} \left\{ \log \left[\frac{\theta^i A p(\nu^*)}{[\beta + I(B)]\sqrt{1 - 2kI(B)/(\eta\phi)}} \right] - \log \lambda + \frac{I(B) \log \lambda}{\rho - n} \right\}.$$
$$(27)$$

The comparison of (27) and (23) immediately reveals that only those households with ability $\theta^i > \theta_0(I)$ have the incentive to invest in education in order to realize

$$Z(\theta^i \geq \theta_0) > Z(\theta^i < \theta_0),$$

where $\theta_0(I)$ is given by (19), with $I = \hat{I}(\theta^i < \theta_0)$ under majority voting for given $\theta_0 > 0.5$. Actually, this means that the minority of skilled workers has to take $\hat{I}(\theta^i < \theta_0)$ and thus $\theta_0[\hat{I}(\theta^i < \theta_0)]$ as given. Finally, even when $I = \hat{I}(\theta^i < \theta_0)$ is perfectly foreseen by all skilled households, they still prefer to become skilled and lose the vote on B rather than working as unskilled and joining the winning majority. Differentiation of (27) with respect to B yields the f.o.c.

$$\frac{dZ(\theta^i \geq \theta_0)}{dB} = \frac{1}{\rho - n} \left[\frac{\frac{(\beta+I)k}{\theta_0\eta\phi} - \theta_0}{(\beta + I)\theta_0} \frac{dI}{dB} + \frac{dI}{dB} \frac{\log \lambda}{\rho - n} \right] = 0, \quad (28)$$

where (19) and (21) have been used. We see that the individual characteristic θ^i cancels out, hence all skilled workers have identical preferences with regard to B. An optimum satisfying this f.o.c. only exists if the first term in square brackets is negative (since $dI/dB < 0$), which is fulfilled if and only if $I < I^{crit}$ holds. From (28) we can derive the aggregate innovation rate desired by all skilled workers in implicit form:[22]

$$\hat{I}(\theta^i \geq \theta_0) = \frac{(\rho - n)(\eta\phi - 2kI)}{(\log \lambda)(\eta\phi - 2kI) + (\rho - n)k} - \beta \quad (29)$$

with $I < \eta\phi/(2k)$ from Fig. 1. Comparison of (29) with (24) gives our first main result:

---

[22] Using the benchmark parameters with the intermediate case of Germany ($\eta/k = 0.3716$), (29) can be transformed into the quadratic equation $I^2 - 0.233337I + 0.004934 = 0$. This has two solutions: the larger one $\hat{I}(\theta^i \geq \theta_0) = 0.2098 > I^{max} = 0.1637$ is not feasible, whereas the smaller one $\hat{I}(\theta^i \geq \theta_0) = 0.0235 < \hat{I}(\theta^i < \theta_0) = 0.0363 < I^{max}$ is feasible.

Proposition 3. *For $I < I^{crit}$, skilled workers (i.e., those individuals who decide to become skilled after a majority decision on the level of firing costs is reached), although not threatened by unemployment risk,*

(i) prefer unambiguously a lower steady-state innovation rate, and

(ii) vote for a higher level of firing costs than unskilled workers.

For $I \geq I^{crit}$, skilled workers vote for zero firing costs.

Given part (i) of Proposition 3, part (ii) follows immediately from $dI/dB < 0$ as stated in Proposition 1. The intuitive reasoning for the surprising finding in part (i) of Proposition 3 is as follows. By voting on the level of firing costs, both worker groups face a trade-off between rising consumption quantity and a slower growth rate of consumer goods quality. On the one hand, larger firing costs reduce the aggregate innovation rate - the growth rate of the quality of consumer goods slows down, which reduces the discounted lifetime utility of both worker groups by the same amount (third term in (23) and (27)). On the other hand, larger firing costs increase labor input in goods production by reducing the unskilled unemployment rate u and increasing the proportion θ_0 of unskilled workers available. Each unskilled worker individually benefits from the decline in u through the increase in expected wage income $w_L(1-u)$ for the given wage rate $w_L \equiv 1$. This effect also benefits skilled workers: a lower unskilled unemployment rate implies higher per-capita consumption expenditure c and thus a larger market for the output of the current quality leader, which raises the reward for innovating ϑ and thus w_H. However, as argued when discussing Fig. 2, an increase in firing costs triggers an *education equilibrium effect* and a *skilled labor demand effect*, and the former dominates the latter if and only if $I < I^{crit}$ holds. Thus, demand for skilled workers declines due to the lower innovation rate, but this is more than offset by the required increase in w_H in order to make the individual with ability $\theta^i = \theta_0$ (with θ_0 now being higher than before) indifferent with respect to his educational choice. Hence, skilled workers benefit from an *additional* gain through stricter employment protection relative to the unskilled. For $I > I^{crit}$, however, both terms in the square brackets in (28) are negative, hence no interior solution exists. Since in this case a decrease in firing costs raises both the growth rate of the quality of consumer goods and the skilled wage rate, skilled workers would vote for zero firing costs (corner solution).

Since skilled workers are still in the minority, the importance of Proposition 3 is not that it explains the observed cross-country variation in firing costs, depending on the proportion of skilled workers in each country.[23] However, the result may nevertheless be relevant in the following sense: as long as $I < I^{crit}$ holds, it offers an argument for why we *should not expect* that the massive increase in the percentage of skilled workers that has been observed in most OECD countries over the last decades, induces political pressure to reduce employment protection levels for less-skilled workers. However, continuous skill upgrading reduces I^{crit} (as shown in Table 1 above), and once $I \geq I^{crit}$ holds, the (relatively large) proportion of skilled workers would vote or lobby for zero firing costs.

At the beginning of this section we argued that in principle, a complete welfare comparison should take into account the transitional period. However, at least when starting from $B_0 < \hat{B}(\theta^i < \theta_0)$, we are confident that taking account for transitional effects would not change our results qualitatively for three reasons. First, a rise in per-capita firing costs (e.g., from B_0 to the level preferred by the unskilled workers) implies an increase in θ_0 (see Fig. 1). Since *fewer* individuals decide to become educated, the education period of length T does not matter for the transition in this case. The required drop in the proportion of skilled workers H/L is achieved by the death of skilled workers, by the birth of unskilled workers who enter immediately the labor market, and by the immediate drop in the innovation rate, which results in declining unskilled unemployment. Second, the immediate decline in the unskilled unemployed rate raises production and consumption quantity of both skilled and unskilled workers. This positive welfare effect dominates in the short run, whereas the negative welfare effect (lower quality growth) arises mainly in the long run. Hence, in this case we do not face the problem that a negative short-run welfare effect more than outweighs possible long-run welfare gains. In the opposite case of $B_0 > \hat{B}(\theta^i < \theta_0)$, this problem arises and could prevent the majority of workers from voting in favor of a reform proposal aimed at reducing firing costs, similar to the failure of the proposal to cut the replacement rate in the model of Joseph and Weitzenblum (2003) that we mentioned earlier. Third, the short-run effect on consumption quantities works in the same direction for skilled and unskilled workers. Hence, there is no reason to believe that due to transitional effects, our result in Proposition 3 should not continue to hold.

---

[23] This conclusion may not hold anymore when considering the different rates of influence held by skilled and unskilled workers in the political process. For instance, voter turnout is usually found to increase with income and, in particular, with education (Wolfinger and Rosenstone, 1980). Moreover, costly lobbying (campaign contributions) may rise with income which is positively related to skills.

5 Determinants of the Level of Firing Costs

5.1 Interactions between Different Types of Labor Market Rigidities

When discussing possible reasons for the persistently higher unemployment rates in many European countries compared to the US, Siebert (1997) stressed the importance of taking account of interactions between different types of labor market rigidities, instead of performing a ceteris-paribus analysis for each friction only:

> "Looking at single institutional characteristics one at a time is never very promising, because the effect of a single institutional arrangement can only be understood in its interaction with other institutional rules. [...] Consequently, the cumulative effect of rules is relevant determining their total impact." (ibid, p. 39).

We therefore analyze the effects of a more efficient matching technology from the viewpoint of both employers and employees, modeled as an increase in the exogenous matching productivity parameter A, on the steady-state equilibrium before and after a response of $\hat{B}(\theta^i < \theta_0)$, respectively. As is obvious from (17a), for given ν^* an increase in A implies the simultaneous reduction of the matching time y. As shown in Fig. 3 (below), for a given level of per-capita firing costs

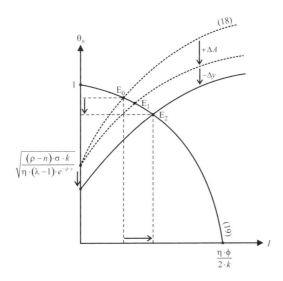

Fig. 3. Steady-state effects of more efficient matching for fixed B in (I, θ_0)-space

B, an increase in A first rotates the curve for (18) clockwise downward. Formally, this follows immediately from (18) when dividing both nominator and denominator by A. Then the resulting decrease in y shifts the entire curve for (18) further downward, including the ordinate intercept (proof for $dI/dy < 0$ is given in Appendix C). The innovation rate increases unambiguously, which implies a decline in θ_0, since more skilled workers are needed for R&D.

The initial positive impact of a rise in A on the innovation rate comes from the reduction in unskilled unemployment, thus u determined in (16) decreases for a given level of I. Lower unemployment implies higher output and thus a larger market for innovating firms. More efficient matching leads to a decrease in the matching time y. This also affects positively the innovation rate because it implies a smaller discount rate on the innovators' future monopoly profits (production can start earlier) at any given value of the reward for innovating ϑ. The net effect on unskilled unemployment is ambiguous since the increase in the innovation rate tends to raise u.

The points $\{E_0, E_1, E_2\}$ in Fig. 4 (below) correspond to those in Fig. 3. Initially, the skilled wage rate increases with rising A due to the drop in unskilled unemployment that raises the profitability of doing R&D (move from E_0 to E_1). The resulting decrease in matching time y triggers an *education equilibrium effect* and a *skilled labor demand*

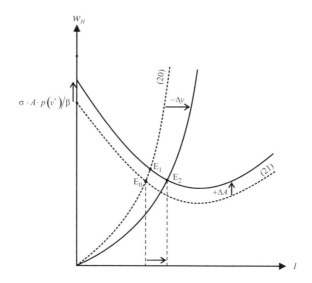

Fig. 4. Steady-state effects of more efficient matching for fixed B in (I, w_H)-space

effect, and the former dominates the latter for $I < I^{crit}$. Thus, demand for skilled workers rises due to the larger innovation rate, but this positive effect on w_H is more than offset by the required decrease in w_H in order to make the individual with ability $\theta^i = \theta_0$ (with θ_0 now being lower than before) indifferent with respect to his educational choice. The required decrease in w_H comes from the fact that an increase in I raises u which reduces $w_L(1 - u)$. Hence, a lower w_H is needed to induce all individuals with $\theta^i > \theta_0$ to become educated (move from E_1 to E_2 in Fig. 4). The net effect on w_H is ambiguous for $I < I^{crit}$, and unambiguously positive for $I > I^{crit}$.

Since the matching time is reduced, the increase in A can be interpreted as an increase in labor market flexibility. This raises unambiguously the level of firing costs preferred by the unskilled workers who form the majority. Formally, $\partial \hat{B}(\theta^i < \theta_0)/\partial A > 0$ follows from (25) whenever $\hat{B}(\theta^i < \theta_0) > 0$ holds. This could be illustrated by help of Fig. 3 as follows: suppose that $I = \hat{I}(\theta^i < \theta_0)$ holds at the initial steady-state equilibrium E_0. After the (unexpected) change in A and y, unskilled workers (i.e., those who decide not to invest in education under the new B) vote for a new value for $\hat{B}(\theta^i < \theta_0)$ such that the curve for (18) rotates counterclockwise around its ordinate intercept until $I = \hat{I}(\theta^i < \theta_0)$ is reestablished at E_0 again. Hence our second main result follows:

Proposition 4. *An exogenous increase in labor market flexibility, ceteris paribus accelerating innovation and economic growth, increases the political support for larger firing costs of unskilled workers (i.e., of those individuals who decide not to become skilled after a majority decision on the level of firing costs is reached for the given new value of A), thereby reducing innovation and growth again.*

Hence, a more flexible labor market with more efficient matching has two effects: first, it induces an increase in the aggregate innovation and growth rate for a given level of firing costs. Second, it increases the level of per-capita firing costs preferred by the majority-winning unskilled workers, which in turn reduces the steady-state innovation and growth rate.[24] The intuition for this result is as follows: for the optimal decision on B, the net effect of an increase in matching efficiency A on the unskilled workers' unemployment rate (which is ambiguous for given B) does not matter. The welfare-maximizing choice of per-capita

---

[24] Suppose that $I < I^{crit}$ holds. Then, skilled workers (i.e., those individuals who would still decide to become skilled under the new $\hat{B}(\theta^i < \theta_0)$) vote for a level of firing costs that exceeds the one preferred by the unskilled by a constant 'markup' as is obvious from comparing (29) and (24). Hence they also increase their demand for firing costs after a rise in A. The intuition is similar to that given for the unskilled workers.

firing costs B results in the *unique* desired innovation rate (24) that is independent of A and y - the marginal effects of a change in B on the lifetime utility derived from consumption quantity and quality growth do not change. Since the increase in A raises the steady-state innovation rate, optimal behavior of the unskilled (as of the skilled) workers is to restore the welfare-maximizing path of I, which requires that firing costs increase accordingly. A positive effect on the level of discounted lifetime utility of all workers will remain after $I = \hat{I}(\theta^i < \theta_0)$ is restored again. This is because it remains the increase in A in the first term in curly brackets of (23) and (27), respectively, and with fixed $I = \hat{I}(\theta^i < \theta_0)$, an increase in A reduces u unambiguously.

Hence, given that the economy starts at $I = \hat{I}(\theta^i < \theta_0)$, an increase in matching efficiency would not change the steady-state innovation and growth rate at all if a once-and-for-all vote on the level of B took place thereafter. In Sect. 6.4 we will argue that $I = \hat{I}(\theta^i < \theta_0)$ is preserved even with repeated voting.

The result presented in this section serves as an example for the interaction of labor market frictions as stressed by Siebert (1997) cited above. Here, one rigidity of the labor market is the non-instantaneous matching of unemployed workers with producing firms as defined by the matching function $Am(V, L)$. More efficient matching works toward an alleviation of this rigidity. However, this intensifies a second labor market rigidity, namely the level of requested firing costs: alleviating one (exogenous) rigidity aggravates the other (endogenous) one.

5.2 The Trade-off between Growth and Employment Protection

In his vintage model of exogenous growth, Saint-Paul (2002) finds that the workers' gains from employment protection are smaller the higher the growth rate, i.e., the faster the rate of creative destruction.[25] The reasoning for his finding is as follows. Employment protection keeps a certain fraction of the workforce in vintages with productivity below that of the most recent vintage, because in his model, firms determine endogenously the optimal exit date which is postponed by larger firing

---

[25] This may be viewed as a contrast to his own empirical findings (Saint-Paul, 1996, pp. 283-86). There, he finds the empirical regularity present in EU countries that, since the 1960s, governments reduced (increased) firing costs at times of low (high) growth. Given that the government did follow the workers' demand for employment protection, two explanations for this apparent contradiction seem plausible. Either the sign of the (theoretical) correlation between growth and requested firing costs should be positive as is found in Saint-Paul's data, or his empirical findings reflect only short-sighted motivation of workers when voting on firing costs. Our model takes a long-run perspective.

costs.[26] Faster growth enlarges the productivity gap between old and new vintages, whereas the opportunity costs of working (that is, the value of being unemployed) are increasing at the current growth rate. Hence, the value of keeping the current employment (and reaping the rent that arises by assumption of match-specific human capital) deteriorates faster with higher economic growth, which reduces support for employment protection by the decisive median voter.

Since the growth rate is endogenous in our model, the comparative static exercise is less straightforward than in Saint-Paul's model. However, to analyze workers' attitudes toward employment protection in a faster growing economy, we can look at the effects of changes to the exogenous parameters closely related to growth, namely a rise in the size of innovations λ and a rise in the R&D productivity parameter η. The marginal effect of a larger size of innovations on the steady-state utility growth rate $\dot{z}/z = I \log \lambda$ is positive for fixed B:

$$\frac{\partial(\dot{z}/z)}{\partial \lambda} = \frac{\partial I_1}{\partial \lambda}(\log \lambda) + \frac{I_1}{\lambda}$$
$$= \frac{1}{2}\left[\left(\frac{P}{2}\right)^2 - Q\right]^{-1/2} \frac{Ap(\nu^*)}{B}\theta_0(\log \lambda) + \frac{I_1}{\lambda} > 0, \quad (30)$$

where
$$I_1 \equiv -P/2 + \sqrt{((P/2)^2 - Q)} > 0$$

with $P > 0$ and $Q < 0$ as defined in Appendix B. Due to $\frac{\partial I_1}{\partial \lambda} > 0$, an increase in λ shifts the curve for (18) downward in Fig. 1 without affecting the curve for (19). Hence, for given B, a larger size of innovations speeds up innovation and growth. However, differentiation of (25) shows that $\partial \hat{B}(\theta^i < \theta_0)/\partial \lambda > 0$ holds.[27] Therefore, the results

---

[26] More precisely, the optimal exit date is determined by equalizing the marginal loss per unit of time (wage minus productivity) to the annuity equivalent of the firing costs. Thus, in Saint-Paul's model, production takes place with several technologies simultaneously, and technical progress improves the efficiency of the production process without affecting the quality of consumer goods. Therefore, the consumption side of the economy can be (and actually is) neglected in his framework. In our model, by contrast (that explains 'creative destruction' *endogenously*), technical progress involves product innovations that result in rising consumer goods quality over time. Since we assume limit pricing behavior of the quality leader, and consumers only buy goods with the lowest quality-adjusted price, consumer goods of different quality levels do not coexist in our framework. Hence, rising firing costs do not extend the lifetime of *old* firms but only the expected incumbency period $1/I$ of the *current* quality leader.

[27] Whereas the nominator of (25) increases unambiguously with rising λ, a *sufficient* condition for that the denominator of (25) declines with rising λ is $1 \geq [k/(\eta\phi)]\{3[(\rho - n)/\log \lambda] - 2\beta\}$. For our benchmark parameter values, the RHS of this inequality takes a value of 0.4254. Moreover, this inequality is satisfied for *any* possible values for λ and η/k considered in Table 1.

of an increase in λ are similar to that of an increase in the matching efficiency (Proposition 4). The only difference in this case is that the growth rate desired by unskilled workers (i.e., by those individuals who do not invest in education under the new $\hat{B}(\theta^i < \theta_0)$) is affected: $\partial \hat{I}(\theta^i < \theta_0)/\partial \lambda = -(\rho - n)/[(\log \lambda)^2 \lambda] < 0$. If each innovation raises product quality to a larger extent, workers would adjust their vote on firing costs as to reduce the desired expected frequency of innovations. This is easily understood by looking at (23): on the one hand, a larger size of innovations raises the marginal utility gain of a slightly increasing innovation rate in terms of higher quality growth (third term in curly brackets of (23)). On the other hand, the marginal utility loss of a rise in I in terms of declining consumption quantity is unaffected (first term in curly brackets of (23)). Therefore, equality between marginal gains and losses is reached through a lower "desired" innovation rate, which requires to vote for a higher B.[28] Hence the steady-state utility growth rate $\dot{z}/z = I \log \lambda$ with voting on firing costs declines:

$$\frac{\partial(\dot{z}/z)}{\partial \lambda}\Big|_{I=\hat{I}(\theta<\theta_0)} = \frac{\partial(\rho - n - \beta \log \lambda)}{\partial \lambda} = -\frac{\beta}{\lambda} < 0, \qquad (31)$$

and $\theta_0[\hat{I}(\theta^i < \theta_0)]$ increases according to (19).

We now discuss the effects of an increase in R&D productivity η. Fig. 5 (page 107) illustrates what happens in this case, both before and after unskilled workers (i.e., those who still remain unskilled after a vote on B for the new value of η) react by adjusting their desired level of firing costs.

The economy starts in the steady-state equilibrium E_0 at which the resulting aggregate innovation rate happens to equal the innovation rate desired by unskilled workers (the majority), $I = \hat{I}(\theta^i < \theta_0)$. A positive R&D-technology shock $+\Delta\eta$ (which was unexpected in the previous vote on B) shifts both the skilled labor full employment curve (19) and the R&D equilibrium curve (18) to the right, with the ordinate (abscissa) intercept of the latter (former) declining (rising). Without voting on firing costs thereafter, the steady-state equilibrium would shift from E_0 to E_1 where the innovation rate has risen unambiguously, whereas the net effect on the threshold ability level is ambiguous. The curve for (19) shifts outward since with a higher R&D productivity, any positive given amount $(1 - \theta_0^2)\phi N/2$ of skilled workers can produce more R&D output than before (formally, θ_0 rises for any given $I > 0$ in (19)). The downward shift of (18) is explained by the fact that expected R&D benefits increase for given skilled labor input (these additional

---

[28] By the second term in curly brackets of (23), consumption quantity is reduced due to higher markup pricing. This, however, does not affect the optimal decision about B.

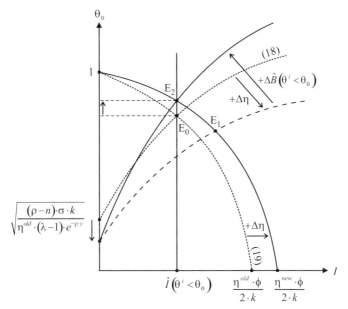

Fig. 5. Steady-state effects of rising $R\&D$ productivity with voting response

benefits will be transferred to a higher skilled wage rate because of free entry in the R&D race).[29] However, since the welfare-maximizing innovation rate given in (24) is unaffected, unskilled workers (i.e., those individuals who decide not to invest in education under a vote on B for the given new η) raise their demand for employment protection in order to restore this level.[30] Hence with voting on B, the curve for (18) rotates counterclockwise around its ordinate intercept like in Fig. 1, and the steady-state equilibrium moves from E_1 to E_2. Relative to the old steady state at E_0, the proportion of unskilled workers has risen because fewer skilled workers than before are needed to produce the same aggregate innovation rate $\hat{I}(\theta^i < \theta_0)$. Hence, in our different framework, Saint-Paul's (2002, p. 699) conclusion that

> "[...] periods of high growth may be a more appropriate time for increasing labor market flexibility [...]"

---

[29] The formal proof is similar to Appendix A. Applying the implicit function theorem to (18) shows that $dI/d\eta > 0$ if and only if condition (11) is fulfilled, which holds necessarily for any positive R&D investment. Therefore, the R&D equilibrium curve shifts downward at any given level of θ_0.

[30] Formally, $\partial\hat{B}(\theta^i < \theta_0)/\partial\eta > 0$ holds not only for our benchmark parameter values but for the whole range of all possible parameter values that result in an interior steady-state solution with $\theta_0 \in]0,1[$ and $\hat{B}(\theta^i < \theta_0) > 0$.

no longer holds. Instead, we state our third main result:

Proposition 5. *Given $I < I^{crit}(I > I^{crit})$, an exogenous positive growth shock – taking the form of a larger size of innovations λ or a higher R&D productivity η – increases political support of all workers (of the individuals who decide to stay unskilled under the new B) for larger firing costs, and raises the proportion of unskilled workers in the new steady-state. In the case of a larger λ, the new desired innovation rate $\hat{I}(\theta^i < \theta_0)$ is lower than before, whereas this rate does not change in the case of a larger η.*

The results of this section could also be viewed as a caveat to the findings of Arnold (2002). He shows that in a North-South model of intraindustry trade with innovation and endogenous growth in the North and (exogenous) imitation by the South, the growth effects of increased Southern imitation depend on Northern labor market flexibility. The latter is modeled by an exogenous parameter denoting the outflow rate from unemployment which equals our job-finding rate $p(\nu)$. In the case of high (low) labor market flexibility (i.e., large (low) $p(\nu)$), increased Southern imitation stimulates (impedes) Northern economic growth. That is, alleviating the (only) labor market distortion in his model tends to support growth-enhancing effects of a change to another exogenous parameter, in that case a rise in the Southern imitation rate.[31] In our model, by contrast, alleviating the exogenous component of labor market rigidity (increase in A) creates political support for another, growth-retarding distortion of the labor market (an increase in firing costs).[32] This effect offsets any potentially growth-enhancing exogenous shocks (as discussed above) or policies like those related to international trade and imitation that could be added to our model: the steady-state utility growth rate with voting on firing costs is fixed at $\dot{z}/z = \hat{I}(\theta^i < \theta_0) \log \lambda = \rho - n - \beta \log \lambda$. Therefore, there is no systematic link anymore in our framework between one particular element

---

[31] In Arnold's model, the negative effects of rising Southern imitation on Northern growth consist of a shortening of product life cycles (harming monopolists' profits and thus innovation incentives) and a rise in frictional unemployment (because imitation reallocates production to the South due to lower marginal labor costs). The positive effect on Northern growth is rooted in the efficiency gain in Southern production, which raises world demand for Northern monopolists' goods and thus their profits, which stimulates innovation incentives.

[32] A notable similarity between Arnold (2002) and our model is that more efficient matching ceteris paribus (that is, for a given level of firing costs in our case) raises the long-run growth rate. However, this result hinges crucially on the presence of scale effects in Arnold's model (a higher total number of employed workers implies an increase in the innovation rate), whereas our model is free of scale effects (I is independent of the size of the total workforce).

of *exogenous* labor market flexibility and the innovation and growth rate.

6 Qualifications and Extensions

6.1 Accounting for Firm Ownership of Workers

Neglecting firm ownership of workers influences obviously our results concerning the level of requested firing costs. Like in Saint-Paul (2002), this assumption is made mainly because it allows us to concentrate on the conflicting interests *among* workers, instead of adding a political conflict between workers and shareholders (which may be identical to workers). Moreover, it allows us to solve our model explicitly for $\hat{B}(\theta^i < \theta_0)$ and to provide a clear discussion of its determinants. As in Saint-Paul's model, taking account of firm ownership of workers would weaken political support for firing costs (the optimal balance between quality growth and consumption quantity is found at a higher desired innovation rate), depending on the relative importance of labor and capital income. This is because the value of firms (thus, $e^{-yr}\vartheta$) depreciates with higher firing costs. If the fraction of financial assets in total income were higher for skilled workers than for the unskilled, this would decrease the demand for firing costs among the former by more than among the latter. However, accounting for equal share ownership among skilled and unskilled workers affects our results in (24) and (29) only quantitatively, without having any impact on Proposition 3. Moreover, Propositions 4 and 5 are not affected at all, even when taking account of an unequal distribution of share ownership across worker types. Finally, since share ownership among workers is much more common in the US than in West European countries, this may provide one explanation for the much lower level of firing costs observed in the US.

6.2 R&D Incentives of Industry Leaders

One may wonder whether introducing firing costs should provide an incentive for quality leader firms to improve their own products. By gaining a quality advantage of size λ^2 instead of λ, they could try to avoid the risk of having to pay the firing costs once being overtaken by an innovating follower firm. However, it turns out that this idea conflicts with the R&D process put forward in Sect. 2.2 above, which is taken from Segerstrom (1998) and Dinopoulos and Segerstrom (1999): it is assumed that *all* firms have the *same* R&D technology, and once a new innovation occurs, the patent attached to the previous leading technology expires and becomes common knowledge. Therefore, quality

followers do not have to "catch up before they can pass" (i.e., they do
not have to copy the current state-of-the-art product before being able
to improve it), contrary to the R&D setup in Aghion et al. (2001).[33]
This means that even if quality leader firms improved their own products, the instantaneous probability of a further quality-augmenting innovation by followers would not change, hence the leader's probability
of having to pay the firing costs does not change. The intuition follows
Grossman and Helpman (1991):

> "[...] we implicitly suppose that potential entrants can, via in-
> spection of the goods on the market, learn enough about the
> state of knowledge to mount their own research efforts, even if
> the patent laws (or the lack of complete knowledge about best
> production methods) prevent them from manufacturing the cur-
> rent generation products. This specification captures in part the
> often noted, public-good characteristics of technology" (ibid, p.
> 47).

Hence, the "Arrow effect" still ensures that industry leaders find it
more profitable to direct their R&D investments toward other industries in which they are quality followers (see Grossman and Helpman,
1991, p. 47, for proof), irrespective of the firing costs. To capture the
empirical fact of significant R&D expenditure of industry leaders, it
would be necessary either to introduce R&D cost advantages for them
relative to follower firms, as in Segerstrom and Zolnierek (1999) and
Segerstrom (2004), or to assume Stackelberg behavior of industry leaders, as in Etro (2004). Both approaches, however, would complicate the
Schumpeterian unemployment mechanism described in Sect. 2.3 considerably, which is beyond the scope of this paper (but might provide
a fruitful subject for future research).

6.3 The Effects of Firing Costs on Hiring

A basic principle of labor economics is that higher firing costs tend to
decrease both hiring and firing of firms, such that the net effect on unemployment becomes ambiguous. This accords with empirical evidence
referred to in footnote 1 above. At first sight, it seems that this paper
does not indicate the negative effect of firing costs on hiring: in (17),
the steady-state vacancy rate is independent of B, and a higher level of
B reduces unambiguously unskilled unemployment due to lower labor
market turnover (declining "Schumpeterian unemployment"). Inspection of equation (13) that describes the process of vacancy creation

---

[33] As noted by Segerstrom (2004), this assumption made by Aghion et al.
(2001) has the counterfactual implication that small firms do not innovate.

reveals that actually, we did account for the negative effect of firing costs on hiring: larger firing costs reduce the aggregate innovation rate (since firms anticipate expected costs of layoffs when deciding on the optimal level of R&D investment), which tends to reduce the number of vacancies posted. However, this effect is completely offset by the induced increase in market size: since the unskilled unemployment rate declines and the proportion of unskilled workers rises with larger firing costs, aggregate production must also increase, which raises unskilled labor demand of innovating firms. That is, larger firing costs reduce the frequency of vacancy postings but once innovation occurs, the number of posted vacancies is higher, reflecting the larger market size for each incumbent monopolist.

This is a knife-edge result that hinges crucially on the assumption of a linear production function

$$Q_t = (1 - u)\theta_0 N_t.$$

Assume now that households use part of their savings to finance the accumulation of a physical capital stock K with $K_t = K_0 e^{nt}$. Note that the capital stock must grow at the population growth rate in order to ensure constant per-capita consumption expenditure, similar to (6), that we need because of constant wage rates. With a Cobb-Douglas production function

$$Q_t = [(1 - u)\theta_0 N_t]^\alpha K_t^{1-\alpha}, \quad 0 < \alpha < 1,$$

the market-size effect of a declining u and a rising θ_0 would be alleviated, and a positive (negative) relationship between the steady-state vacancy rate and the aggregate innovation rate (the level of firing costs) would result. To show this, we first use the new production function (that equals total consumption) in (14) and solve this equation for the new steady-state unskilled unemployment rate in implicit form:

$$u = \frac{(1-u)^\alpha K_0^{1-\alpha} I}{\beta \theta_0^{1-\alpha}} + 1 - \frac{Ap(\nu^*)}{\beta}. \tag{32}$$

In (32), θ_0 is determined by a new R&D equilibrium condition replacing (18), and by (19) for skilled labor full employment. Equation (32) reduces to (16) for $\alpha = 1$, and it still implies a positive long-run relationship between innovation and unskilled unemployment. Then, using (32) and the new production function in (13) gives the new steady-state vacancy rate

$$\nu^* = \frac{\frac{(1-u)^\alpha e^{ny}(I+\beta)}{\theta_0^{1-\alpha}} - Ap(\nu^*)}{\beta - \delta} K_0^{1-\alpha}, \tag{33}$$

which reduces again to (17) for $\alpha = 1$. Now, an increase in firing costs has two effects on ν^*. First, by reducing the innovation rate, ν^* declines which is the expected negative effect on hiring that vanishes in the linear-production case. Second, by reducing the unskilled unemployment rate, ν^* somewhat rises again. This second effect is weakened indirectly, however, by the first: a lower vacancy rate reduces the job-finding rate $p(\nu^*)$ due to the monotonous matching function and therefore tends to raise u according to (32) again. Overall, a net negative effect of rising firing costs on the steady-state vacancy rate will prevail, which somewhat weakens the market-size effect referred to above. Hence, after a rise in firing costs, the reduction (increase) in u (θ_0) is alleviated, with the extent depending on the size of α.

It turns out that this extension of the model does not affect our main results qualitatively. The crucial point in the logic of Proposition 3 is that for $I < I^{crit}$, skilled workers realize additional benefits from higher firing costs relative to the unskilled because the *education equilibrium effect* dominates the *skilled labor demand effect*. This reasoning and thus Proposition 3 still hold. Proposition 4 also remains valid since $dI/dA > 0$ and $dI/dB < 0$ continue to hold. All workers still face the same trade-off between consumption quantity and consumption quality growth. However, with the new production function, the increase in consumption quantity after a marginal rise in firing costs is smaller than before. This is because the negative effects of firing costs on hiring alleviate the net reduction in unskilled unemployment. Since the negative effect of a marginal reduction in the innovation rate on workers' utility in terms of quality growth is unchanged, they vote for a lower level of B than in the linear-production case. Hence, for a given output level, the innovation rate $\hat{I}(\theta^i < \theta_0)$ that is realized after the vote on B is larger than with the old production function. Finally, by a similar argument, the logic of Proposition 5 is also not affected qualitatively by this extension of our model.

6.4 Accounting for Repeated Voting

In general, with repeated voting on a policy issue, there may be important general-equilibrium feedback effects that affect voting behavior in the future, which, with forward-looking voters, can influence voting behavior today. In particular, rational voters will take into consideration that their vote today may change the distribution of workers tomorrow, which could induce strategic voting. This in turn could lead to situations of multiple politico-economic equilibria. In their introductory section, Hassler et al. (2003) provide a broad overview over the relevant literature on these issues.

Fortunately, things are much simpler in our framework. First of all, since all unskilled and all skilled workers have the same preferences about firing costs, respectively, there are only two possible political outcomes: $\hat{B}(\theta^i < \theta_0)$, preferred by all unskilled workers and given in (25), and $\hat{B}(\theta^i \geq \theta_0) > \hat{B}(\theta^i < \theta_0)$, preferred by all unskilled workers if $I < I^{crit}$ (or, alternatively, $\hat{B}(\theta^i \geq \theta_0) = 0$ if $I \geq I^{crit}$). Second, these two desired levels of per-capita firing costs are unique, respectively. Third, the proportion θ_0 of unskilled workers is a smoothly increasing function of B as can be seen from Fig. 1. Then, all we need to ensure $B = \hat{B}(\theta^i < \theta_0)$ as the unique political outcome with repeated voting (irrespective of the frequency of voting) is to assume that $\theta_0 > 0.5$ holds (which can be stated in terms of fundamental parameters, see footnote 21).

7 Conclusions

This paper contributes to the literature on the growth effects of labor market flexibility from a political economy point of view within the setup of a standard Schumpeterian endogenous growth model without scale effects. Given the rigidity of non-instantaneous matching of unskilled workers with vacancies posted by new quality leader firms, we analyze both general equilibrium consequences of and political demand for firing costs. We find that although firing costs reduce the steady-state innovation and growth rate, all workers vote for positive firing costs (if the innovation rate falls short of a critical level) by evaluating a trade-off between the quantity of consumption and the growth of the quality of consumer goods. If the innovation rate is below the critical level, skilled workers (i.e., those individuals who still invest in education after the majority-winning unskilled workers have decided on firing costs) even vote for larger firing costs than unskilled workers, although only the latter can become unemployed. Moreover, we find that workers increase their demand for firing costs in the case of more efficient matching on the labor market. Hence, alleviating a labor market rigidity that is exogenous to our framework aggravates the rigidity that is determined endogenously by majority voting.

We can derive two major insights from our analysis. First, contrary to the conclusion of Saint-Paul (2002), our results do not support the view that employment protection is likely to be lower in fast growing economies. Once the aggregate innovation and growth rate is made endogenous in a neo-Schumpeterian framework, all workers have an individually 'optimal' rate of creative destruction. The median voter's (single-peaked) preferences for this rate of innovation are realized by adjusting the endogenous labor market rigidity accordingly. If the exogenous component of labor market rigidity or other exogenous parameters change in a way to increase innovation and long-run growth, workers vote for *more* employment protection. Second, our results suggest that the interplay between labor market flexibility and economic growth tends to be more complicated than reflected in popular statements like 'a flexible labor market tends to support economic growth'. This may well hold for all defining elements of labor market flexibility taken as an aggregate (hence it holds in the model of Arnold, 2002, where there is just one type of labor market rigidity). However, because some of those elements are endogenous to the political process and interact with other elements as illustrated for example by our model, it seems to be questionable to explain cross-country variations in economic growth by differences in a single aspect of labor market rigidity.

Our results are unlikely to change qualitatively once one extends the analysis to cover the case of incomplete unemployment insurance. This would introduce unemployed workers' preferences for firing costs that differ from those of unskilled employed workers. However, it seems justifiable to assume that the median voter is still an unskilled employed worker who mainly cares about expected wage earnings.[34]

An interesting extension of our analysis would be to add the possibility for firms to escape firing costs by outsourcing the production of consumer goods to a foreign country. Alternatively, instead of firing costs, one could also analyze the preferences of different worker groups for unemployment benefits within our dynamic setting.

Appendix

A. The Proof of $dI/d\theta_0 > 0$ in (18)

To prove that the curve for (18) is upward sloping in Fig. 1, we write

$$f(I, \theta_0) \equiv I - \frac{\eta e^{-\rho y} Ap(\nu^*)\theta_0^2(\lambda - 1) - (\rho - n)\sigma Ap(\nu^*)k}{\sigma Ap(\nu^*)k + (\beta + I)\eta e^{-\rho y}\theta_0 B} = 0 \quad (A.1)$$

---

[34] Saint-Paul (1996) distinguishes five groups of individuals (skilled workers, unskilled and semi-skilled workers, short-term unemployed, long-term unemployed, and capitalists) and argues that

> "typically, the decisive voter will be considered as a member of [the] group [of] unskilled and semi-skilled employed workers. This is meant to be a relatively broad group, including workers without a college degree, who make up more than 70% of the workforce in most European countries" (ibid, p. 275).

and apply the implicit function theorem:

$$\frac{dI}{d\theta_0} = -\frac{\partial f/\partial \theta_0}{\partial f/\partial I}$$

$$= -\frac{-[2\eta e^{-\rho y}Ap(\nu^*)\theta_0(\lambda - 1)]den + nom(\beta + I)e^{-\rho y}\eta B}{den^2 + nom\ e^{-\rho y}\theta_0\eta B},$$

$$\text{(A.2)}$$

where nom and den denote nominator and denominator of (18), respectively. Using $den/nom = 1/I$, (A.2) takes a positive value if and only if

$$2Ap(\nu^*)\theta_0(\lambda - 1) > I(\beta + I)B \qquad \text{(A.3)}$$

is fulfilled. By using $\beta + I = Ap(\nu^*)/(1-u)$ from (16) and subsequently $\theta_0(1-u) = c/\lambda$ from (6), condition (A.3) can be restated as follows:

$$2c(\lambda - 1)/\lambda > IB. \qquad \text{(A.4)}$$

This is fulfilled because of our assumption (11).

B. Proof of Proposition 1

Equation (18) can be solved for

$$I^2 + \underbrace{\left[\frac{\sigma Ap(\nu^*)k}{e^{-\rho y}\eta\theta_0 B} + \beta\right]}_{\equiv P}I + \underbrace{\frac{Ap(\nu^*)}{B}\left[\frac{(\rho - n)\sigma k}{e^{-\rho y}\eta\theta_0} - \theta_0(\lambda - 1)\right]}_{\equiv Q} = 0. \quad \text{(A.5)}$$

This quadratic equation yields two roots

$$I_{1,2} = -P/2 \pm \sqrt{(P/2)^2 - Q},$$

of which only

$$I_1 = -P/2 + \sqrt{(P/2)^2 - Q}$$

is positive. Moreover, there are no complex solutions since $Q < 0$ immediately follows from looking at the ordinate intercept of (18) in Fig. 1. Thus, I_1 is the only feasible solution. Differentiating this with respect to B gives

$$\frac{dI_1}{dB} = \frac{P - \beta}{2B} + \frac{1}{2}[(P/2)^2 - Q]^{-\frac{1}{2}}\left(P\frac{\beta - P}{2B} + \frac{Q}{B}\right). \qquad \text{(A.6)}$$

The derivative in (A.6) is negative if and only if

$$[(P/2)^2 - Q]^{-\frac{1}{2}}\left[\frac{P(P - \beta)}{2} - Q\right] > P - \beta,$$

which can be rewritten as

$$\frac{P}{2} - \frac{Q}{P - \beta} > [(P/2)^2 - Q]^{\frac{1}{2}} = I + \frac{P}{2}, \tag{A.7}$$

where the equality on the RHS follows from our definition in (A.5). Simplifying and substituting for P and Q in (A.7) finally gives the condition

$$I < \frac{e^{-\rho y}\eta\theta_0^2(\lambda - 1)}{\sigma k} - (\rho - n). \tag{A.8}$$

Note that the RHS of (A.8) equals (18) for $B = 0$. Since (18) can be written as

$$I = \frac{\frac{e^{-\rho y}\eta\theta_0^2(\lambda-1)}{\sigma k} - (\rho - n)}{1 + \frac{(\beta+I)e^{-\rho y}\eta\theta_0 B}{\sigma A p(\nu^*)k}}, \tag{A.9}$$

(A.8) follows immediately. Hence, we have shown that an increase in firing costs reduces the value for the innovation rate I defined implicitly in (18), given any feasible value for θ_0. Thus, the curve for (18) shifts to the left as depicted in Fig. 1, whereas the curve for (19) is not affected. This proves Proposition 1.

C. The Proof of $dI/dy < 0$ in (18)

In order to show that the curve for (18) shifts downward again after the induced decline in the matching time y as shown in Fig. 3, we use (A.1) and implicit differentiation:

$$\frac{dI}{dy} = \frac{\partial f/\partial y}{\partial f/\partial I}$$
$$= -\frac{-[-\rho\eta e^{-\rho y}Ap(\nu^*)\theta_0^2(\lambda - 1)]den + nom[-\rho(\beta + I)\eta e^{-\rho y}\theta_0 B]}{den^2 + nom\, e^{-\rho y}\theta_0\eta B}.$$
$$\tag{A.10}$$

Using $den/nom = 1/I$, (A.10) takes a negative value if and only if

$$c(\lambda - 1)/\lambda > IB$$

is satisfied, which is our assumption in (11). Therefore, a reduction in y shifts the curve for (18) downward in Fig. 3, whereas the curve for (19) is not affected. Thus, $dI/dy < 0$ follows immediately.

Acknowledgements

The author would like to thank seminar participants of the University of Dortmund (in particular Christian Bayer), participants of the DEGIT VIII conference, Helsinki, May 30-31, 2003 (in particular Volker Grossmann, Ingrid Kubin and Omar Licandro), and participants of the annual meeting of Verein für Socialpolitik, Zurich, September 30 - October 3, 2003, for helpful discussion. The constructive comments of an anonymous referee are gratefully acknowledged. The usual disclaimer applies.

References

Aghion, P., Harris, C., Howitt, P., and Vickers, J. (2001): "Competition, Imitation and Growth with Step-by-Step Innovation." *Review of Economic Studies* 68: 467-492.

Aghion, P., and Howitt, P. (1992): "A Model of Growth through Creative Destruction." *Econometrica* 60: 323-351.

Aghion,P., and Howitt, P. (1994): "Growth and Unemployment." *Review of Economic Studies* 61: 477-494.

Aghion, P., and Howitt, P. (1998): *Endogenous Growth Theory*. Cambridge, Mass.: MIT Press.

Arnold, L. G. (2002): "On the Growth Effects of North-South Trade: the Role of Labor Market Flexibility." *Journal of International Economics* 58: 451-466.

Dinopoulos, E., and Segerstrom, P. S. (1999): "A Schumpeterian Model of Protection and Relative Wages." *American Economic Review* 89: 450-472.

Dinopoulos, E., and Thompson, P. (1996): "A Contribution to the Empirics of Endogenous Growth." *Eastern Economic Journal* 22: 389-400.

Etro, F. (2004): "Innovation by Leaders." *Economic Journal* 114: 281- 303.

Grossman, G. M., and Helpman, E. (1991): "Quality Ladders in the Theory of Growth." *Review of Economic Studies* 58: 43-61.

Hassler, J., Rodriguez Mora, J. V., Storesletten, K., and Zilibotti, F. (2003): "The Survival of the Welfare State." *American Economic Review* 93: 87-112.

Jones, C. I. (1995): "R&D-Based Models of Economic Growth." *Journal of Political Economy* 103: 759-784.

Jones, C. I. (1999): "Growth: With or Without Scale Effects?" *American Economic Review, Papers and Proceedings* 89: 139-144.

Joseph, G., and Weitzenblum, T. (2003): "Optimal Unemployment Insurance: Transitional Dynamics vs. Steady State." *Review of Economic Dynamics* 6: 869-884.

OECD (1999): *Employment Outlook*. Paris.

OECD (2003): *Education at a Glance*. Paris.

Reinberg, A., and Hummel, M. (2003): "Geringqualifizierte: In der Krise verdrängt, sogar im Boom vergessen." *IAB Kurzbericht* Nr. 19, Institut für Arbeits- und Berufsforschung der Bundesanstalt für Arbeit, Germany.

Saint-Paul, G. (1996): "Exploring the Political Economy of Labor Market Institutions." *Economic Policy: A European Forum* 23: 263-315.

Saint-Paul, G. (2002): "The Political Economy of Employment Protection." *Journal of Political Economy* 110: 672-704.

Segerstrom, P. S. (1998): "Endogenous Growth Without Scale Effects." *American Economic Review* 88: 1290-1310.

Segerstrom, P. S. (2004): *Intel Economics*. Mimeo, Stockholm School of Economics.

Segerstrom, P. S., Anant, T. C. A., and Dinopoulos, E. (1990): "A Schumpeterian Model of the Product Life Cycle." *American Economic Review* 80: 1077-1092.

Segerstrom, P. S., and Zolnierek, J. (1999): "The R&D Incentives of Industry Leaders." *International Economic Review* 40: 745-766.

Şener, M. F. (2000): "A Schumpeterian Model of Equilibrium Unemployment and Labor Turnover." *Journal of Evolutionary Economics* 10: 557-583.

Şener, M. F. (2001): "Schumpeterian Unemployment, Trade and Wages." *Journal of International Economics* 54: 119-148.

Siebert, H. (1997): "Labor Market Rigidities: At the Root of Unemployment in Europe." *Journal of Economic Perspectives* 11: 37-54.

Steger, Thomas M. (2003): "The Segerstrom Model: Stability, Speed of Convergence and Policy Implications." *Economics Bulletin* 15: 1-8.

Wolfinger, R. E., and Rosenstone, S. (1980): *Who Votes?* New Haven: Yale University Press.

Address of author: – Wolf-Heimo Grieben, University of Dortmund, Department of Economics, Vogelpothsweg 87, 44221 Dortmund, Germany (email: w.grieben@wiso.uni-dortmund.de)

J. Econ. (2005) Suppl. 10: 119-142

Journal of Economics
Zeitschrift für Nationalökonomie

Printed in Austria

White-Collar Employment, Inequality, and Technological Change

Volker Grossmann

Received January 29, 2003; Revised version received July 19, 2004
© Springer-Verlag 2005

This paper develops a R&D-based growth model to examine the relationship between technological change, growth, welfare and the demand for skill-intensive, analytical activities (e.g., product development, quality-control, and design of advertising campaigns). Results are consistent with evidence on rising employment shares of skilled, white-collar workers and increases in the skill premium in the US or UK. Moreover, accounting for a simultaneous decrease in overhead labor requirements (e.g., administrative staff), the analysis suggests that recent technology shifts have no systematic impact on firm sizes and on the economy's rate of growth. This sheds some light into the "Solow-productivity paradox".

Keywords: analytical skills, skill premium, R&D-based growth, white-collar employment

JEL classification: O31, O33, J21, J31.

1 Introduction

There is now a broad consensus that in the 1980s and 1990s the structure of labor demand has shifted in favor of skilled workers, and that this shift can largely be attributed to technological advances. However, understanding the interplay between new technologies and the structure of labor demand requires to shed light into the decision of firms how to allocate workers with different skills to different tasks. For instance, contrary to earlier notions of "skill-biased technological change" (SBTC), computer users per se do not seem to have gained more from computerization than workers using a pencil (DiNardo and Pischke, 1997). In fact, administrative workers, who nowadays use computers more intensively than most other group, seem to be clear losers of the recent technological revolution (e.g. Berman, Bound and Grichilis,

1994). Such evidence demonstrates that the mere observation that shifts in the labor demand structure are related to the emergence of new information and communication technologies (ITC) is not a very useful hypothesis.

This paper attempts to draw a more differentiated picture of the relationship between technological change, growth and the structure of employment by hypothesizing that computerization has favored skill-intensive, analytical activities like product development, quality-control, design of customer services, and promotion of products by advertising campaigns. These tasks require much analytical thinking and are based on efficient flows of information about markets and customers. Creation and analysis of such information are favored by new ITC. New ITC allow marketing managers to assemble, store and analyze customer data like demographics and purchase habits ('data mining'). In turn, 'data warehouses' enable firms to design and keep track of marketing campaigns and to target consumers more effectively than by mass-media advertising (e.g. Bresnahan, 1999; Shapiro and Varian, 1999). Moreover, enhanced possibilities to do research on consumers' preferences, the emergence of computer-aided design and more efficient interactions between design, production and marketing help firms to improve the quality of products.

I develop a non-scale endogenous growth model which allows for both types of demand-enhancing tasks, R&D, performed in-house in order to improve the quality of goods, and advertising, which is viewed as promotional activity.[1] Firms can freely enter the economy but have to cover the costs for non-production labor from subsequent profits under monopolistic competition. This is because R&D and advertising activities are incurred prior to product market competition, and thus give rise to endogenous sunk cost. Moreover, firms have to incur fixed overhead labor requirements in terms of both skilled or unskilled workers, which may be interpreted to include administrative staff.

First, I show that an increase in the effectiveness of skill-intensive, quality-improving (R&D) or promotional activities fosters a reallocation of skilled workers from production-related activities towards these analytical, demand-enhancing tasks. This shift in the employment structure is consistent with evidence provided by the empirical literature on SBTC, which shows a clear upward trend in the share of skilled, white-collar workers like managers and professionals (e.g., Berman, Bound and Grichilis, 1994; Berman, Bound and Machin, 1998; Machin and van Reenen, 1998; see also Falkinger and Grossmann, 2003). More-

---

[1] See Grossmann (2003) for an extensive discussion of this modelling approach and the mechanisms which arise from introducing promotional activity in a quality-ladder growth model featuring in-house R&D. In that paper, however, I do neither allow for heterogenous agents nor for wage inequality.

over, the wage-bill of firms for skilled, white-collar workers unambiguously increases, endogenously implying higher sunk costs of firms. Consequently, the number of firms declines, and thus, firm sizes increase. In contrast, an equiproportionate decrease in the fixed overhead labor requirements (e.g., a decrease in administrative overhead costs) neither affects aggregate employment in demand-enhancing tasks nor relative wages, and, as usual, raises the number of firms. Interestingly, however, a decrease in fixed costs reduces the rate of growth. Although somewhat surprising at the first glance, this result is consistent with the empirical evidence that larger firms conduct more R&D (e.g. Cohen and Levin, 1989; Cohen and Klepper, 1996).

In sum, the analysis suggests that a rising effectiveness of demand-enhancing tasks, together with a decline in overhead requirements, leads to both shifts in the employment structure towards skilled, white-collar workers and rising skill premia, however, without affecting firm sizes and growth in a systematic way. Hence, the proposed theory is consistent with two further empirical regularities. First, it sheds some light into the so-called "Solow productivity paradox" ("...you can see the computer age everywhere but in the productivity statistics", Solow, 1987). Empirical evidence suggests that the administrative staff in firms has declined significantly.[2] Although this may raise welfare due to an increase in product variety, a positive relationship between firm size and R&D activity gives rise to a growth-retarding effect of declining overhead costs. This serves as a counteracting force to a positive impact of an increase in the effectiveness of R&D on growth. As a result, productivity may not increase.[3] Second, despite the merger wave in the 1980s and 1990s, there is no clear evidence on rising firm sizes (e.g. Pryor, 2001).

The model also points to an interesting interplay between R&D and advertising incentives of firms. Besides an increase in the effectiveness of R&D, also a more effective advertising technology, even if intensifying a wasteful competition among firms, may raise both growth and welfare. This is because higher sunk costs incurred for advertising are associated with an increase in firm sizes. Firm size, in turn, is positively related to innovation activity in the proposed framework. As a counteracting effect, however, due to the assumption that promotional activity

---

[2] For instance, Falkinger and Grossmann (2003, Tab. 1) show that the U.S. employment share of workers in administrative occupations in the manufacturing sector has declined from 12.8 percent in 1983 to 9.1 percent in 2000. In producer services (banking, insurance, real estate, legal services etc.), the decline in the employment share of administrators was even more pronounced, having decreased from 35.1 to 19.5 percent during that time period.

[3] However, evidence suggests that it has done so in the second half of the 1990s (contrary to the evidence in the 1980s and early 1990s) - at least in the US (e.g. Stiroh, 2002).

is skill-intensive, an increase in the demand for advertising raises the skill premium. This gives a disincentive for firms to hire researchers, leaving the relationship between advertising incentives and innovation activity ambiguous. If an increase in the effectiveness of advertising raises growth, however, it may also raise welfare, despite a decline in product variety which is triggered by higher advertising outlays.

Most theoretical studies on SBTC do not account for differences in tasks performed by production-related and non-production labor. (See Acemoglu, 2002, for an comprehensive review of this literature.) An exception is an interesting, related model by Nahuis and Smulders (2002), who argue that an increase in the supply of skilled workers fosters a shift towards a more knowledge-intensive production process, requiring more non-production workers. As a result, if the intertemporal return from innovations can be appropriated by firms to a sufficiently large degree, the skill premium permanently rises. In contrast to their study, the present analysis focusses on technological changes regarding analytical tasks, rather than on skill supply. Other growth models focussing on labor reallocation towards innovation activity and shifts in relative wages are developed by Grossmann (2000) and Thesmar and Thoenig (2001). However, their contributions differ from the present one in that they do not consider *in-house* R&D and do not allow for advertising. Moreover, Grossmann (2002) examines an ideal variety model which shows that standard notions of skill-biased process innovations are typically not consistent with a rise in skill premia when allowing for skill-intensive, quality-improving tasks.

Other related literature, although not addressing wage inequality and advertising, is concerned with the relationship between R&D and concentration. Smulders and van de Klundert (1995) first formalized the empirical finding that big firms can spread the cost of R&D over a larger volume of sales in a growth model (see also Peretto, 1998, 1999),[4] which plays a crucial role for the impact of a change in fixed costs and advertising on growth in the present paper.

Finally, alternative explanations of the Solow productivity paradox refer to measurement problems of both output (particularly in service industries) and quality-improvements of goods, as well as costs of adjustment to new technologies (for a comprehensive discussion, see Triplett, 1999). Regarding adjustment costs, Bas and Nahuis (2002) argue that skilled labor is temporarily withdrawn from production in order to accumulate knowledge after the introduction of a new general purpose technology, resulting in both higher wage inequality and (for some time) lower productivity growth.

---

[4] Cohen and Klepper (1996) provide a simple IO model which rests on the cost-spreading hypothesis, and present empirical evidence in favor of it.

The plan of the paper is as follows. Sect. 2 presents the model. The equilibrium analysis is provided in Sect. 3. Sect. 4 summarizes the main hypotheses on a shift in the demand for analytical skills. Sect. 5 examines the impact of an improvement in the advertising technology on welfare. The last section concludes. Proofs are relegated to an appendix.

2 The Model

Consider an economy which is populated by L individuals with infinite lifetimes, each supplying one unit of labor in each period $t = 0, 1, 2, ...$ (i.e., there is no population growth). There is a segmented and perfectly competitive labor market with two types of labor, L^S skilled and L^U unskilled workers (i.e., $L = L^S + L^U$), which differ in their analytical ability. There exists a (positive) representative consumer (who chooses aggregate market demand when endowed with aggregate resources) with intertemporal utility function

$$U = \sum_{t=0}^{\infty} \rho^t \ln C_t, \tag{1}$$

$0 < \rho < 1$, where C_t is a consumption index, which is given by

$$C_t = \left(\int_0^{n_t} (q_t(i)x_t(i))^{\frac{\sigma-1}{\sigma}} \, di \right)^{\frac{\sigma}{\sigma-1}} \tag{2}$$

$\sigma > 1$. $x_t(i)$ denotes the quantity of good $i \in \mathcal{N}_t \equiv [0, n_t]$ consumed in period t, whereas $q_t(i)$ will be referred to as its perceived quality. Each firm produces exactly one variety of the horizontally differentiated product in monopolistic competition. The measure n_t is referred to as the "number of firms" at date t and is endogenously determined.

Firms have a constant-returns to scale production technology. To keep the analysis as simple as possible, assume that the production function F for differentiated goods is of the Cobb-Douglas type:[5]

$$x_t(i) = F(l_t^S(i), l_t^U(i)) = a l_t^S(i)^\alpha l_t^U(i)^{1-\alpha}, \tag{3}$$

$a > 0$, $0 < \alpha < 1$, where $l_t^S(i)$ and $l_t^U(i)$ denote skilled and unskilled production-related labor in firm $i \in \mathcal{N}_t$, respectively, $t \geq 0$.

---

[5] This specification is inconsequential for the main results of the paper (as discussed below), and allows to derive all results analytically. The crucial assumption is the linear-homogeneity of the production function.

There are two types of demand-enhancing, non-production activities: quality-improving tasks performed in-house ("R&D") and promotional tasks ("advertising"). These activities are more skill-intensive than production-related tasks. For simplicity, suppose they can only be performed by skilled labor. For instance, R&D may be interpreted as product innovations or improvement of customer services whereas advertising may be viewed as framing of product characteristics in accordance with consumers' desires. Both (in-house) R&D labor investments and advertising costs have to be incurred *one period in advance* of production, i.e., are sunk in the production period.[6] Formally, perceived product quality $q_t(i)$ of variety i in any period $t > 0$ evolves according to

$$q_t(i) = \begin{cases} \bar{S}_{t-1} g(l^R_{t-1}(i)) h(l^A_{t-1}(i)/\bar{l}^A_{t-1}) & \text{if } g(l^R_{t-1}(i)) \geq 1, \\ \bar{S}_{t-1} h(l^A_{t-1}(i)/\bar{l}^A_{t-1}) & \text{otherwise,} \end{cases} \tag{4}$$

where $l^R_{t-1}(i)$ and $l^A_{t-1}(i)$ denote the amount of R&D and advertising labor of firm $i \in \mathcal{N}_t$ employed in $t-1$, respectively, and

$$\bar{l}^A_{t-1} = \frac{1}{n_t} \int_0^{n_t} l^A_{t-1}(i)di, \tag{5}$$

$t \geq 1$, is the *average* amount of advertising labor of firms producing consumption goods in t. Both $g(\cdot)$ and $h(\cdot)$ are increasing functions. Note that, if all firms allocate the same amount of labor to advertising (i.e., $l^A_{t-1}(i) = \bar{l}^A_{t-1} > 0$ for all i), no firm gains, compared to a situation without advertising. That is, engaging in promotional activity is a form of wasteful competition.[7]

$$\bar{S}_{t-1} = \bar{S}_{t-2} \frac{1}{n_{t-1}} \int_0^{n_{t-1}} g(l^R_{t-2}(i))di \tag{6}$$

reflects an intertemporal knowledge spillover effect from previous investments of firms in R&D. Regarding intellectual property rights, (4) and (6) imply that innovations are proprietary knowledge for one period only. Moreover, (4) and (6) borrow from Young (1998) in modelling "equivalent innovations". That is, if all firms invest the same amount in R&D at date $t-2$, i.e., if $l^R_{t-2}(i) = l^R_{t-2}$ for all i, we have

---

[6] The assumption that current R&D spending of a firm is effective in the subsequent (production) period follows Young (1998).

[7] The modelling strategy that only the relative advertising effort matters for a firm's success in affecting perceived quality is similar to the game-theoretic literature on "contest success functions" (Skaperdas, 1996), applied here to a general equilibrium model with monopolistically competitive firms.

$\bar{S}_{t-1} = \bar{S}_{t-2}g(l_{t-2}^R)$, according to (6). That is, the number of firms conducting research at date $t - 2$, n_{t-1}, does not affect research capabilities of firms in the subsequent period. Intuitively, this means that firms come up with similar solutions to similar problems at the same time. In the model of Young (1998), this assumption eliminates the empirically problematic feature of many endogenous growth models that the economy's growth rate depends on population size ("scale effect").[8] As will become apparent in Sect. 3.3, in the present model the steady-state growth rate depends on the relative supply of skilled labor, L^S/L^U, but not on population size L.

The number of firms n_0 in the initial period is historically given. Moreover, for simplicity, assume $q_0(i) = \bar{S}_0 > 0$, $i \in \mathcal{N}_0$, for the firms' initial product quality. Also specify

$$g(l^R) = \left(l^R\right)^\kappa, \quad h(l^A/\bar{l}^A) = \left(l^A/\bar{l}^A\right)^\eta, \tag{7}$$

$\kappa > 0$, $\eta > 0$. The parameters κ and η are referred to as "effectiveness of R&D" and "effectiveness of advertising", respectively.

There is free entry of firms into the economy, with a large number of ex ante identical potential entrants. At all times, firms have to incur fixed labor requirements $f^S(\geq 0)$ and $f^U > 0$ in terms of skilled and unskilled labor, respectively, prior to production. These fixed labor requirements may be interpreted as including administrative staff (e.g., concerning tasks like supervising, billing, auditing etc.). Although, in general, administrative tasks are not literally independent of output, it is plausible to assume that bureaucracy costs have a fixed component, which is the crucial element in the present context. As outlined in the introduction, recent developments suggest that technological change has reduced these overhead costs. In $t - 1$, firms which produce final output in period t issue bonds or shares in a perfect asset market in order to finance fixed (labor) costs as well as non-production labor costs for R&D and advertising.

3 General Equilibrium

Let us choose unskilled labor as numeraire and denote the (relative) wage rate of skilled labor in period t by ω_t. The representative con-

---

[8] See Jones (1995) and Young (1998) for more discussion.

sumer's budget constraint in period $t \geq 0$ then reads[9]

$$A_{t+1} = (1 + r_t)A_t + \omega_t L^S + L^U - E_t, \tag{8}$$

where A_t denotes the value of asset holdings in t, E_t is consumption expenditure and r_t is the (endogenous) interest rate between $t - 1$ and t. Utility maximization implies that consumption spending evolves according to Euler equation

$$E_t = (1 + r_t)\rho E_{t-1}, \tag{9}$$

$t > 0$. Moreover, the demand function for good i in period t is given by

$$x_t^D(i) = q_t(i)^{\sigma-1} \frac{E_t}{P_t} \left(\frac{p_t(i)}{P_t} \right)^{-\sigma}, \tag{10}$$

where $p_t(i)$ is the price of good i in t. The price index

$$P_t \equiv \left(\int_0^{n_t} \left(\frac{p_t(i)}{q_t(i)} \right)^{1-\sigma} di \right)^{\frac{1}{1-\sigma}} \tag{11}$$

is defined such that the CES-index C_t, given by (2), equals real consumption expenditure in period t, i.e., $C_t = E_t/P_t$.

Cost minimization implies that the (relative) wage rate for skilled labor fulfills

$$\omega_t = \frac{\alpha}{1-\alpha} \frac{l_t^U(i)}{l_t^S(i)}, \tag{12}$$

and marginal production cost are given by

$$c_t = \frac{(\omega_t)^\alpha}{a\alpha^\alpha(1-\alpha)^{1-\alpha}}, \tag{13}$$

according to production technology (3). Profits of firm i in period t are given by $\pi_t(i) = (p_t(i) - c_t)x_t^D(i)$. Thus, using (10), output prices by the monopolistically competitive firms are set according to the well-known formula

$$p_t(i) = p_t = \frac{\sigma}{\sigma - 1} c_t \tag{14}$$

for all $i \in \mathcal{N}_t$ and $t \geq 0$ (Dixit and Stiglitz, 1977).

---

[9] Initial income from asset holdings $(1 + r_0)A_0$ is exogenously given for consumers. In addition to budget constraint (8), the representative consumer also has to observe both a standard transversality condition, which is given by $\lim_{T \to \infty} A_{T+1}/\prod_{t=1}^{T}(1 + r_t) = 0$, and non-negativity constraints, $E_t \geq 0$, $A_{t+1} \geq 0$, $t \geq 0$.

Non-production labor costs of any firm $i \in \mathcal{N}_t$ equal

$$\omega_{t-1}\left(l_{t-1}^R(i) + l_{t-1}^A(i) + f^S\right) + f^U.$$

(Recall that unskilled labor is numeraire.) To avoid only mildly interesting case distinctions, let us focus the analysis on the case $g(l_{t-1}^R(i)) \geq 1$. Thus, at time $t-1$, the firm value $V_{t-1}(i)$ of firm $i \in \mathcal{N}_t$ is given by

$$\max_{l_{t-1}^R(i), l_{t-1}^A(i)} \left\{ \frac{p_t - c_t}{1 + r_t} x_t^D(i) - \omega_{t-1}\left(l_{t-1}^R(i) + l_{t-1}^A(i) + f^S\right) - f^U \right\}$$

(15)

$$\text{s.t. } x_t^D(i) = \left[\bar{S}_{t-1} g(l_{t-1}^R(i)) h\left(\frac{l_{t-1}^A(i)}{\bar{l}_{t-1}^A} \right) \right]^{\sigma - 1} \frac{E_t}{P_t} \left(\frac{p_t}{P_t} \right)^{-\sigma},$$

according to (4), (10) and (14). Note that, since each single firm has measure zero (i.e., there are no strategic interactions among firms), P_t, E_t and $\bar{l}_{t-1}^A$ are taken as given in the optimization problem of firms. Using (7), it is easy to show that under

$$(\kappa + \eta)(\sigma - 1) < 1,$$

(AA)

product demand $x_t^D(i)$ as stated in (15), and thus each firm's objective function at date $t-1$, is strictly concave as function of $(l_{t-1}^R(i), l_{t-1}^A(i))$. As all potential entrants are identical, the analysis focusses on symmetric equilibria; that is, for all $i \in \mathcal{N}_t$, we have $l_{t-1}^R(i) = l_{t-1}^R$, $l_{t-1}^A(i) = l_{t-1}^A = \bar{l}_{t-1}^A$, $V_{t-1}(i) = V_{t-1}$, $t \geq 1$, and $l_t^S(i) = l_t^S$, $l_t^U(i) = l_t^U$, $x_t^D(i) = x_t^D$, $t \geq 0$.

Recall that we focus on $g(l_{t-1}^R) \geq 1$, and thus, under (7), $l_{t-1}^R \geq 1$. Moreover, as will become apparent, $l_{t-1}^A > 0$ under (AA). Thus, the first-order conditions of maximization program (15) can be written as equality:

$$\frac{p_t - c_t}{1 + r_t} x_t^D(\sigma - 1) \frac{g'(l_{t-1}^R)}{g(l_{t-1}^R)} = \omega_{t-1},$$

(16)

$$\frac{p_t - c_t}{1 + r_t} x_t^D(\sigma - 1) \frac{h'(1)}{h(1)} \frac{1}{l_{t-1}^A} = \omega_{t-1}.$$

(17)

Conditions (16) and (17) simply state that marginal benefits and marginal costs of R&D and advertising employment, respectively, are equalized. Combining (16) with (17), and using (7), the following first result is implied.

Lemma 1. *For any $t \geq 1$, we have $l_{t-1}^A / l_{t-1}^R = \eta / \kappa$ in symmetric equilibrium.*

Hence, the ratio of advertising employment to R&D employment is time-invariant. It decreases with the effectiveness of R&D, κ, and increases with the effectiveness of advertising, η.

In symmetric equilibrium, the following conditions must hold under free entry, clearing of goods markets as well as clearing of labor markets for skilled and unskilled workers, respectively.[10]

$$V_{t-1} = \frac{p_t - c_t}{1 + r_t} x_t^D - \omega_{t-1} \left(l_{t-1}^R + l_{t-1}^A + f^S \right) - f^U = 0, \ t \geq 1; \ (18)$$

$$x_t^D = a \left(l_t^S \right)^{\alpha} \left(l_t^U \right)^{1-\alpha}, \ t \geq 0; \tag{19}$$

$$L^S = n_{t-1} l_{t-1}^S + n_t \left(l_{t-1}^R + l_{t-1}^A + f^S \right), \ t \geq 1; \tag{20}$$

$$L^U = n_{t-1} l_{t-1}^U + n_t f^U, \ t \geq 1. \tag{21}$$

We are now ready to study the general equilibrium implications of both changes in incentives of firms to incur costs for R&D and advertising, reflected by κ and η, respectively, and shifts in fixed labor requirements f^S, f^U. (Equilibrium values are denoted by superscript (*) throughout the paper.)

3.1 Relative Wages

Which kind of technological changes are consistent with a rise in wage inequality, as observed particularly in Anglo-American economies throughout the 1980s and most of the 1990s? The following result provides an answer. (All results are proven in appendix.)

Proposition 1. *(Wage inequality) Under (AA), in equilibrium, the (relative) wage rate of skilled labor is time-invariant, i.e., $\omega_t = \omega^*$ for all $t \geq 0$, where ω^* increases with κ and η, and is homogenous of degree zero as function of (f^S, f^U).*

An increase in κ or η makes skilled labor more effective in analytical non-production tasks. This gives firms incentives to reallocate skilled labor from production to non-production activities, leaving skilled labor a scarcer resource. Consequently, the relative wage rate ω^* increases, in line with the empirical evidence for the US and UK in the 1980s and (at least) the early 1990s.

Moreover, an equiproportionate change in f^S and f^U (leaving f^S/f^U unchanged) has no impact on ω^*. In fact, one can show that this property holds for any constant-returns to scale technology for the production of final goods, represented by function F. One way to understand

---

[10] According to Walras' law, these conditions imply that also the asset market clears.

this is that equilibrium production labor inputs per firm, l^S and l^U, are inversely related to the number of firms, which - not surprisingly - is increasing in both f^S and f^U (as will become apparent below). Thus, technological change which reduces fixed labor requirements in the same proportion (i.e., an equiproportionate decrease in f^S and f^U) cannot explain a change in wage inequality.

The absence of transitional dynamics in the model is not confined to the relative wage, ω. Formally, the underlying reason for this property lies in the linear spillover effect in the evolution of perceived quality (4), which leads to a time-invariant interest rate. In sum, we obtain the following.

Corollary 1. *Under (AA), the equilibrium interest rate immediately jumps to a steady state level, with $r_t = (1 - \rho)/\rho$ for all $t \geq 1$. Moreover, in equilibrium, E, p, n, l^R, l^A, l^S and l^U are time-invariant from period 1 onwards, whereas $l_0^S \neq l_t^S$ and $l_0^U \neq l_t^U$ whenever $n_0 \neq n_t$, $t \geq 1$.*

Let us denote $E_{t-1} = E^*$, $p_{t-1} = p^*$, $n_t = n^*$, $l_{t-1}^R = l^{R*}$, $l_{t-1}^A = l^{A*}$, $l_t^S = l^{S*}$, and $l_t^U = l^{U*}$ for equilibrium values in $t \geq 1$; moreover, denote $l_0^S = l_0^{S*}$ and $l_0^U = l_0^{U*}$ regarding the equilibrium at period 0.

3.2 Number and Size of Firms

Recall that there are two types of sunk costs in the model: endogenous costs for R&D and advertising labor as well as the exogenous overhead costs f^S and f^U in terms of skilled and unskilled labor, respectively (e.g. for administration). As usual, sunk costs give rise to economies of scale which determine the equilibrium number of firms, n^*, and thus, firm sizes, L/n^*, under free entry. This is reflected in the following result:

Proposition 2. *(Firm size) Under (AA), for any $t \geq 1$, steady state firm size, L/n^*, increases with the effectiveness of R&D or advertising, κ or η, respectively; moreover, L/n^* is linear homogenous as function of (f^S, f^U).*

As usual, an increase in exogenous fixed costs, reflected by labor requirements f^S and f^U, reduces the number of firms n^*, and thus, raises firm sizes L/n^*. More interestingly, since an increase in R&D or advertising incentives, κ or η, raise demand for skilled, white-collar workers, sunk costs (i.e., the wage-bill for white-collar workers) endogenously rise, in turn raising firm sizes.

3.3 Innovations and Growth

What are the determinants of innovation activity and economic growth? Let ϑ_t denote the growth rate of real consumption $C_t = E_t/P_t$; i.e., define $\vartheta_t \equiv (C_t - C_{t-1})/C_{t-1}$. We obtain the following result.

Proposition 3. *(R&D, advertising and growth) Under (AA), for any $t > 1$:*

(i) *The economy's growth rate is given by $\vartheta_t = \vartheta^* = g(l^{R*}) - 1 = (l^{R*})^\kappa - 1$;*

(ii) *both l^{R*} and ϑ^* are increasing in κ, whereas the impact of η on l^{R*} and ϑ^* is ambiguous;*

(iii) *l^{R*} is linear-homogenous as function of (f^S, f^U), i.e., an equipro- portionate increase in f^S and f^U raises ϑ^*;*

(iv) *l^{R*} is homogenous of degree zero as function of (L^S, L^U), i.e., an equiproportionate increase in L^S and L^U does not affect ϑ^*; both l^{R*} and ϑ^* are increasing in L^S/L^U;*

(v) *l^{A*} is increasing in η and linear-homogenous as function of (f^S, f^U), whereas the impact of κ on l^{A*} is ambiguous.*

Not surprisingly, according to part (i) of Proposition 3, the steady-state growth rate ϑ^* rises when l^{R*} rises. The intuition of part (ii) is as follows. A shift in the effectiveness of R&D, κ, raises l^{R*} by increasing the marginal benefit of innovation activity, which is given by the left-hand side of first-order condition (16). An increase in the effectiveness of advertising, η, has two counteracting effects on R&D labor per firm, l^{R*}. On the hand, an increase in η endogenously raises the firms' sunk costs for advertising. This positively affects innovation activity *per firm*, since the marginal benefit to invest in R&D increases when firms be- come larger (i.e., when x^D increases, all other things equal).[11] Second, however, it raises the wage rate ω^* for skilled labor, according to Propo- sition 2. This means that researchers become more expensive, implying a disincentive to invest in R&D. A priori, it is not clear which effect dominates. Regarding part (iii), again, due to a positive relationship between firm size and innovation incentives (and the constant-returns- to-scale production technology), technological change which induces an equiproportionate *decrease* in f^S and f^U *lowers* the economy's rate of growth. This result is related to an absence of a "scale effect" regarding the rate of growth in the model, which is established in part (iv). That is, ϑ^* is independent on population size $L = L^S + L^U$ of the economy, although being positively affected by relative skill supply L^S/L^U. If, to

---

[11] This mechanism, which relies on a positive relationship between innova- tion activity and firm size, has been extensively studied e.g. in Smulders and van de Klundert (1995) and Peretto (1998, 1999). For empirical support, see e.g. Cohen and Levin (1989) and Cohen and Klepper (1996).

the contrary, the number of firms, and thus the scale of the economy, would matter for growth, then a decrease in exogenous fixed costs may spur growth by raising the number of firms. Finally, comparative-static results regarding advertising employment per firm, l^{A*}, are analogous to the results regarding l^{R*}.

3.4 Aggregate White-collar Employment of Skilled Labor

As argued in the introduction, the observed increase in the employment share of skilled, white-collar workers, particularly in managerial and professional occupations, has been taken as evidence for the hypothesis of SBTC. Under the interpretation of f^S as skilled, administrative staff, the aggregate equilibrium employment of skilled, white-collar workers is given by $\Gamma^* \equiv n^* \left(l^{R*} + l^{A*} + f^S \right)$.[12]

Proposition 4. (Skilled, white-collar employment) Under (AA), for any $t \geq 0$, total skilled, white-collar employment, Γ^*, is increasing in both κ and η, and homogenous of degree zero as function of (f^S, f^U).

Proposition 4 shows that an increase in the demand for skilled labor, when triggered by a higher κ or η, is not only reflected by a higher skill premium, ω^*, and higher R&D and advertising activity *per firm*, l^{R*} and l^{A*}, but also in higher *aggregate* white-collar employment of skilled labor, Γ^*. That is, despite the negative impact of an increase in R&D and advertising incentives on the number of firms (Proposition 2), there is a reallocation towards skilled, white collar employment in the aggregate. In contrast, an equiproportionate decline in administrative staff, f^S and f^U, has no impact on Γ^*.

In sum, an empirical prediction of our analysis, which explicitly distinguishes between production-related and non-production activities of skilled labor, is that computerization has increased the demand for analytical skills in non-production activities (which are reflected in sunk costs). The analysis is thus capable to shed light into the sources of observed shifts in the labor demand structure. This is further discussed in the next section.

4 The Shift in Demand for Analytical Skills

Theorem 1 summarizes the main hypotheses suggested by the preceding analysis.

---

[12] Defining $\Gamma_t \equiv n_{t+1} \ l_t^R + l_t^A + f^S$, $t \geq 0$ (recall that n_{t+1} is the number of firms which produce consumption goods in $t+1$, requiring investments at date t) yields $\Gamma_t = \Gamma^*$ for all $t \geq 0$, according to Corollary 1.

Theorem 1. *Provided that (AA) holds, we obtain:*

(a) *An increase in the effectiveness of R&D or advertising (κ or η, re-spectively) together with an equiproportionate decrease in overhead labor requirements (f^S and f^U) raises relative wages, w^*, and the employment share of skilled, white-collar workers, Γ^*, without af-fecting firm sizes, L/n^*, and the growth rate, ϑ^*, in a systematic way.*

(b) *Fiercer wasteful competition for customers by advertising (i.e., an increase in η) may have a positive impact on growth.*

Empirical evidence shows that computerization has not favored computer users per se, but, in contrast, has led to a substitution of employees in administrative occupations by computerized routines. In the present model, this is reflected by a decrease in f^S and f^U. At the same time, computerization has enabled firms to create and analyze large customer databases (e.g., Bresnahan, 1999). This has opened up new possibilities for market research, contributing to a better under-standing of consumer behavior. In turn, firms were enabled to find out how to frame product characteristics more effectively in their advertis-ing campaigns, to keep track of advertising campaigns, and to target potential customers more directly. These developments are reflected by an increase in η. Maybe even more important, more effective market research, the emergence of computer-aided design, and more efficient in-formation flows between production, development and marketing units have helped to improve the quality of products and services, which is reflected by an increase in κ. Under these hypotheses, part (a) of Theo-rem 1 suggests that computerization has raised both the skill premium and total employment in demand-enhancing activities by raising de-mand for analytical skills (since both w^* and Γ^* increase with κ and η, whereas being unrelated to equiproportionate decreases in f^S and f^U). However, computerization is neither systematically related to firm sizes nor to economic growth.

According to part (b) of Theorem 1, higher spending on promotional activities (triggered by an increase in η), although modelled as being completely wasteful from a social point of view, may raise the economy's rate of growth. This result is due to the (empirically well-supported) properties of the model that higher sunk costs (e.g., for advertising) raise firm size, and, in turn, larger firms conduct more R&D. However, there is a counteracting effect since advertising incentives are positively related to the wage rate of skilled labor, in turn leaving researchers more expensive.

As a remark, the assumption that innovation activity affects prod-uct quality, q_t, rather than productivity is made merely for the sake of concreteness. Alternatively, treating R&D as *productivity-enhancing* activity (e.g., reorganization of production, development of management techniques, creation of an internal human capital stock), rather than being related to the quality of goods, may formally lead to exactly identical results. To see this, suppose that (alternatively to (4)) perceived quality can be affected by advertising only, i.e., let $q_t(i) = h(l_{t-1}^A(i)/\bar{l}_{t-1}^A)$. Moreover, let the production function (similar to (3)) be given by $x_t(i) = A_t(i)l_t^S(i)^\alpha l_t^U(i)^{1-\alpha}$, where the total factor productivity of firm i is given by $A_t(i) = \bar{S}_{t-1}g(l_{t-1}^R(i))$ if $g(l_{t-1}^R(i)) \geq 1$ (and $A_t(i) = \bar{S}_{t-1}$ otherwise). Suppose that everything else remains the same. It is straightforward to show that, under this modification, all formal results remain *exactly* valid. Only the type of innovation activity has changed from affecting q_t to affecting A_t. For instance, similar to the creation of customer databases which raise the potential to improve the quality of goods, computerization has also allowed to assemble data on the internal organization of a firm (Bresnahan, 1999). In turn, analytical skills are needed to draw conclusions from these extended possibilities to improve production processes (and thus, to raise A_t). Again, this raises the demand for skilled, white-collar workers. According to part (a) of Theorem 1, however, the overall impact of technological change on productivity growth is generally ambiguous, consistent with the "Solow-productivity paradox".

5 Welfare Effects of Advertising

According to part (b) of Theorem 1, advertising incentives, measured by η, may raise growth. A natural question to ask is whether an increase in η may also raise intertemporal welfare in equilibrium, U^*, despite lowering product variety unambiguously.

This section examines the relative importance of declining product variety versus potentially growth-enhancing effects of a more effective advertising technology for welfare. In order to show that an increase in η *may* increase welfare, an example suffices. For gaining some insight into the plausibility of such an outcome, however, the only simplification made here is to specify $f^S = 0$. In this case, the following can be stated.

Proposition 5. *(Advertising and welfare.) Suppose $f^S = 0$ and (AA) hold. Then the impact of an increase in η on welfare U^* may generally be positive or negative. It is negative if η is sufficiently high.*

As apparent from the proof in the appendix, both possibilities, a positive or negative relationship between the effectiveness of advertising, η, and welfare, U^*, occur under plausible parameter values. The result that an increase in η may raise welfare can be led back to the feature of the model that firm size and the marginal return to R&D are positively related, and may be more than a theoretical peculiarity.[13] It is ultimately a consequence of complex interactions between several market imperfections in the model: imperfect goods markets, a positive intertemporal externality of R&D, and a negative (static) externality of advertising.

6 Conclusion

This paper has developed a R&D-based growth model to examine the relationship between relative wages of skilled labor, the structure of employment in production-related and analytical tasks, firm sizes, economic growth, and welfare. It has been argued that the emergence of new ITC has favored skill-intensive, analytical activities, which are related to sunk costs of firms. For the sake of concreteness, the analysis has focussed on demand-enhancing activities like product development, quality-control, design of customer services, and advertising. As outlined, however, the results equally apply for a study of productivity-enhancing activities.

It has been shown that higher incentives to invest in R&D or advertising lead to a reallocation of skilled labor towards these analytical tasks, in turn, raising relative wages of skilled labor. In contrast to the standard literature on SBTC, which does not distinguish between production-related and non-production tasks, results are not only consistent with a rising skill premium in (fairly) flexible labor markets like the US and the UK, but also with rising employment shares in managerial and professional activities. Empirical evidence also suggests that the administrative staff, although fairly intensive computer users, has been downsized considerably. Accounting for this decrease in overhead labor requirements, in addition to hypothesizing a higher effectiveness of analytical tasks, the analysis suggests that recent technology shifts have neither a systematic impact on firm sizes nor on the economy's rate of growth. The latter is consistent with the "Solow productivity paradox" which refers to the puzzle that computerization did not seem to have helped boosting productivity in a significant way at least until the mid 1990s.

Finally, the interplay between innovation activity and promotional activity has been examined. In particular, it has been shown that higher advertising incentives, although intensifying a wasteful competition in

---

[13] In Grossmann (2003), a potentially positive welfare effect of improvements in the advertising technology cannot occur when an interior solution to the social planning optimum exists. One can check, however, that this is not the case in the present context.

the model, may lead to faster growth. This result rests on the sunk cost nature of advertising spending together with the property that larger firms have higher incentives to innovate, all other things equal. In addition, and even more surprising, this mechanism gives rise to a potentially positive impact of a technology-related increase in advertising incentives on welfare.

Appendix

A. Proof of Proposition 1

Note that $h(1) = 1$, according to (7). Thus, (4) implies that $q_t(i) = q_t = \bar{S}_{t-1} g(l_{t-1}^R)$ for all i in symmetric equilibrium. Hence, together with $p_t(i) = p_t$ from (14), equations (10) and (11) imply that demand for each differentiated good is given by

$$x_t^D = \frac{E_t}{n_t p_t}. \tag{A.1}$$

Substituting Euler equation (9) into (A.1), and using (14), leads to

$$\frac{p_t - c_t}{1 + r_t} x_t^D = \frac{\rho}{\sigma} \frac{E_{t-1}}{n_t}. \tag{A.2}$$

Next, note that substituting (A.2) into free entry condition (18) implies

$$\frac{\rho}{\sigma} \frac{E_{t-1}}{n_t} = \omega_{t-1} \left(l_{t-1}^R + l_{t-1}^A + f^S \right) + f^U. \tag{A.3}$$

Moreover, substituting (7) and (A.2) into first-order condition (16) yields

$$\frac{\rho}{\sigma} \frac{E_{t-1}}{n_t} (\sigma - 1)\kappa = \omega_{t-1} l_{t-1}^R. \tag{A.4}$$

Now substitute (A.3) into (A.4) and use $l_{t-1}^A = \eta l_{t-1}^R / \kappa$ from Lemma 1 to obtain

$$\omega_{t-1} l_{t-1}^R = \frac{\kappa(\sigma - 1) \left(\omega_{t-1} f^S + f^U \right)}{1 - (\kappa + \eta)(\sigma - 1)}. \tag{A.5}$$

Substitution of (A.5) into (A.4) then leads to

$$\frac{E_{t-1}}{n_t} = \frac{\sigma \left(\omega_{t-1} f^S + f^U \right)}{\rho \left[1 - (\kappa + \eta)(\sigma - 1) \right]}, \tag{A.6}$$

$t \geq 1$. Moreover, combining equilibrium condition (19) with (A.1), using (12)-(14), and rearranging terms yields

$$n_{t-1} l_{t-1}^U = E_{t-1} \frac{(\sigma - 1)(1 - \alpha)}{\sigma} \tag{A.7}$$

for any $t \geq 1$. Substituting (A.7) into labor market clearing condition (21) and using (A.6) then leads to

$$\frac{1}{n_t} = \frac{1}{L^U} \left[\frac{(\sigma - 1)(1 - \alpha)\left(\omega_{t-1}f^S + f^U\right)}{\rho\left[1 - (\kappa + \eta)(\sigma - 1)\right]} + f^U \right]. \qquad (A.8)$$

This gives a first relationship between n_t and ω_{t-1}. Next, note that (12) implies $l_{t-1}^U = \omega_{t-1}l_{t-1}^S(1 - \alpha)/\alpha$, $t \geq 1$. Substituting this into (A.7) and rearranging terms yields

$$n_{t-1}l_{t-1}^S = \frac{E_{t-1}}{\omega_{t-1}} \frac{\alpha(\sigma - 1)}{\sigma}. \qquad (A.9)$$

Substituting (A.9) and $l_{t-1}^A = l_{t-1}^R \eta/\kappa$ from Lemma 1 into labor market clearing condition (20), and substituting both (A.5) and (A.6) into the resulting expression, eventually leads to a second relationship between n_t and ω_{t-1}:

$$\frac{1}{n_t} = \frac{1}{L^S} \left[\frac{(\sigma - 1)[\alpha + \rho(\kappa + \eta]\left(\omega_{t-1}f^S + f^U\right)}{\rho\left[1 - (\kappa + \eta)(\sigma - 1)\right]\omega_{t-1}} + f^S \right]. \qquad (A.10)$$

Combining (A.8) and (A.10) then proves that the relative wage is time-invariant in equilibrium, i.e., $\omega_{t-1} = \omega^*$ for all $t \geq 1$, where ω^* is implicitly given by

$$0 = (\sigma - 1)[\alpha + \rho(\kappa + \eta] \left(\frac{f^S}{f^U} + \frac{1}{\omega^*} \right) + \frac{f^S}{f^U}\rho\left[1 - (\kappa + \eta)(\sigma - 1)\right] -$$
$$\frac{L^S}{L^U} \left[(\sigma - 1)(1 - \alpha) \left(\omega^* \frac{f^S}{f^U} + 1 \right) + \rho\left[1 - (\kappa + \eta)(\sigma - 1)\right] \right]. \qquad (A.11)$$

Thus, applying the implicit function theorem,

$$\frac{\partial \omega^*}{\partial \kappa} = \frac{\rho\left(\frac{L^S}{L^U} + \frac{1}{\omega^*} \right)}{\frac{\alpha + \rho(\kappa + \eta)}{(\omega^*)^2} + (1 - \alpha)\frac{L^S}{L^U}\frac{f^S}{f^U}} > 0, \qquad (A.12)$$

and, similarly, $\partial \omega^*/\partial \eta > 0$. Finally, (A.11) implies that ω^* is homogenous of degree zero as function of (f^S, f^U). This concludes the proof.

B. Proof of Corollary 1

First, according to (A.8) [or (A.10)], $\omega_{t-1} = \omega^*$ implies that the number of firms is time-invariant, $n_t = n^*$, $t \geq 1$. Thus, according to

(A. 6), $E_{t-1} = E^*$ for all $t \geq 1$. Combining this with (9) confirms the expression for the interest rate, r_t. Also note that

$$p_t = p^* = \frac{\sigma\,(\omega^*)^\alpha}{(\sigma-1)a\alpha^\alpha(1-\alpha)^{1-\alpha}} \qquad (A.\,13)$$

for all $t \geq 0$, according to (13), (14), and $\omega_t = \omega^*$, i.e., output prices are time-invariant in equilibrium. Moreover, $\omega_{t-1} = \omega^*$, $t \geq 1$, implies that l^R and l^A are time-invariant, according to (A. 5) and Lemma 1, respectively. Moreover, $n_t = n^*$, $E_{t-1} = E^*$ for all $t \geq 1$ imply that l_t^U, and, together with $\omega_t = \omega^*$, also l_t^S is constant from period 1 onwards, according to (A. 7) and (A. 9), respectively. (A. 7) and (A. 9) also imply that $l_0^U \neq l_t^U$ and $l_0^S \neq l_t^S$, respectively, if $n_0 \neq n_t$, $t \geq 1$. This concludes the proof.

C. Proof of Proposition 2

The result immediately follows from (A. 8) [or (A. 10)] and Proposition 1.

D. Proof of Proposition 3

To prove part (i), first, confirm by using the expression for the price index (11) together with $E_t = E^*$, $p_t = p^*$ and $n_{t+1} = n^*$, $t \geq 0$, that ϑ_t equals the growth rate of perceived quality q_t. Since, using $h(1) = 1$,

$$q_t = \bar{S}_{t-1}g(l^{R*})h(1) = \bar{S}_0 g(l^{R*})^t,$$

in symmetric equilibrium, according to (4) and (6), q_t and thus ϑ_t grow with rate $g(l^{R*}) - 1$. This confirms part (i). Note from part (i) that the effects on l^{R*} immediately imply the effects on ϑ^*, which are thus not stated separately in the following proofs of parts (ii)-(iv). To prove part (ii), note that (A. 5) and $\omega_{t-1} = \omega^*$ imply

$$l^{R*} = \frac{\kappa(\sigma-1)\left(f^S + \frac{f^U}{\omega^*}\right)}{1-(\kappa+\eta)(\sigma-1)}. \qquad (A.\,14)$$

Using both (A. 11) and (A. 12), it is tedious but straightforward to confirm that $\partial l^{R*}/\partial\kappa > 0$. In contrast, $\partial l^{R*}/\partial\eta >, =, < 0$ is possible, which confirms part (ii). Part (iii), which states that l^{R*} is linear-homogenous as function of $\left(f^S, f^U\right)$, follows from (A. 14) and the fact that ω^* is homogenous of degree zero as function of $\left(f^S, f^U\right)$. Part (iv) follows from (A. 14) and the fact that ω^* is homogenous of degree zero as function of (L^S, L^U) and is decreasing in L^S/L^U, according to (A. 11). By analogy, the results regarding $l^{A*} = l^{R*}\eta/\kappa$ (recall Lemma 1) follow from the results regarding l^{R*}, which confirms part (v). This concludes the proof.

E. Proof of Proposition 4

Using (A. 14) and $l^{A*} = l^{R*}\eta/\kappa$ from Lemma 1, one obtains

$$l^{R*} + l^{A*} + f^S = \frac{(\kappa + \eta)(\sigma - 1)\frac{f^U}{\omega^*} + f^S}{1 - (\kappa + \eta)(\sigma - 1)}. \tag{A.15}$$

Moreover, using $\omega_{t-1} = \omega^*$, (A. 8) implies

$$n^* = \frac{L^U \rho \left[1 - (\kappa + \eta)(\sigma - 1)\right]}{(\sigma - 1)(1 - \alpha)\left(\omega^* f^S + f^U\right) + f^U \rho \left[1 - (\kappa + \eta)(\sigma - 1)\right]}. \tag{A.16}$$

Recall that $\Gamma^* = n^* \left(l^{R*} + l^{A*} + f^S\right)$. According to (A. 15) and (A. 16), and making use of (A. 11), we thus get

$$\Gamma^* = \frac{\frac{(\kappa+\eta)(\sigma-1)}{\omega^*} + \frac{f^S}{f^U}}{(\sigma - 1)\left[\alpha + \rho(\kappa + \eta)\right]\left(\frac{f^S}{f^U} + \frac{1}{\omega^*}\right) + \frac{f^S}{f^U}\rho\left[1 - (\kappa + \eta)(\sigma - 1)\right]}. \tag{A.17}$$

Homogeneity of degree zero of Γ^* as function of (f^S, f^U) immediately follows from (A. 17) and Proposition 1. Using (A. 17) and $\partial\omega^*/\partial\kappa > 0$ or $\partial\omega^*/\partial\eta > 0$, respectively, the impact of an increase in κ or η on Γ^* is straightforward but tedious to confirm. This concludes the proof.

F. Proof of Proposition 5

First, note that $f^S = 0$ implies

$$\omega^* = \frac{L^U}{L^S} \frac{(\sigma - 1)\left[\alpha + \rho(\kappa + \eta)\right]}{(\sigma - 1)(1 - \alpha) + \rho\left[1 - (\kappa + \eta)(\sigma - 1)\right]}, \tag{A.18}$$

$$n^* = \frac{L^U}{f^U} \frac{\rho\left[1 - (\kappa + \eta)(\sigma - 1)\right]}{(\sigma - 1)(1 - \alpha) + \rho\left[1 - (\kappa + \eta)(\sigma - 1)\right]}, \tag{A.19}$$

and

$$l^{R*} = \frac{\kappa f L^S}{L^U} \frac{(\sigma - 1)(1 - \alpha) + \rho\left[1 - (\kappa + \eta)(\sigma - 1)\right]}{\left[\alpha + \rho(\kappa + \eta)\right]\left[1 - (\kappa + \eta)(\sigma - 1)\right]}, \tag{A.20}$$

according to (A. 11), (A. 14) and (A. 16). Moreover, combining (2)-(6) and observing Corollary 1, one obtains that, for all $t \geq 1$,

$$C_t = a\bar{S}_0 g(l^{R*})^t (n^*)^{\frac{\sigma}{\sigma-1}} (l^{S*})^\alpha (l^{U*})^{1-\alpha}$$

in equilibrium (recall $h(1) = 1$). Thus, using (7) and (12),

$$\ln C_t = t\kappa \ln l^{R*} + \frac{\sigma}{\sigma-1} \ln n^* + \ln l^{U*} - \alpha \ln \omega^* + const., \qquad \text{(A. 21)}$$

$t \geq 1$. Analogously, observing $q_0(i) = \bar{S}_0$ for all $i \in \mathcal{N}_0$,

$$C_0 = a\bar{S}_0(n_0)^{\frac{\sigma}{\sigma-1}} (l_0^{S*})^\alpha (l_0^{U*})^{1-\alpha}$$

in equilibrium, and thus,

$$\ln C_0 = \ln l_0^{U*} - \alpha \ln \omega^* + const. \qquad \text{(A. 22)}$$

according to (2) and (12). Now, substituting (A. 21) and (A. 22) into (1), and making use of both

$$\sum_{t=0}^{\infty} \rho^t = 1/(1-\rho)$$

and

$$\sum_{t=1}^{\infty} \rho^t t = \rho/(1-\rho)^2,$$

leads to

$$U^* = \ln l_0^{U*} + \frac{1}{1-\rho} \left(\rho \ln l^{U*} - \alpha \ln \omega^* + \frac{\rho\sigma}{\sigma-1} \ln n^* + \frac{\rho\kappa}{1-\rho} \ln l^{R*} \right)$$
$$+ const. \qquad \text{(A. 23)}$$

Next, setting $f^S = 0$ in (A. 6), combining the resulting expression with (A. 19), and observing Corollary 1, yields

$$E^* = \frac{\sigma L^U}{(\sigma-1)(1-\alpha) + \rho\left[1 - (\kappa+\eta)(\sigma-1)\right]}. \qquad \text{(A. 24)}$$

Combining $E_{t-1} = E^*$ as given in (A. 24) with (A. 7) leads to

$$l_0^{U*} = \frac{1}{n_0} \frac{(\sigma-1)(1-\alpha)L^U}{(\sigma-1)(1-\alpha) + \rho\left[1 - (\kappa+\eta)(\sigma-1)\right]}. \qquad \text{(A. 25)}$$

Moreover, according to (A. 7), (A. 19) and (A. 24),

$$l^{U*} = \frac{(\sigma-1)(1-\alpha)f^U}{\rho\left[1 - (\kappa+\eta)(\sigma-1)\right]}. \qquad \text{(A. 26)}$$

Now, substituting (A. 18), (A. 19), (A. 20), (A. 25) and (A. 26) into (A. 23), and manipulating the resulting expression, one can show that

$$U^* = const. + \frac{\rho\kappa}{1-\rho}\ln\kappa$$

$$+\frac{\rho\left[1 - \kappa(\sigma-1) - \rho\right]}{(\sigma-1)(1-\rho)^2}\left(\ln\left[1 - (\kappa+\eta)(\sigma-1)\right] - \ln f^U\right)$$

$$-\frac{\alpha(1-\rho) + \rho\kappa}{(1-\rho)^2}\ln\left[\alpha + \rho(\kappa+\eta)\right]$$

$$-\frac{(1-\rho)(\sigma-1)(1-\alpha) + \rho\left[1 - \kappa(\sigma-1) - \rho\right]}{(\sigma-1)(1-\rho)^2}\times$$

$$\ln\left((\sigma-1)(1-\alpha) + \rho\left[1 - (\kappa+\eta)(\sigma-1)\right]\right) \qquad (A. 27)$$

From this, it is easy to derive that

$$\frac{\partial U^*}{\partial\eta} = -\frac{\rho}{(1-\rho)^2}\left(\frac{\alpha(1-\rho) + \rho\kappa}{\alpha + \rho(\kappa+\eta)} + \right. \qquad (A. 28)$$

$$\left.\frac{(\sigma-1)^2(1-\alpha)\left[\eta(1-\rho) - \rho\kappa\right]}{\left[1 - (\kappa+\eta)(\sigma-1)\right]\left((\sigma-1)(1-\alpha) + \rho\left[1 - (\kappa+\eta)(\sigma-1)\right]\right)}\right).$$

Thus, $\partial U^*/\partial\eta < 0$ if, e.g., $\eta(1-\rho) \geq \rho\kappa$. In contrast, if, for instance, $\eta = 0.1$, $\kappa = 0.2$, $\sigma = 4$, (i.e., $1 - (\kappa+\eta)(\sigma-1) = 0.1$, thus fulfilling assumption (AA)), $\rho = 0.9$ and $\alpha = 0.5$, then $\partial U^*/\partial\eta > 0$, according to (A. 28). This confirms the result.

Acknowledgements

I am grateful to an anonymous referee for very valuable comments. This paper has also benefited from discussions with Henning Bohn, Josef Falkinger, Volker Meier, and seminar participants at the University of Zurich and the conference on "Dynamics, Economic Growth, and International Trade" (DE-GIT VIII) 2003, Helsinki.

References

Acemoglu, D. (2002): "Technical Change, Inequality, and the Labor Market." *Journal of Economic Literature* 40: 7-72.

Berman, E., Bound J., and Z. Grichilis (1994): "Changes in the Demand for Skilled Labor within U.S. Manufacturing: Evidence from the Annual Survey of Manufactures." *Quarterly Journal of Economics* 109: 367-397.

Berman, E., Bound J., and S. Machin (1998): "Implications of Skill-Biased Technological Change: International Evidence." *Quarterly Journal of Economics* 113: 1245-1279.

Bresnahan, T.F. (1999): "Computerisation and Wage Dispersion: An Analytical Reinterpretation." *Economic Journal* 109: F390-F415.

Cohen, W.M., and Levin R.C. (1989): "Empirical Studies of Innovation and Market Structure." In: Schmalensee, R., Willig, R. D. (Eds.), *Handbook of Industrial Organization, Vol. II.* North-Holland, Amsterdam, ch. 18.

Cohen, W.M., and Klepper S. (1996): "A Reprise of Firm Size and R&D." *Economic Journal* 106: 925-951.

DiNardo, J.E., and Pischke J.-S. (1997): "The Returns to Computer Use Revisited: Have Pencils Changed the Wage Structure too?" *Quarterly Journal of Economics* 112: 291-303.

Dixit, A., and Stiglitz J.E. (1977): "Monopolistic Competition and Optimum Product Diversity." *American Economic Review* 67: 297-308.

Falkinger, J., and Grossmann V. (2003): "Workplaces in the Primary Economy and Wage Pressure in the Secondary Labor Market." *Journal of Institutional and Theoretical Economics* 159: 523-544.

Grossmann, V. (2000): "Skilled Labor Reallocation, Wage Inequality, and Unskilled Unemployment." *Journal of Institutional and Theoretical Economics* 156: 473-500.

Grossmann, V. (2002): "Quality Improvements, the Structure of Employment, and the Skill-Bias Hypothesis Revisited." *Topics in Macroeconomics* 2: http://www.bepress.com/bejm/topics/vol2/iss1/art2/.

Grossmann, V. (2003): Contest for Attention in a Quality-Ladder Model of Endogenous Growth, *CESifo Working Paper* No. 1003.

Jacobs, B., and Nahuis R. (2002): "A General Purpose Technology Explains the Solow Paradox and Wage Inequality." *Economics Letters* 74: 243-250.

Jones, C.I. (1995): "R&D-Based Models of Economic Growth." *Journal of Political Economy* 103: 759-784.

Machin, S., and van Reenen J. (1998): "Technology and Changes in Skill Structure: Evidence from Seven OECD Countries." *Quarterly Journal of Economics* 113: 1215-1244.

Nahuis, R., and Smulders S. (2002): "The Skill Premium, Technological Change and Appropriability." *Journal of Economic Growth* 7: 137-56.

Peretto, P.F. (1998): "Technological Change, Market Rivalry, and the Evolution of the Capitalist Engine of Growth." *Journal of Economic Growth* 3: 53-80.

Peretto, P.F. (1999): "Firm Size, Rivalry, and the Extent of the Market in Endogenous Technological Change." *European Economic Review* 43: 1747-1773.

Pryor, F.L. (2001): "Will Most of Us be Working for Giant Enterprises by 2028?" *Journal of Economic Behavior and Organization* 44: 363-382.

Shapiro, C., and Varian H.R. (1999): *Information Rules.* Boston: Harvard Business School Press.

Skaperdas, S. (1996): "Contest Success Functions." *Economic Theory* 7: 283-290.

Smulders, S., and van de Klundert T. (1995): "Imperfect Competition, Concentration and Growth With Firm-Specific R&D." *European Economic Review* 39: 139-160.

Solow, R.M. (1987): "We'd Better Watch Out." *New York Times Book Review* (July 12), 36.

Stiroh, K.J. (2002): "Information Technology and the U.S. Productivity Revival: What Do the Industry Data Say?" *American Economic Review* 92: 1559-1576.

Thesmar, D., and Thoenig M. (2001): "Creative Destruction and Firm Organization Choice." *Quarterly Journal of Economics* 116: 1201-1237.

Triplett, J.E. (1999): "The Solow Productivity Paradox: What Do Computers Do to Productivity?" *Canadian Journal of Economics* 32: 309-34.

Young, A. (1998): "Growth Without Scale Effects." *Journal of Political Economy* 106: 41-63.

Address of author: – Volker Grossmann, Socioeconomic Institute, University of Zurich, Zürichbergstr. 14, 8032 Zurich, Switzerland (e-mail: volker.grossmann@wwi.unizh.ch)

J. Econ. (2005) Suppl. 10: 143-166

Journal of Economics
Zeitschrift für Nationalökonomie
Printed in Austria

Indeterminacy and Labor Augmenting Externalities

Aditya Goenka and Odile Poulsen

Received September 26, 2003; Revised version received July 14, 2004
© Springer-Verlag 2005

We study a two-sector model of economic growth with labor augmenting external effects. Using general specifications of the technologies, we derive necessary and sufficient conditions for local indeterminacy. We show that, when the investment good sector is capital intensive at the private level, the necessary condition for the growth ray to be indeterminate is that the cost of forgoing consumption is not too high. When the consumption good sector is capital intensive, indeterminacy requires that the depreciation of the capital stock is not too low and that utility is not too concave.

Keywords: Indeterminacy, externalities, two-sector growth model, factor intensities.

JEL Classification: C62, E32, O41.

1 Introduction

It is a well known fact that in dynamic economies equilibria can be indeterminate. Indeterminacy refers to a situation where starting from a given initial condition, there exist a continuum of capital sequences all converging to the same balanced growth path. It is important to understand indeterminacy in models of economic growth. In their examination of the uniqueness and stability properties of the Lucas model, Benhabib and Perli (1994, p. 113) write:

> "Why would two countries like South Korea and Philippines, whose wealth and endowments were quite close not so long ago differ so drastically in their recent experience? (...) variations in growth experiences may be the result of indeterminacy of equilibria, where different countries follow different trajectories towards a balanced growth path."

Indeterminacy of equilibria means that otherwise similar agents have different expectations about future economic events and hence coordinate beliefs in different ways. This gives rise to different saving and growth rates. Hence, as Boldrin and Rustichini (1994, p. 324) note,

> "Given the extent to which models of this form are now used for the purpose of empirically assessing the economic sources of growth, it seems important to clarify the matter. If indeterminacy is present the interpretation of many simple estimations, obtained by pooling data together from a variety of different countries, can be questioned as there is no reason to believe that these countries should be moving along the same equilibrium path."

The contribution of the paper is to add further results to the literature on indeterminacy. We derive necessary and sufficient conditions for the growth ray to be locally indeterminate in a two-sector model of economic growth when either of the sectors has a higher capital ratio than the other (the sector with the highest capital-labor ratio is said to be capital intensive). To derive the results we restrict the preference structure, but use a general specification of the technologies (under a specific externality structure).

The model is a two-sector growth model (Uzawa, 1963; Srinivasan, 1964) with spillovers (Romer, 1986). One sector produces a pure consumption good and the other produces a pure investment good. In addition to the labor and capital inputs provided by the representative consumer, each sector's productivity is affected by the aggregate capital stock. This provides a positive externality a la Harrod (Uzawa, 1961) in the production of both sectors through learning by doing (Arrow, 1962; Sheshinski, 1967). The setting is the same as in Drugeon, Poulsen and Venditti (2003) except that time is discrete.

Let us look at the literature to understand how indeterminacy can arise in a two-sector growth model. Indeterminacy occurs when an equilibrium is stable. Stiglitz and Uzawa (1969) remark that a sufficient condition for the uniqueness and stability of a steady state are that (1) the elasticity of substitution in each sector is greater than one, (2) the capital intensity in the consumption good sector is greater than the capital intensity in the investment good sector (see also Burmeister and Dobell, 1970). In a recent contribution, Jensen (2003) shows that if the elasticity of substitution in both sectors is different, then the above condition on the factor intensity in both sectors is not feasible. Benhabib and Nishimura (1998) present further evidence that factor intensity plays a crucial role in determining the uniqueness and stability in a two-sector growth model. They examine the occurrence of indeterminate equilibria in a framework where external effects from capital and labor are sector specific, social returns are constant and private returns are decreasing. Both production functions are Cobb-Douglas and utility is linear. They show that under these assumptions the steady state is locally indeterminate if the investment good sector is labor intensive from the private level but capital intensive from the social level. By comparing the results of Benhabib and Nishimura (1998) and Benhabib, Nishimura and Venditti (2002), we see that there also exists a difference between models in continuous and discrete time. The latter[1] show that if the model is in discrete rather than continuous time, the steady state can be indeterminate even if the consumption good sector is labor intensive both from the social and private perspective[2]. These conditions are on the technology. Thus, one may think that the preferences of the representative consumer may also affect the properties of the dynamics. Benhabib, Meng, and Nishimura (2000) extend the result of Benhabib and Nishimura (1998) to the non-linear utility case in a three-sector setting. Hence, assumptions on concavity of the utility do not seem to be an important source of indeterminacy. What is the role of the nature of the externality in affecting the dynamics? Harrison and Weder (2002) show by introducing aggregate externalities in the Benhabib and Nishimura (1998) framework that neither the aggregate external effects from capital nor the sector specific external effects from labor play a role in determining the indeterminacy property of the model. Nishimura and Venditti (2001) show that if external effects are purely intersectoral the steady state can be indeterminate if the investment good sector is more capital intensive at the private level if the representative agent is not too impatient. To sum up, the research on indeterminacy has identified the following economic fundamentals as important sources of indeterminacy:

1. The degree of private and social returns.

2. The types of externalities (are external effects sector specific, intersectoral or aggregate? Do they affect both labor and capital?).

3. The allocation of inputs between sectors.

4. The use of specific functional forms for the technology.

5. The time structure of the model (whether time discrete or continuous).

However, these results are open to the criticism that they lack generality since specific functional forms for both the utility and production

---

[1] In Benhabib, Nishimura and Venditti (2002) the labor supply is also assumed to be inelastic whereas Benhabib and Nishimura (1998) assume it is elastic. However, labor elasticity does not play a crucial role in establishing the indeterminacy results.

[2] This is because in continuous time the steady state is indeterminate if the roots of the characteristic polynomial are negative. In discrete time they need to be less than one in absolute value. They can be either positive or negative. See Sect. 4 for a more detailed discussion.

functions are employed, and since the externality must be of a certain type. Our paper is an attempt to address this criticism. In order to improve the understanding of the mechanisms behind indeterminacy, we adopt a more general specification of the economic fundamentals: our production functions exhibit constant private returns and increasing social returns. The utility function is restricted to be of the CES class. The CES utility function is compatible with the existence of a balanced growth ray. Externalities come from the aggregate capital stock and are Harrod-Neutral. Harrod-Neutral or labour augmenting technical change is the canonical form of technical change as it is compatible with the existence of a growth ray. This last assumption allows us to show that the production possibility frontier is homogenous of degree one and to focus on the allocation of inputs between sectors. Our results show that the necessary condition for the balanced growth ray to be indeterminate may be satisfied if either of the two productive sector is capital intensive at the private level and utility is not too concave.

We also examine whether the nature of the time structure has any implications for indeterminacy. In the continuous time model of Drugeon, Poulsen and Venditti (2003) local indeterminacy is ruled out when the consumption good sector is capital intensive at the private level. In the discrete time model studied here, however, indeterminacy can result in this case (see the discussion in Sect. 4).

Sect. 2 formulates the model. Sect. 3 gives the main results on indeterminacy. Sect. 4 interprets the results and Sect. 5 concludes.

2 The Model

The economy is populated by a continuum of identical consumers indexed by h, where $h \in [0, 1]$. All consumers are infinitely lived and rational. Each consumer h is initially endowed with an equal fraction of the aggregate capital stock $k_0^h = \bar{k}$, and a single unit of labor. These productive resources are allocated optimally between the two productive sectors of the economy. The representative consumer maximizes his (discounted) intertemporal welfare. At any point of time (which is discrete), welfare is measured by a utility function of current consumption per capita $u(c_t)$. The function u is concave, twice continuously differentiable and strictly increasing. In keeping with the literature, we assume the following restriction on the utility function:

Assumption 1.

$$u(c) = \frac{c^\alpha}{\alpha},$$

where $0 < \alpha \leq 1$.

The representative consumer discounts future consumption. This is expressed by a positive discount factor β, where $0 < \beta < 1$. At time $t = 0$, the representative consumer, thus, maximizes

$$U_0 = \sum_{t=0}^{\infty} \beta^t \frac{c_t^{\alpha}}{\alpha}. \tag{1}$$

We omit the time subscripts whenever they are not necessary. The production side is composed of two sectors. Sector 1 produces the consumption good, c, while sector 2 produces the investment good, y. Each sector consists of a continuum of identical firms. As we will look at the behavior of a representative firm in each sector, these will be indexed by i with $i = 1, 2$. The inputs, capital, k and labor, l, are freely mobile between sectors. The representative firm in sector i produces output using a non negative amount of capital, k^i, a non negative amount of labor, l^i, and faces an externality from the aggregate capital stock in any given period, X, where $X = \int_0^1 k(h)dh$. Thus,

$$c = F^1(k^1, l^1, X), \tag{2}$$

$$y = F^2(k^2, l^2, X). \tag{3}$$

The key restriction in the model is that spillovers are labor augmenting or, technical change is Harrod-Neutral:

Assumption 2. $F^i : \Re_+^3 \to \Re_+$, $i = 1, 2$ is continuous. For a given $X \in \Re_+$:

(i) $F^i(., ., .)$ is of class C^2 on $\Re_{++} \times \Re_{++} \times \Re_+$;

(ii) $F^i(., ., X)$ is homogenous of degree one and strictly increasing over $\Re_{++} \times \Re_{++}$;

(iii) $F_{11}^i(., l^i, X) < 0$, for all $k^i \in \Re_{++}$ and $\lim_{k^i \to 0} F_1^i(k^i, l^i, X) = \infty$;

(iv) $F_{22}^i(k^i, ., X) < 0$, for all $l^i \in]0, 1]$ and $\lim_{l^i \to 0} F_2^i(k^i, l^i, X) = +\infty$.

We restrict the spillovers to be labor augmenting:

Assumption 3. (*Harrod-Neutrality*)

$F^i(k^i, l^i, X) = \mathcal{F}^i(k^i, l^i X)$, $i = 1, 2$, where $\mathcal{F}^i(., .)$ is homogenous of degree 1 in k^i and $l^i X$.

Harrod (1937) introduced this form of labor augmenting technological progress and it has been extensively used by the learning by doing literature[3]. For any given sequence of externalities $\{X_t\}$, define

---

[3] See Arrow (1962), Uzawa (1961), Sheshinski (1967), Romer (1986) and Lucas (1988).

the production possibility frontier, $T(k, y, X)$. It is the value function of the maximization problem in which the representative firm in the consumption good sector chooses its output level given the existing technical constraint, full employment of inputs, and the aggregate capital stock X. In other words,

$$T(k, y, X) = \max_{\{k^1, l^1\}} \mathcal{F}^1(k^1, l^1 X) \tag{4}$$

subject to

$$y = \mathcal{F}^2(k^2, l^2 X),$$
$$k = k^1 + k^2,$$
$$1 = l^1 + l^2,$$
$$k^i \geq 0, \ l^i \geq 0, \ i = 1, 2.$$

For all given $X \geq 0$, it is assumed:[4]

Assumption 4. $T(k, y, X)$ is of class C^2 on $\Re_{++} \times \Re_{++} \times \Re_+$.

The investment resource constraint for this economy is $k_{t+1} = y_t + (1 - \delta)k_t$, where $0 < \delta \leq 1$ is the depreciation rate of capital in every period. Using a standard argument it can be shown that for any given $X \geq 0$, $T(k, y, X)$ is concave. Define the set of feasible interior solutions to (4) as

$$D(X_t) = \{(k_t, k_{t+1}) \in \Re_+ \times \Re_+ :$$
$$(1 - \delta)k_t \leq k_{t+1} \leq \mathcal{F}^2(k_t, X_t) + (1 - \delta)k_t, \text{ for all } X_t \in \Re_+\}.$$

This set is non-empty and convex.

Now, define the indirect utility function, $V(k_t, k_{t+1}, X_t)$, where

$$V(k_t, k_{t+1}, X_t) = [T(k_t, k_{t+1} - (1 - \delta)k_t, X_t)]^\alpha / \alpha.$$

Then, the reduced form model is:

$$\max_{\{k_t\}_{t=0}^\infty} \sum_{t=0}^\infty \beta^t V(k_t, k_{t+1}, X_t),$$

$$k_0 = \bar{k},$$
$$(k_t, k_{t+1}) \in D(X_t), \tag{5}$$
$$\{X_t\} \text{ given.}$$

---

[4] The following assumption is satisfied, for instance, by Cobb-Douglas production functions.

An *interior solution* to Problem (5) satisfies the following sufficient conditions[5]:

$$V_2(k_t, k_{t+1}, X_t) + \beta V_1(k_{t+1}, k_{t+2}, X_{t+1}) = 0, \tag{6}$$

$$\lim_{t \to \infty} \beta^t k_t V_1(k_t, k_{t+1}, X_t) = 0, \tag{7}$$

$$\sum_{t=0}^{t=\infty} \beta^t V(k_t, k_{t+1}, X_t) < \infty. \tag{8}$$

Equation (6) is the Euler equation, equation, (7) the transversality condition and equation (8) the summability condition.

An *equilibrium path* $\{k_t\}$, is an interior solution to Problem 5 along which the sequence of externalities $\{X_t\}$ satisfying $\{k_t\{X_t\}\} = \{X_t\}$ for all $t \geq 0$. We do not consider the question of existence to this fixed point problem. A detailed treatment of this issue is beyond the scope of this paper. Romer (1983) and Mitra (1998) both address the existence issue of the fixed point problem $\{k_t\{X_t\}\} = \{X_t\}$ for all $t \geq 0$ in a slightly different framework. Here, we assume that there exists an equilibrium path $\{k_t\}$ such that $\{k_t\{X_t\}\} = \{X_t\}$.

Benhabib and Nishimura (1985) show that the sign of T_{21} is positive (negative) if the investment good sector is more (less) capital intensive than the consumption good sector. The consumption good sector is said to be more capital intensive if the capital-labor ratio in the consumption good sector is higher than the capital-labor ratio in the investment good sector. In other words, the consumption good sector is more capital intensive if[6] $k^1/l^1 > k^2/l^2$. Under Harrod-Neutrality and the assumptions above, Drugeon and Venditti (1998) establish that $k^i(k_t, y_t, X_t)$ and $l^i(k_t, y_t, X_t)$, $i = 1, 2$, are homogenous of degree 1 and 0, respectively. From this it follows that $T(k_t, y_t, X_t)$ is homogenous of degree 1. Under Assumption 1, the indirect utility function, $V(k_t, k_{t+1}, X_t)$, is homogenous of degree α. Following the slightly dif-

---

[5] A proof of this can be found in Boldrin, Nishimura, Shigoka and Yano (2001).

[6] In an economy where production functions are both Cobb Douglas the factor intensity are related to the factor shares. Suppose that

$$c_t = \mathcal{A}(k_t^1)^\sigma (l_t^1 X_t)^{1-\sigma}, \quad y_t = \mathcal{B}(k_t^2)^\mu (l_t^2 X_t)^{1-\mu}.$$

Then *Harrod-Neutrality* implies that the difference in factor intensity can then be computed as

$$\frac{k^2}{l^2} > \frac{k^1}{l^1} \text{ if and only if } \mu > \sigma.$$

ferent continuous time model of Drugeon, Poulsen and Venditti (2003)[7], a similar characterization can be made in the discrete time environment with externalities:

Lemma 1. *Let Assumptions 1-4 be satisfied. Then* $T(k_t, y_t, X_t)$ *is homogenous of degree 1. Furthermore,*

$$T_{21} = \frac{\mathcal{F}_{12}^1 \mathcal{F}_{12}^2 q \mathcal{F}^2 l^1}{\Delta k^2 k^1} \left(\frac{k^1}{l^1} - \frac{k^2}{l^2} \right), \tag{9}$$

$$T_{22} = T_{21} \frac{l^2}{\mathcal{F}^2} \left(\frac{k^1}{l^1} - \frac{k^2}{l^2} \right) < 0, \tag{10}$$

$$T_{23} = -T_{21} \frac{k^1}{l^1 X} + \frac{2l^2}{\mathcal{F}_1^2} \left(\mathcal{F}_{12}^1 + q \mathcal{F}_{12}^2 \right), \tag{11}$$

where

$$\Delta = -\frac{\mathcal{F}_{12}^1 (\mathcal{F}^1)^2 (\mathcal{F}_1^2)^2}{(\mathcal{F}_1^1)^2 k^1 l^1 X} - \frac{\mathcal{F}_{12}^1 (\mathcal{F}^2)^2 \mathcal{F}_1^1}{\mathcal{F}_1^2 k^2 l^2 X} < 0.$$

Proof: See Drugeon and Venditti (1998) and Drugeon, Poulsen and Venditti (2003). ////

Corollary 1. *Suppose the consumption good sector is capital intensive. Then* $T_{23} > 0$.

3 Indeterminacy

In this section we address existence and stability of the growth ray. In the previous section an equilibrium path $\{k_t\}$ was defined as an interior solution to Problem 5 along which the sequence of externalities $\{X_t\}$ satisfying $\{k_t\{X_t\}\} = \{X_t\}$ for all $t \geq 0$. The question of existence to the fixed point problem is beyond the scope of this paper. Assuming that such a solution exists, the existence of a growth ray is established.

3.1 Existence of a Growth Ray

The *growth factor* of capital is defined as $k_{t+1}/k_t = \gamma_t$. Define the maximum feasible growth factor as $\overline{\gamma}$. $\underline{\gamma}$ is the minimum feasible growth rate. Under Harrod-Neutrality, $\overline{\gamma} = \mathcal{F}^2(1,1) + 1 - \delta$ and $\underline{\gamma} = 1 - \delta$. To ensure existence of an interior growth ray, we assume the following:

Assumption 5. $\beta \left[\mathcal{F}_1^2(k^2(1, \delta, 1), l^2(1, \delta, 1)) + 1 - \delta \right] > 1.$

---

[7] The technology is defined at a point of time and whether time is continuous or discrete does not significantly affect these properties. See Poulsen (2001) for details in the discrete time case.

Thus, the growth rate of capital is equal to $\gamma_t - 1$. To ensure existence of an interior growth ray with endogenous growth we need $\overline{\gamma} > 1$. This amounts to assuming that $\mathcal{F}^2(1,1) > \delta$. This complies with the results of Jensen (2003) who shows that the technology parameter in the capital good sector plays a crucial role for deciding whether growth is bounded or not. A growth ray is now defined in terms of a growth factor.

Definition 1. *An equilibrium path* $\{k_t\}$ *is a growth ray if there exists a growth factor* $\gamma \in [1-\delta, \overline{\gamma}]$ *such that for all* $t \geq 0$, $k_t = \gamma^t k_0$, *where* $k_0 \neq 0$.

An equilibrium path is a solution to Problem 5 if it solves equations (6)-(8).[8] Under Harrod-Neutrality these equations can be rewritten along a growth ray as:

$$\gamma_t^{1-\alpha} V_2(1, \gamma_t, 1) + \beta V_1(1, \gamma_{t+1}, 1) = 0, \tag{12}$$

$$\lim_{t \to \infty} \beta^t k_t^\alpha V_1(1, \gamma_t, 1) = 0, \tag{13}$$

$$\sum_{t=0}^{t=\infty} \beta^t V(1, \gamma_t, 1) < \infty. \tag{14}$$

The transversality condition (13) is satisfied along a growth ray if the following assumption holds:

Assumption 6. $\beta \overline{\gamma}^\alpha < 1$.

Proposition 1. *Let Assumptions 1-6 be satisfied. Then there exists an interior growth ray,* $\widetilde{\gamma} \in (1, \overline{\gamma})$ *if* $\mathcal{F}^2(1,1) > \delta$ *and*

$$\beta[\mathcal{F}_1^2(k^2(1, \widetilde{\gamma}+1-\delta, 1), l^2(1, \widetilde{\gamma}+1-\delta, 1)) - 1 + \delta] > 1.$$

Proof: We first show that $T_3 > 0$. From the definition of $T(k, y, X)$

$$T_3 = \mathcal{F}_1^1 \frac{\partial k^1}{\partial X} + X \mathcal{F}_2^1 \frac{\partial l^1}{\partial X} + l^1 \mathcal{F}_2^1. \tag{15}$$

By definition, $y = \mathcal{F}^2(k^2, l^2 X)$, so

$$0 = \mathcal{F}_1^2 \frac{\partial k^2}{\partial X} + \mathcal{F}_2^2 \frac{\partial l^2}{\partial X} + l^2 \mathcal{F}_2^2. \tag{16}$$

---

[8] For more details the reader is referred to Boldrin, et al. (2001) and Mitra (1998).

Under the full employment of productive resources

$$\frac{\partial k^1}{\partial X} = -\frac{\partial k^2}{\partial X}, \tag{17}$$

$$\frac{\partial l^1}{\partial X} = -\frac{\partial l^2}{\partial X}. \tag{18}$$

Furthermore, the envelope theorem implies that $T_2(k, y, X) = -q$, and by definition,

$$q = \frac{\mathcal{F}_1^1}{\mathcal{F}_1^2} = \frac{\mathcal{F}_2^1}{\mathcal{F}_2^2}. \tag{19}$$

Substituting (17), (18) and (19) into (15), and using (16), we get

$$T_3 = q\mathcal{F}_2^2. \tag{20}$$

We now show that there exists an interior growth ray. Using the Euler theorem on homogenous functions

$$c_t = k_t T_1(k_t, y_t, X_t) + y_t T_2(k_t, y_t, X_t) + X_t T_3(k_t, y_t, X_t).$$

From (20),

$$c_t > k_t T_1(k_t, k_{t+1} - (1-\delta)k_t, X_t) + [k_{t+1} - (1-\delta)k_t]T_2(k_t, k_{t+1}$$
$$- (1-\delta)k_t, X_t)$$
$$> k_t [T_1(1, \gamma_t - (1-\delta), 1) + [\gamma_t - (1-\delta)]T_2(1, \gamma_t - (1-\delta), 1)].$$

The Euler equation along a growth ray, γ, is

$$\gamma^{1-\alpha} V_2(1, \gamma, 1) + \beta V_1(1, \gamma, 1) = 0. \tag{21}$$

Along a growth ray, (21) simplifies to

$$\frac{\gamma^{1-\alpha}}{\beta} - (1-\delta) = -\frac{T_1(1, \gamma - (1-\delta), 1)}{T_2(1, \gamma - (1-\delta), 1)}$$

or, $\varepsilon(\gamma) = \sigma(\gamma)$. Both these are continuous functions of γ. At $\bar{\gamma}$, we have

$$0 > T_1(1, \bar{\gamma} - (1-\delta), 1) + [\bar{\gamma} - (1-\delta)]T_2(1, \bar{\gamma} - (1-\delta), 1).$$

This can be written as

$$\bar{\gamma} - (1-\delta) > -\frac{T_1(1, \bar{\gamma} - (1-\delta), 1)}{T_2(1, \bar{\gamma} - (1-\delta), 1)}. \tag{22}$$

Thus $\sigma(\bar{\gamma}) < \bar{\gamma} - (1-\delta)$, and so

$$\sigma(\bar{\gamma}) - \varepsilon(\bar{\gamma}) < \frac{\bar{\gamma}(\beta\bar{\gamma}^\alpha - 1)}{\beta\bar{\gamma}^\alpha}.$$

It follows that, under Assumption 6, $\sigma(\bar{\gamma}) - \varepsilon(\bar{\gamma}) < 0$. For a growth ray to exist it is sufficient that $\sigma(1) - \varepsilon(1) > 0$. This inequality is satisfied if and only if

$$-\frac{T_1(1,\delta,1)}{T_2(1,\delta,1)} = \beta[\mathcal{F}_1^2(k^2(1,\delta,1),l^2(1,\delta,1)) - 1 + \delta] > 1.$$

This is true under Assumption 5. ////

3.2 Local Indeterminacy

In what follows we show that, under certain conditions on the utility function and the depreciation rate, local indeterminacy can arise no matter which sector is capital intensive at the private level. A word of caution is necessary here. A growth ray is said to be indeterminate if in every neighborhood we can find another growth ray, i.e. the growth ray is not locally unique.

Definition 2. *A growth ray $k_t = \gamma^t k_0$ is locally indeterminate if for every $\epsilon > 0$, there exists another equilibrium sequence $\{k'_t\}$ with $\gamma'_t = k'_{t+1}/k'_t$ such that $|k_1 - k'_1| < \epsilon$ with $k_0 = k'_0$.*

Drugeon, Poulsen and Venditti (2003) show that the allocation of productive resources between the two sectors affects the uniqueness property of the growth ray. Furthermore, a necessary condition for the occurrence of multiple growth ray is that the investment good sector is capital intensive at the private level when evaluated at the growth ray. The multiplicity result is not affected by the time structure of the model. We therefore refer the reader to this paper for a more detailed exposition.

For a system of dimension two, indeterminacy occurs when the two roots of the characteristic polynomial are inside the unit circle. We see, from (12), that in our model the dynamic system is of dimension 1^9. Therefore, if the root associated with (12) is within $(-1, 1)$, then the growth ray will be locally indeterminate. Before we derive the local indeterminacy result we establish the next lemma.

Lemma 2. *Let Assumptions 1-6 be satisfied. Then:*

$$V_{21} = T^{\alpha-2}\{(\alpha - 1)T_2[T_1 - (1 - \delta)T_2] + T[T_{21} - (1 - \delta)T_{22}]\}, (23)$$
$$V_{23} = T^{\alpha-2}[(\alpha - 1)T_2T_3 + TT_{23}]. \tag{24}$$

---

[9] We could instead choose to linearize the Euler equation (equation 12). In this case the system is of dimension two. One of the roots of this system is always equal to unity. See the discussion in Sect. 4.2.

Furthermore, no matter which sector is the most capital intensive,
$V_{21} + V_{23} > 0$ *for all* $\gamma_t \in (1 - \delta, \bar{\gamma})$.

Proof: By definition

$$V(k_t, k_{t+1}, X_t) = [T(k_t, k_{t+1} - (1 - \delta)k_t, X_t)]^\alpha / \alpha.$$

Under Assumption 4 we can compute the following derivatives:

$$V_1 = T^{\alpha-1}[T_1 - (1 - \delta)T_2],$$
$$V_{21} = T^{\alpha-2}\{(\alpha - 1)T_2[T_1 - (1 - \delta)T_2] + T[T_{21} - (1 - \delta)T_{22}]\},$$
$$V_2 = T^{\alpha-1}T_2,$$
$$V_{23} = T^{\alpha-2}[(\alpha - 1)T_2T_3 + TT_{23}].$$

Using the expressions of V_{21} and V_{23}, derived in Lemma 2:

$$V_{21}+V_{23} = T^{\alpha-2}\{(\alpha-1)T_2[T_1-(1-\delta)T_2+T_3]+T[T_{21}-(1-\delta)T_{22}+T_{23}]\}.$$

Along a growth ray, $T_1 - (1 - \delta)T_2 = -\beta^{-1}\gamma^{1-\alpha}T_2$. So,

$$V_{21}+V_{23} = T^{\alpha-2}\{(1-\alpha)T_2[\beta^{-1}\gamma^{1-\alpha}T_2-T_3]+T[T_{21}-(1-\delta)T_{22}+T_{23}]\}.$$

Under Assumptions 1-6, $T_2[\beta^{-1}\gamma^{1-\alpha}T_2 - T_3] > 0$ and $-(1-\delta)T_{22} > 0$. Thus using (11), the sign of $T_{21} + T_{23}$ is

$$T_{21} + T_{23} = T_{21}\left(1 - \frac{k^1}{l^1 X}\right) + \frac{2l^2(\mathcal{F}_{12}^1 + q\mathcal{F}_{12}^2)}{\mathcal{F}_1^2}.$$

Under Assumption 2, $2l^2(\mathcal{F}_{12}^1 + q\mathcal{F}_{12}^2)/\mathcal{F}_1^2 > 0$. It follows that $V_{21} + V_{23} > 0$ if $T_{21} + T_{23} > 0$. And $T_{21} + T_{23} > 0$ if $T_{21}\left(1 - k^1/l^1 X\right) \geq 0$. So, if $T_{21}\left(1 - k^1/l^1 X\right) \geq 0$, then $V_{21} + V_{23} > 0$. Along a growth ray

$$1 - \frac{k^1}{l^1 X} = \frac{l^1 k - k^1}{l^1 k} = \frac{l^2}{k}\left(\frac{k^2}{l^2} - \frac{k^1}{l^1}\right).$$

Hence, on using (9), we obtain

$$T_{21}\left(1 - \frac{k^1}{l^1 X}\right) = \frac{\mathcal{F}_{12}^1 \mathcal{F}_{12}^2 q \mathcal{F}^2 l^1 l^2}{\Delta k^1 k^2 k}\left(\frac{k^2}{l^2} - \frac{k^1}{l^1}\right)^2 \geq 0. \qquad \text{////}$$

We can now show that, if the investment good sector is more capital intensive, then the growth ray is indeterminate if utility is not too concave. When the investment good sector is more capital intensive for all $\gamma_t \in (1 - \delta, \bar{\gamma})$, we know from Lemma 1 that $T_{21} > 0$ and $T_{22} < 0$ for all $\gamma_t \in (1 - \delta, \bar{\gamma})$. So, $T_{21} - (1 - \delta)T_{22} > 0$. If the investment good sector is more capital intensive $V_{21} > 0$ for all $\gamma_t \in (1 - \delta, \bar{\gamma})$. The sign of T_{23} is, however, ambiguous. In this case, the sign of V_{23} is ambiguous, too.

Proposition 2. *Let Assumptions 1-6 be satisfied. Let the investment good sector be more capital intensive. Then,*
(*i*) *A necessary condition for the growth ray to be locally indeterminate is*

$$T_{23}(1, \gamma + 1 - \delta, 1) < 0$$

$$\Longleftrightarrow T_{21} \frac{k^1}{l^1}\bigg|_{(1,\gamma+1-\delta,1)} > \frac{2l^2}{\mathcal{F}_1^2} \left(\mathcal{F}_{12}^1 + q\mathcal{F}_{12}^2\right)\bigg|_{(1,\gamma+1-\delta,1)}. \qquad (25)$$

(*ii*) *A necessary and sufficient condition for the growth ray to be locally indeterminate is*

$$-\frac{TT_{23} + (\alpha - 1)T_2 T_3}{T[T_{12} - (1-\delta)T_{22}] + (\alpha - 1)T_2[T_1 - (1-\delta)T_2]}\bigg|_{(1,\gamma+1-\delta,1)}$$
$$> 1 - \beta\gamma^{\alpha}.$$

Proof: (*i*) Suppose that the investment good sector is more capital intensive, i.e. suppose that $k^2/l^2 > k^1/l^1$. Under Harrod-Neutrality (Assumption 3) the Euler equation reduces to

$$\gamma^{1-\alpha} V_2(1, \gamma, 1) + \beta V_1(1, \gamma, 1) = 0.$$

Then, along an equilibrium growth ray γ, we have

$$\left[(1-\alpha)\gamma^{-\alpha} V_2(1,\gamma,1) + \gamma^{1-\alpha} V_{22}(1,\gamma,1)\right] d\gamma_t + \beta V_{12}(1,\gamma,1) d\gamma_{t+1} = 0. \qquad (26)$$

From the Euler theorem on homogenous functions

$$(\alpha - 1)V_2(1,\gamma,1) = V_{21}(1,\gamma,1) + V_{22}(1,\gamma,1)\gamma + V_{23}(1,\gamma,1).$$

Hence (26) reduces to

$$\left[V_{21}(1,\gamma,1) + V_{23}(1,\gamma,1)\right] d\gamma_t + \beta\gamma^{\alpha} V_{12}(1,\gamma,1) d\gamma_{t+1} = 0,$$

and

$$\frac{d\gamma_{t+1}}{d\gamma_t} = \frac{V_{21}(1,\gamma,1) + V_{23}(1,\gamma,1)}{\beta\gamma^{\alpha} V_{12}(1,\gamma,1)}. \qquad (27)$$

From Lemma 2 it follows that if $k^2/l^2 > k^1/l^1$ for all $\gamma_t \in (1-\delta, \overline{\gamma})$, then

$$\frac{d\gamma_{t+1}}{d\gamma_t} > 0 \text{ for all } \gamma \in (1-\delta, \overline{\gamma}).$$

The growth ray is locally indeterminate if and only if

$$\frac{d\gamma_{t+1}}{d\gamma_t} < 1. \qquad (28)$$

Condition (28) holds if and only if

$$\frac{1}{\beta\gamma^\alpha} + \frac{V_{23}(1,\gamma,1)}{\beta\gamma^\alpha V_{12}(1,\gamma,1)} < 1.$$

Under Assumption 6 a necessary condition for (28) to hold is again

$$\frac{V_{23}(1,\gamma,1)}{V_{12}(1,\gamma,1)} < 0. \tag{29}$$

However, if $k^2/l^2 > k^1/l^1$, then from, Lemma 1, we have $T_{21} > 0$ and $T_{22} < 0$. Thus, if the investment good sector is more capital intensive, then $V_{21} > 0$. So (29) reduces to $V_{23} < 0$. Looking at (24) we see that a necessary condition for this to be true is that

$$T_{23}(1,\gamma+1-\delta,1) < 0.$$

(ii) A necessary and sufficient condition for (28) to be satisfied is

$$-\frac{V_{23}(1,\gamma,1)}{V_{12}(1,\gamma,1)} > 1 - \beta\gamma^\alpha,$$

or, using (23) and (24),

$$-\left.\frac{TT_{23} + (\alpha-1)T_2 T_3}{T\left[T_{12} - (1-\delta)T_{22}\right] + (\alpha-1)T_2\left[T_1 - (1-\delta)T_2\right]}\right|_{(1,\gamma+1-\delta,1)}$$
$$> 1 - \beta\gamma^\alpha. \qquad\qquad ////$$

We see that for the necessary and sufficient condition for local indeterminacy to be satisfied utility cannot be too concave. This implies that the marginal utility of consumption is relatively inelastic. The cost in utils of producing additional capital stock is given by V_2. Hence the necessary and sufficient condition says that the increase in V_2 due to the positive external effects must be lower than the decrease in V_2 due to the current capital stock, but not too low. This result is also obtained by Drugeon, Poulsen, and Venditti (2003) in a continuous time framework.

In discrete time, when the consumption good sector is more capital intensive for all $\gamma_t \in (1-\delta,\overline{\gamma})$, we know from Lemma 1 that $T_{21} < 0$, $T_{22} < 0$ and $T_{23} > 0$ for all $\gamma_t \in (1-\delta,\overline{\gamma})$. Thus, if the consumption good sector is more capital intensive for all $\gamma_t \in (1-\delta,\overline{\gamma})$, then $V_{23} > 0$ for all $\gamma_t \in (1-\delta,\overline{\gamma})$ and the sign of V_{21} is ambiguous. We show in the next proposition that when the consumption good sector is more capital intensive, a necessary condition for the growth ray γ to be locally indeterminate is that $V_{21}(1,\gamma,1) < 0$.

Proposition 3. *Let Assumptions 1-6 be satisfied. Let the consumption good sector be more capital intensive Then,*
(i) A necessary condition for the growth ray to be locally indeterminate is

$$T\left[T_{12} - (1-\delta)T_{22}\right] + (\alpha - 1)T_2\left[T_1 - (1-\delta)T_2\right]\big|_{(1,\gamma+1-\delta,1)} < 0. \quad (30)$$

(ii) A necessary and sufficient condition for the growth ray to be locally indeterminate is

$$-\frac{TT_{23} + (\alpha-1)T_2T_3}{T\left[T_{12} - (1-\delta)T_{22}\right] + (\alpha-1)T_2\left[T_1 - (1-\delta)T_2\right]}\Bigg|_{(1,\gamma+1-\delta,1)}$$
$$< 1 + \beta\gamma^\alpha.$$

Proof: (i) Suppose that the consumption good sector is more capital intensive i.e. suppose that $k^1/l^1 > k^2/l^2$. Under Harrod-Neutrality (Assumption 3) we can show as in the Proof of Proposition 2 that if $V_{12}(1,\gamma,1) \neq 0$ we have

$$\frac{d\gamma_{t+1}}{d\gamma_t} = \frac{V_{21}(1,\gamma,1) + V_{23}(1,\gamma,1)}{\beta\gamma^\alpha V_{12}(1,\gamma,1)}.$$

From the results of Lemma 2 it follows that if $k^1/l^1 > k^2/l^2$ for all $\gamma_t \in (1 - \delta, \overline{\gamma})$, then

$$\frac{d\gamma_{t+1}}{d\gamma_t} < 0 \text{ for all } \gamma \in (1 - \delta, \overline{\gamma}).$$

The growth ray is locally indeterminate if and only if

$$\frac{d\gamma_{t+1}}{d\gamma_t} > -1. \quad (31)$$

Since $V_{12} = V_{21}$, (31) holds if and only if

$$\frac{1}{\beta\gamma^\alpha} + \frac{V_{23}(1,\gamma,1)}{\beta\gamma^\alpha V_{12}(1,\gamma,1)} > -1.$$

Under Assumption 6, we have $\beta\gamma^\alpha < 1$. So a necessary condition for (31) to hold is

$$\frac{V_{23}(1,\gamma,1)}{V_{12}(1,\gamma,1)} < 0. \quad (32)$$

However, if $k^1/l^1 > k^2/l^2$, then, from Lemma 1, we have $T_{21} < 0$, $T_{22} < 0$ and $T_{23} > 0$ for all $\gamma_t \in (1 - \delta, \overline{\gamma})$. Hence, if the consumption good sector is more capital intensive for all $\gamma_t \in (1-\delta, \overline{\gamma})$, then $V_{23} > 0$. Then, (32) reduces to $V_{21} < 0$, i.e. to

$$T\left[T_{12} - (1-\delta)T_{22}\right] + (\alpha - 1)T_2\left[T_1 - (1-\delta)T_2\right]\big|_{(1,\gamma+1-\delta,1)} < 0.$$

(*ii*) A necessary and sufficient condition for (31) to be satisfied is

$$-\frac{V_{23}(1,\gamma,1)}{V_{12}(1,\gamma,1)} < 1 + \beta\gamma^\alpha,$$

or, using (23) and (24),

$$-\frac{TT_{23} + (\alpha - 1)T_2 T_3}{T\left[T_{12} - (1-\delta)T_{22}\right] + (\alpha - 1)T_2\left[T_1 - (1-\delta)T_2\right]}\bigg|_{(1,\gamma+1-\delta,1)}$$
$$< 1 + \beta\gamma^\alpha. \hspace{4cm} ////$$

The necessary and sufficient condition for local indeterminacy requires again that the marginal utility of consumption is relatively inelastic. The cost in utils of producing additional capital stock is given by V_2. Hence the necessary and sufficient condition says that the decrease in V_2 due to the positive external effects must be lower than the increase in V_2 due to the current capital stock, but not too low.

4 Interpretation

4.1 Interpretation of the Main Result

With generic functional forms we cannot compute explicitly the social factor intensities. However, suppose we used Cobb-Douglas production functions. Then it can be shown that when the investment sector is more capital intensive at the private level, it is also more intensive at the social level[10]. Hence it is not clear to us how this affects the Stolper-Samuelson theorem[11]. To understand the mechanisms behind indeterminacy we propose the following interpretation following Benhabib and Nishimura (1998), Benhabib Nishimura, and Venditti (2002) and Nishimura and Venditti (2001). Assume, for simplicity, that the depreciation of the capital stock is total. Suppose that the investment good sector is more capital intensive at the private level. Starting from

---

[10] Details are available from the authors upon request.

[11] The Stolper-Samuelson theorem has been shown to work through private factor intensities when externalities are intersectoral by Nishimura and Venditti (2002). It works through social factor intensities when external effects are sector specific as shown by Benhabib and Nishimura (1998).

an equilibrium, suppose that the price of investment increases exogenously above its equilibrium level. The rate of investment will then also increase above its initial level. The Rybczynski theorem tells us that the output of the investment sector will increase above its equilibrium value. Under Harrod Neutrality compute the following partial derivative:

$$\frac{\partial \mathcal{F}_1^2(k^2, l^2)}{\partial y} = \mathcal{F}_{11}^2 \frac{\partial k^2}{\partial y} + \mathcal{F}_{12}^2 \frac{\partial l^2}{\partial y}.$$

From the Euler theorem on homogenous functions this simplifies to

$$\frac{\partial \mathcal{F}_1^2(k^2, l^2)}{\partial y} = \mathcal{F}_{11}^2 \left(\frac{\partial k^2}{\partial y} - \frac{k^2}{l^2 X} \frac{\partial l^2}{\partial y} \right).$$

Drugeon and Venditti (1998) have shown under Harrod-Neutrality

$$\frac{\partial k^2}{\partial y} = -\frac{\mathcal{F}_{12}^1 \mathcal{F}^1}{q l^1 X \Delta} - \frac{\mathcal{F}_{12}^2 q \mathcal{F}^2}{l^2 X \Delta}, \tag{33}$$

$$\frac{\partial l^2}{\partial y} = -\frac{\mathcal{F}_{12}^1 \mathcal{F}^1}{q k^1 X \Delta} - \frac{\mathcal{F}_{12}^2 q \mathcal{F}^2}{k^2 X \Delta}, \tag{34}$$

where

$$\Delta = -\frac{\mathcal{F}_{12}^1 (\mathcal{F}^1)^2 (\mathcal{F}_1^2)^2}{(\mathcal{F}_1^1)^2 k^1 l^1 X} - \frac{\mathcal{F}_{12}^2 (\mathcal{F}^2)^2 \mathcal{F}_1^1}{\mathcal{F}_1^2 k^2 l^2 X} < 0.$$

It follows that

$$\frac{\mathcal{F}_{12}^1 \mathcal{F}^1}{q \Delta k^1} \left(\frac{k^2}{l^2} - \frac{k^1}{l^1} \right) \lesseqgtr 0 \text{ if and only if } \frac{k^2}{l^2} \gtreqless \frac{k^1}{l^1}.$$

And consequently we have

$$\frac{\partial \mathcal{F}_1^2(k^2, l^2)}{\partial y} \gtreqless 0 \text{ if and only if } \frac{k^2}{l^2} \gtreqless \frac{k^1}{l^1}.$$

As the output of the investment sector increases, the marginal productivity of capital in the investment good sector will increase. This validates the beliefs of higher returns from capital. How do prices and output react? By definition

$$T_{11} = \frac{\partial r}{\partial k} = \mathcal{F}_{11}^1 \left(1 - \frac{\partial k^2}{\partial k} \right) - \mathcal{F}_{12}^1 \frac{\partial l^2}{\partial k} X$$

$$= -\mathcal{F}_{11}^1 \left(\frac{\partial k^2}{\partial k} - \frac{k^1}{l^1} \frac{\partial l^2}{\partial k} \right) + \mathcal{F}_{11}^1.$$

Drugeon and Venditti (1998) show that

$$\frac{\partial k^2}{\partial k} = \frac{\mathcal{F}_{11}^1 \mathcal{F}_2^2 \mathcal{F}^1}{q l^1 X \Delta}, \quad \frac{\partial l^2}{\partial k} = \frac{\mathcal{F}_{11}^1 \mathcal{F}_1^2 \mathcal{F}^1}{q l^1 X^2 \Delta}.$$

Hence

$$T_{11} = -\frac{(\mathcal{F}_{11}^1)^2(\mathcal{F}^1)^2}{q^2(l^1)^2 X^2 \Delta} + \mathcal{F}_{11}^1. \tag{35}$$

Reducing to the same denominator and substituting for Δ, (35) reduces to

$$\frac{\mathcal{F}_{11}^1 \mathcal{F}_{12}^2 (\mathcal{F}^2)^2 (\mathcal{F}_1^1)^3 k^1 l^1}{\mathcal{F}_{12}^1 (\mathcal{F}^1)^2 (\mathcal{F}_1^2)^3 k^2 l^2 + \mathcal{F}_{12}^2 (\mathcal{F}^2)^2 (\mathcal{F}_1^1)^3 k^1 l^1} < 0.$$

It follows that $T_{11} < 0$ when either of the two sector is capital intensive. Furthermore

$$T_{21} = -\frac{\partial q}{\partial r}\frac{\partial r}{\partial k} > 0, \; T_{22} = -\frac{\partial q}{\partial r}\frac{\partial r}{\partial y} < 0, \; T_{23} = -\frac{\partial q}{\partial r}\frac{\partial r}{\partial X}.$$

It follows that

$$\frac{\partial q}{\partial r} > 0, \; \frac{\partial r}{\partial y} < 0, \; \frac{\partial r}{\partial X} > 0.$$

Since $T_{23} + T_{21} > 0$, we have

$$-\frac{\partial q}{\partial r}\left(\frac{\partial q}{\partial r} + \frac{\partial r}{\partial X}\right) > 0.$$

It follows that

$$dq = -(T_{21}dk_t + T_{22}dy_t + T_{23}dX_t)$$
$$= \frac{\partial q}{\partial r}\left(\frac{\partial r}{\partial k} + \frac{\partial r}{\partial y} + \frac{\partial r}{\partial X}\right) < 0.$$

The price of capital will fall. We must now check that the output sequence does not become explosive. We saw above that the output of the investment good increases more than proportionally as a result of the Rybczynski theorem. This means that $k_{t+1} > k_t$. Everything else being equal, there is now more capital available to produce more consumption. As the demand for capital increases in the consumption good sector, the relative price for capital increases. As a result the demand for labor increases. The output of the consumption good sector will increase next period. It follows that $y_{t+2} < y_{t+1}$.

Suppose now that the consumption good sector is more capital intensive at the private level. Starting from an equilibrium, suppose that the price of investment increases exogenously above its equilibrium level. The rate of investment will also increase above its initial level. The Rybczynski theorem tells us that the output of the investment sector will decrease above its equilibrium value. Under Harrod Neutrality we have shown that the marginal productivity of capital is decreasing when the consumption good sector is more capital intensive.

The marginal productivity of capital will increase as y decreases validating the expectations of a higher rate of return. We have to check that the sequence of prices does not explode. Recall that

$$\frac{dq}{dk} = \frac{dq}{dr}\left(\frac{dr}{dk} + \frac{dr}{dy}\frac{dy}{dk} + \frac{dr}{dX}\right).$$

However

$$\frac{dy}{dk} = \mathcal{F}_1^2 \frac{\partial k^2}{\partial k} + \mathcal{F}_2^2 \frac{\partial l^2}{\partial k} X.$$

Using the expression of the partial derivatives derived in (33) and (34) we get

$$\frac{dy}{dk} = \frac{2\mathcal{F}_{11}^1 \mathcal{F}_2^2 \mathcal{F}^1}{q l^1 X \Delta} > 0.$$

Since $dr/dy < 0$, it follows that dq/dk is negative when the consumption good sector is capital intensive. Hence the sequence of prices does not explode.

4.2 Discrete versus Continuous Time

As there is indeterminacy when the consumption sector is capital intensive in our model - something that cannot happen in the continuous time formulation of Drugeon, Poulsen and Venditti (2003) - we comment on this difference using a more general, dynamical systems, perspective. Drugeon, Poulsen, and Venditti (2003) show that the characteristic equation obtained by linearizing the Euler equation admits two real roots, θ_1 and θ_2. However, since $\theta_1 = 0$, the growth ray is locally indeterminate if

$$\theta_2 = \rho - (1-\sigma)\gamma - \frac{V_{23}}{V_{22}} < 0.$$

Since $V_{22} = T^{\alpha-2}\{(\alpha-1)T_2 T_2 + T T_{22}\} < 0$, this condition reduces to $V_{23} < 0$. Looking at the expression obtained for V_{23} in Lemma 2 we see that, as in the discrete time version, the continuous time version requires[12] $T_{23} < 0$. Hence using the expression of T_{23} obtained in Lemma 1 this reduces to condition (25) of Proposition 2. Thus indeterminacy can be obtained when the capital good sector is capital intensive. However, when the consumption good sector is capital intensive, $T_{23} > 0$ (Corollary 1) and indeterminacy is ruled out if the consumption good is more capital intensive.

---

[12] This condition is also obtained by Drugeon and Venditti (2001) in a model with intersectoral effect and optimal growth.

To compare our results with those of Drugeon, Poulsen and Venditti (2003), linearize the Euler equation (equation 12) in the discrete time model. One of the roots of the characteristic polynomial is equal to one. The other root is

$$\frac{1}{\beta\gamma^\alpha} + \frac{V_{23}}{\beta\gamma^\alpha V_{21}}.$$

Indeterminacy therefore requires that this root lies within $(-1, 1)$. A necessary condition for this to be true is that V_{23}/V_{21} is negative. However, the sign of V_{21} can be positive if the investment good sector is capital intensive or negative if the consumption good sector is capital intensive, depreciation of the existing capital stock is not too low and utility is not too concave (with linear utility the condition reduces to T_{23}/T_{21} and the the sign of T_{21} depends on the factor intensity difference). The sign of V_{23} can be negative if the investment good sector is capital intensive and if utility is not too concave or positive if the consumption good sector is capital intensive. Hence one cannot rule out that for some economies the growth ray is indeterminate if the consumption good sector is capital intensive. Thus, the difference in the models of continuous and discrete time hinges on different cross-partials.

The choice between using a discrete or a continuous time formulation rests on both mathematical issues as well as on logical issues. At one level is the question what is the proper representation of evolution of the economic system. There are differing viewpoints (see for example the discussion in Day, 1994) on this and in many economic models this is resolved by using the more convenient analytical formulation of the problem. From a mathematical point of view, using a discrete system is at one level easier to understand and illustrate as the dynamics are generated by iterating a map (Hirsch, Smale and Devaney, 2004). However, there is a key way in which the continuous and discrete time formulations differ. The differential equations accumulate continuous changes over finite intervals. The difference equations implicitly treats the rate of change as constant for the interval. If the rate of change is in fact constant then there is no difference between the two representations (Day, 1994). A more serious distinction is that in the continuous time formulation, orbits are continuous curves in the state space. This limits the nature of the dynamics (Day, 1994; Guckenheimer and Holmes, 1983). Orbits in discrete systems are sequences of discrete points, thus allowing richer dynamics even in a finite interval.

One can ask in what circumstances, if we take the length of the time interval to be infinitesimally small, will the discrete system converge to the continuous system. The intuition is that, in the limit, the two will coincide if the systems are hyperbolic (i.e., none of the eigenvalues have zero real parts in the continuous time formulation, and none are equal to unity in the discrete time formulation). In fact, most of the results on the structural stability of dynamical systems have been derived for the hyperbolic case (see for example Chapter 7 in Shub, 1987). In this case the dynamics are not sensitive to small perturbations of the system. The question of consistency of a discrete time representation of the dynamics with a true continuous time model is an issue that arises in numerical solutions of dynamical systems. It is addressed in detail in the monograph of Godunov and Ryabenkii (1987). The problem is to take a discrete time approximation to the continuous time system and analyze whether the solutions to the discrete time system converge to the solutions of the continuous time system as the time partition is made increasing finer. For the convergence to hold the discrete time system should be robust to perturbations. A sufficient condition for this to be true is that the equilibria are stable and hyperbolic (Chapter 5, Godunov and Ryabenkii, 1987).

It turns out that in the model under consideration, the balanced growth ray is non-hyperbolic both in the discrete and in the continuous time formulation. This is not due to any degeneracy in the model. We use general functional forms, CES utility functions, the canonical nature of technical change, and the learning by doing externality. Given that the system is non-hyperbolic, a richer class of dynamics are possible than would otherwise be the case. There could be a discrete time analogue of the Drugeon, Poulsen and Venditti paper which gives the same results as in the continuous time version. That is not the aim of our research. We take the view that the discrete time specification is a well specified model in its own right. The fact that it delivers a wider set of conditions for instability than the continuous time case should make one re-examine what is the correct way to model a given economic problem.

5 Concluding Comments

We consider a two-sector economy with Harrod-Neutral aggregate external effects. Contrary to earlier contributions we do not use any specific functional forms for the production technologies. We show that the necessary condition for the growth ray to be indeterminate can be satisfied if either of the two sectors is capital intensive provided that the cost of shifting consumption is not too high and when capital does not depreciate too slowly. These results show that indeterminacy in growth model is a phenomenon that is valid in models with generic functional forms for the production functions. Our future research agenda is to analyze if indeterminacy can result with generic functional forms for technologies in a setting where externalities can come both from labor and capital. We plan to investigate if indeterminacy is a robust phenomenon with sector specific and intersectoral externalities coming both from labor and capital.

Acknowledgements

We thank Jean-Pierre Drugeon, Bjarne S. Jensen, Gerhard Sorger, Steve Spear and Alain Venditti for comments and suggestions. We have benefited from comments made by two anonymous referees and the members of the audience during presentations at the 6th Spring Meeting for Young Economists (Copenhagen, 2001), the XIth General Equilibrium Workshop (Athens, 2002), ESEM 2002 (Venice) and DEGIT VIII (Helsinki, 2003). Odile Poulsen acknowledges financial support from the Danish Research Council, grant 212.2269.01.

References

Arrow, K.J. (1962): "The Economic Implications of Learning by Doing." *Review of Economic Studies* 29: 155-173.

Benhabib, J., and Nishimura, K. (1985): "Competitive Equilibrium Cycles." *Journal of Economic Theory* 35: 284-306.

Benhabib, J., and Nishimura, K. (1998): "Indeterminacy and Sunspots with Constant Returns." *Journal of Economic Theory* 81: 58-96.

Benhabib, J., Nishimura, K., and Venditti, A. (2002): "Indeterminacy and Cycles in Two-Sector Discrete Time Models." *Economic Theory* 20: 217-235.

Benhabib, J., Meng, Q., and Nishimura, K. (2000): "Indeterminacy under Constant Return to Scale in Multisector Economies." *Econometrica* 68: 1541-1548.

Benhabib, J., and Perli, R. (1994): "Uniqueness and Indeterminacy: On the Dynamics of Endogenous Growth." *Journal of Economic Theory* 63: 113-142.

Boldrin, M., and Rustichini, A. (1994): "Growth and Indeterminacy in Dynamic Models with Externalities." *Econometrica* 62: 323-429.

Boldrin, M., Nishimura K., Shigoka, T. and Yano, M. (2001): "Chaotic Equilibrium Dynamics in Endogenous Growth Models." *Journal of Economic Theory* 96: 97-132.

Burmeister, E., and Dobell, A.R. (1970): *Mathematical Theories of Economic Growth.* New York: Macmillan.

Day, R.H. (1994): *Complex Economic Dynamics*, vol.1. Cambridge: MIT Press.

Drugeon, J.P., and Venditti, A. (2001): "Intersectoral External Effects, Multiplicities and Indeterminacies." *Journal of Economic Dynamics and Control* 25: 765-787.

Drugeon, J.P., and Venditti, A. (1998): "Intersectoral External Effects, Multiplicities and Indeterminacies II: The Long -Run Growth Case", Working Paper 98A20, GREQAM.

Drugeon, J.P., Poulsen O., and Venditti, A. (2003): "On Intersectoral Allocations, Factor Substitutability and Multiple Long-Run Growth Paths." *Economic Theory* 21: 175-183.

Godunov, S.K., and Ryabenkii, V.S. (1987): *Difference Schemes: An Introduction to the Underlying Theory.* Amsterdam: North Holland.

Guckenheimer, J., and Holmes, P. (1983): *Nonlinear Oscillations, Dynamical Systems and Bifurcation of Vector Fields.* New York: Springer Verlag

Harrison, S.G., and Weder, M. (2002): "Tracing Externalities as Sources for Indeterminacy." *Journal of Economics Dynamics and Control* 26: 851-867.

Harrod, R. (1937): "Review of Joan Robinson's *Essays in the Theory of Unemployment.*" *Economic Journal* 47: 326-330.

Hirsch, M.W., Smale, S., and Devaney, R.L. (2004): *Differential equations, Dynamical Systems and an Introduction to Chaos.* Amsterdam: Elsevier.

Jensen, B. (2003): "Walrasian General equilibrium Allocations and Dynamics in Two-Sector Growth Models." *German Economic Review* 4: 53-87.

Lucas, R. (1988): "On the Mechanics of Economic Development." *Journal of Monetary Economics* 22: 3-42.

Mitra, T. (1998): "On Equilibrium Dynamics under Externalities in a Model of Economic Development." *Japanese Economic Review* 49: 85-107.

Nishimura, K., and Venditti, A. (2001): "Intersectoral Externalities and Indeterminacy." *Journal of Economic Theory* 105: 140-158.

Poulsen, O. (2001): "Indeterminacy in a Two-Sector Discrete Time Model with Labor augmenting External Effects. " Unpublished Ph.D. Thesis, University of Essex.

Romer, P. (1986): "Increasing Returns and Long Run Growth." *Journal of Political Economy,* 94: 1002-1037.

Romer, P. (1983): "Dynamic Competitive Equilibria with Externalities, Increasing Returns and Unbounded Growth." Unpublished Ph.D. Thesis, University of Chicago.

Sheshinski, E. (1967): "Optimal Accumulation with Learning by Doing." In *Essays on the theory of optimal economic growth,* edited by K. Shell. Cambridge: MIT Press, 31-52.

Shub, M. (1987): *Global Stability of Dynamical Systems.* New York: Springer Verlag.

Srinivasan, T.N. (1964): "Optimum Savings in a Two-Sector Model of Economic Growth." *Econometrica* 32: 358-373.

Stiglitz, J.E., and Uzawa, H. (eds), (1969): *Readings in the Modern Theory of Economic Growth.* Cambridge MA: MIT Press.

Uzawa, H. (1961): "Neutral Inventions and the Stability of Growth Equilibrium." *Review of Economic Studies* 28: 117-124.

Uzawa, H. (1963): "On a Two-Sector Model of Economic Growth, II." *Review of Economic Studies* 30: 105-118.

Addresses of authors: – Aditya Goenka, Department of Economics, University of Essex, Wivenhoe Park, Colchester CO4 3SQ, United Kingdom (e-mail: goenka@essex.ac.uk); and Department of Economics, National University of Singapore, Block AS2, Level 6, 1 Arts Link, Singapore 117570 (email: ecsadity@nus.edu.sg); – Odile Poulsen, Department of Economics, Aarhus School of Business, Silkeborgvej 2, 8000 Aarhus C, Denmark (e-mail: odp@asb.dk)

J. Econ. (2005) Suppl. 10: 167-194

Journal of Economics
Zeitschrift für Nationalökonomie
Printed in Austria

Geography and Institutions: Plausible and Implausible Linkages

Ola Olsson

Received September 26, 2003; Revised version received August 2, 2004
© Springer-Verlag 2005

In recent years, empirical investigations have shown that various aspects of physical geography are closely related to the quality of a country's economic institutions. For instance, distance from the equator in latitude degrees is positively correlated to both institutional quality and to levels of economic development. In order to reach a better understanding for this type of regularities, this article reviews the growing empirical literature on geography and institutions, as well as a large body of older and newer theoretical works on the social impacts of geography. It is argued that the most plausible candidates for explaining the broadest cross-continental variance in institutional quality are those focusing on historical differences in biogeographical potential for early agriculture and on the importance of disease geography for European colonization strategy.

Keywords: geography, institutions, topography, geology, biogeography, climate, development.

JEL Classification: N40, N50, P33.

1 Introduction

Recent research on long-run economic development has shown that geography is a central factor for understanding the current distribution of prosperity across the world. However, for many decades, economists used to start their analysis by just taking as given certain patterns of trade, comparative advantage, and institutions like private property rights and a benevolent executive. Because of this neglect of both geographical factors and institutions, economic theory largely failed to account for the enormous international differences in income.

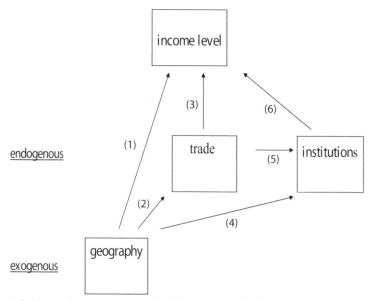

Fig. 1. Linkages between income level, trade, institutions, and geography.

During the last six or seven years, geography has re-entered the research agenda as an ultimate factor in theories of economic development. Scholars in the field have, however, had very different hypotheses about the precise chain of causality. The main views are represented in Fig. 1 above, based upon Rodrik et al (2004). The most obvious linkage is probably the direct influence of various aspects of geography on production (linkage 1). The key scholar in this tradition is Jeffrey Sachs and his coauthors who have studied the effects of mean temperature, distance to the coast, photosynthetic potential, amount of arable land, and prevalence of diseases on agricultural production in developing countries (Bloom and Sachs, 1998; Gallup et al, 1999; Sachs, 2001; Masters and McMillan, 2001). An older influential study that among other things discusses the implications of poor soil quality for agriculture in the tropics is Kamarck (1976).

The second chain of influence goes from geography to patterns of trade (linkage 2). Countries that are geographically well placed for trade with other countries should have a higher income level than landlocked ones and countries isolated by oceans or deserts, this hypothesis maintains (linkage 3). The most important work in this field is probably Frankel and Romer (1999).

Proponents of the third and perhaps most subtle hypothesis argue that institutions like private property rights, free trade, and the rule-of-law are the primary determinants of levels of economic development (linkage 6). However, the quality of a society's institutions is in turn strongly influenced by its geography. Climate, topography, geology, and biogeography all contribute to mould the rules that societies live by (linkage 4). Most of the major research efforts during the last two or three years have focussed on this connection and has shown that it appears to be the one that has the greatest empirical support (Acemoglu, Johnson, and Robinson (henceforth AJR), 2001, 2002a; Easterly and Levine, 2003; Olsson and Hibbs, 2003; Rodrik et al, 2004; Galor et al, 2004).[1] An even more complex causal chain has also been suggested from geography to trade to institutions (linkage 5; AJR, 2002b)[2]. This increased interest in the social effects of geography can also be found among prominent historians like Felipe Fernandez-Armesto who suggests a redefinition of the concept civilization as a relationship between man and nature (Fernandez-Armesto, 2000). A recent influential contribution about geography and long-run development is Jared Diamond (1997).

The broad aim of this review article is to look more closely into the specific linkage between geography and institutions with trade as a possible mediate factor (linkages 2, 4, and 5). The main motivation for this interest is my assertion that the important new empirical contributions in this field often report empirical relationships without a comprehensive theory of how or why geography affects institutions.[3] This might in turn be a consequence of a deficient knowledge of or interest in the major works on the social influence of geography among current writers as well as readers. References are sometimes made in passing to older works like Montesquieu (1750), Huntington (1915), and Wittfogel (1957). But these theories have for so long been in disrepute among academic writers on economic development that most people are only dimly aware of what they actually propose. This article attempts to remedy that situation.

As an illustration of a statistical relationship that until recently has confounded researchers, let us consider Fig. 2 (next page), which shows institutional quality (using a measure called GADP, taken from Hall and Jones (1999) and discussed further below) on the vertical axis

---

[1] During the last years, there has been an ongoing debate between proponents of the pure "geography" tradition and the "institutional" tradition. Sachs (2003) is one of the more recent additions to this literature.

[2] Other recent papers that belong to this category are Galor and Mountford (2003) and Alcala and Ciccone (2004).

[3] AJR (2001, 2002b) and Olsson and Hibbs (2003) arguably do have a theory behind their findings.

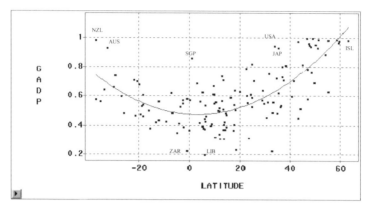

Fig. 2. Average institutional quality 1985-95 (GADP) as a function of latitude degrees for 136 countries. Fitted non-linear OLS curve with $R^2 = 0.51$. GADP from Hall and Jones (1999), LATITUDE from Olsson and Hibbs (2003).

and latitude degrees on the horizontal axis for 136 countries. Latitude degree is an often used variable in empirical studies since it is naturally correlated with several geographical indicators such as temperature, hours of sun, and type of vegetation. As the fitted non-linear regression line suggests, countries further away from the equator (such as Australia and New Zealand at -30 in the Southern Hemisphere and most Western European countries in the Northern Hemisphere at around +50) tend to have "better" institutions than countries near the equator. According to the data, former Zaire and Liberia, both near the equator, had the worst institutions in the world. The fit for this simple non-linear relationship is amazingly high; $R^2 = 0.51$. Is this just a spurious relationship or is there a structural explanation underlying the results?

As will be discussed at length below, there are two explanations for this broad pattern that appear to be more plausible than others. First, the emergence of sedentary agriculture was first initiated in mid-latitude areas where the biogeographical potential in terms of suitable plants and animals for domestication was most favorable, which in turn induced a sustained process of institutional development (Jared Diamond, 1997). The second explanation traces institutional differences in formerly colonized countries to the colonial strategy used by the colonists. In regions where the disease environment allowed white settlers to settle down, strong private property institutions were created whereas harmful, "extractive" institutions emerged in places where diseases prevented permanent settlements (AJR, 2001).

This article contributes to the existing literature in the following ways. It is the first article to survey and compare the recent empirical contributions with a focus on their results regarding geography and institutions. Further, it presents a critical review of older and more recent theories in the field on the basis of a geographical categorization distinguishing between four central geographical aspects; climate, topography, geology, and biogeography. Lastly, the usefulness of existing theories for future research are evaluated.

2 The Variables

The word geography is an imprecise term with numerous connotations. In the literature on geography and economic institutions, several aspects of physical geography have been suggested to have one effect or the other on human behavioral rules. In order to facilitate a discussion, I have chosen to divide the geographical characteristics into four subgroups, as shown in Table 1 below.[4] The first aspect of geography according to this classification is climate, or conditions above the ground surface. Among the climatic characteristics are mean temperature, precipitation, sunlight, humidity, winds, and currents. Not only average levels might play a role but also the variation in these levels with extremes (in parenthesis) such as floods, drought, storms, or blizzards.

Table 1. Aspects of geography

	Non-biological aspects		Biological aspects
Climate	**Topography**	**Geology**	**Biogeography**
temperature	mountain	soil	flora
precipitation (floods, drought)	plateau	mineral	fauna
sunlight	river	gas	type of vegetation (jungle, steppe, desert)
humidity	lake	oil	(disease vectors)
winds (storms)	ocean	earthquakes	
ocean currents	island, penisula	volcanoes	

The second category concerns topography, or the general, non-biological conditions of the ground surface. Any particular spot on earth

---

[4] Since I am not a geographer by profession, this categorization might strike some readers as questionable. Nevertheless, it serves the purposes of my literature survey in the following sections.

might be described as being part of a mountain, plateau, island, ocean, and so on. More specific characteristics are also important such as the shape and orientation of a continent's landmass or the size, navigability, and seasonal variation of rivers. These are regarded as topographical features.[5]

The third category describes relevant non-biological conditions existing or originating from below the ground. Here we find geological aspects such as the character of the soil and the quantity and quality of existing minerals, as well as the prevalence of active volcanoes and earthquakes.

The three categories mentioned so far are all non-biological in the sense that they refer to non-organical conditions. The fourth category is concerned with biology, or the geography of living organisms (excluding human beings). Biogeography describes the spatial distribution of plants and animals and the types of vegetation that are created by combinations of flora and fauna, for instance steppe, taiga, rain forest, or desert. Within this category, I also include medical geography that deals with micro-organisms like virus and bacteria and the disease vectors that facilitate the diffusion of these micro-organisms to and among humans. The geographical distribution of virus and disease vectors depend in turn primarily on animals and climate.

In general, there are of course many associations between the four categories above. For instance, rain forests - which implies a specific type of biogeographical features - are generally found in lowland plateaus (topography) with highly weathered soils (geology) and are associated with high precipitation, high temperature, and high humidity (climate).

The other key variable in this investigation is institutions. In line with North (1990), I use the standard definition of an institution as a formal or informal behavioral rule that is in some way related to economic life. Among the most important economic institutions are the right to private property, the right to form associations, free exchange of goods and services, and various constraints on the executive against random confiscations. Also included are more general aspects such as the rule-of-law in society, political stability and accountability, the absence of corruption, and norms encouraging thriftiness and entrepreneurship. "Good institutions" therefore really refers to a cluster of institutions that strengthen the incentives towards production, investment and exchange rather than consumption and various types of rent seeking (Hall and Jones, 1999; AJR, 2001).

---

[5] Admittedly, this is not an ideal term for the general character of the land since topography is often exclusively used to describe elevation. For lack of a better word, I will use it nonetheless.

3 Empirical Evidence

Several recent articles document a strong link between various aspects of geography and the quality of countries' institutions (Table 2 below gives an overview of some key empirical contributions). However, these results are usually not the outcome of investigations with a stated focus on linkages between geography and institutions, but are rather a by-product of analyses where levels of income per capita is the ultimate dependent variable. For instance, Hall and Jones (1999) was one of the first studies to show that absolute distance from the equator in latitude degrees (the absolute value of the measure used in Fig. 2) was positively related to the quality of institutions. In their empirical model, distance from the equator was used as one of four primary instruments for "social infrastructure" in regressions with income per worker as the dependent variable.

Table 2. Earlier empirical studies on geography and institutions

Study	Geography variable	Institutions variable	Base sample
Hall and Jones (1999)	Distance from equator	Social infrastructure	127 countries
AJR (2001)	Settler mortality	Risk of expropriation	64 ex-colonies
AJR (2002b)	Access to Atlantic	Constraint on executive	
Easterly and Levine (2003)	Dist., Settler mort., Crops/Minerals dummy	Kaufmann measure	72 countries
Rodnik et.al. (2004)	Dist., Settler mort., alt. measures	Kaufmann measure	80 countries
Olsson and Hibbs (2003)	Bio Conditions, Geo Conditions	GADP	112 countries

Hall and Jones' index of social infrastructure was created by combining a measure of trade openness from Sachs and Warner (1995) with data on institutional quality distilled from a private company providing assessments of risk to potential international investors.[6] Following Knack and Keefer (1995), Hall and Jones (1999) used five particular categories from the greater data set and calculated the average value for each category for the period 1986-95. The five categories were intended to capture the following institutional characteristics: (i) law and

---

[6] The firm's name is Political Risk Services and their publication is called "International Country Risk Guide".

order, (ii) bureaucratic quality, (iii) corruption, (iv) risk of expropriation, and (v) government repudiation of contracts. They then calculated
an equal-weighted average of these variables and referred to this measure as "Government anti-diversion policies" (GADP). How this GADP
variable was correlated with geography was not reported in the paper
(since that was not what the authors were interested in), but by using
Hall and Jones' (1999) data, we obtain the U-shaped curve in Fig. 2.

AJR (2001) constructed a similar setup but with some notable and
important differences. Also their primary objective was to demonstrate
the link between institutions and levels of economic development while
explicitly recognizing the problem of joint endogeneity between institutions and income levels. Although the article contains several fascinat-
ing results, the key contribution was probably their use of a superior
instrument for measures of institutional quality; settler mortality rates
during colonial times in countries colonized by Europeans.[7] In short,
AJR:s conjecture was that European colonizers did not create permanent settlements in places with high settler mortality and therefore did
not install good institutions like strong property rights. In "Neo Eu-
ropes" like Australia, where settler mortality was low, the reverse was
true.

Data on settler mortality was collected from works by the historian Philip Curtin. The major sources of settler mortality during these
times, causing roughly 80 percent of all deaths, were malaria and yellow fever. Both illnesses are transmitted by mosquito vectors. Although
AJR argued that the prevalence of malaria and yellow fever depended
to a great extent on very local climatic features - implying that rough
geographic measures such as distance from the equator or temperature
were unlikely to account for the variation in mortality rates - their measure of settler mortality might certainly be regarded as a geographical
variable according to the reasoning above. Their theory will be discussed further below.

The central empirical finding for the purpose of this article was that
settler mortality, as predicted, had a clear negative relationship with
AJR:s measure of institutional quality; risk of expropriation (Hall and
Jones' (1999) fourth category). Furthermore, when distance from the
equator was included as an independent variable alongside settler mortality in a regression of institutional quality, settler mortality retained
its positive and significant relationship whereas distance turned out to
be insignificant (AJR, 2001, Table 3). Hence, the results suggested that

---

[7] Olsson and Hibbs (2003), AJR (2001), McArthur and Sachs (2001) and
others have argued that distance from the equator is flawed as an instrument
for institutions in a regression on income levels since it is likely that a country's latitudinal position is strongly related to agricultural productivity, and
hence has a direct effect on income levels.

distance from the equator is not the key to understanding institutional variation but that it is correlated with one or more true causal variables like settler mortality. This supremacy of institutions over geography was also established in a later related paper (AJR, 2002a).

However, for reasons discussed further below, it turns out that when AJR's (2001) sample is disaggregated into continental subsamples, settler mortality is no longer a significant determinant of institutions in the African and Latin American subsamples.[8] In consequence, settler mortality is problematic as an instrumental variable for institutions in disaggregated analyses where income per capita is the dependent variable (Olsson, 2004).

Results similar to AJR (2001) were obtained by Easterly and Levine (2003). The preferred measure of institutional quality in Easterly and Levine is the average of six indicators reported by Kaufmann et al (1999); (i) voice and accountability, (ii) political instability and violence, (iii) government effectiveness, (iv) regulatory burden, (v) rule of law, and (vi) corruption. Easterly and Levine's primary geography variables are distance from equator and settler mortality as in AJR (2001). Unlike AJR, Easterly and Levine (2003, Table 3) find that when settler mortality and latitude are included as independent variables, both have significant impacts on institutions with the expected signs. Thus, the influence of distance from equator appears to be conditional on what institutional measure that is used. A geography-related (dummy) variable, taking on the value of 1 if any of eleven particular crops or minerals is produced in a country, also appears to have a positive impact on institutions.[9] Beyond its effect on institutions, Easterly and Levine show that geography does not seem to have a direct effect on levels of income.

The setup in Rodrik et al's (2004) investigation with regard to the links between geography and institutions is almost identical to that in Easterly and Levine (2003). The same institutional and geographical measures are used with the difference that the former use a somewhat larger sample of countries. This does not change the result that institutional quality is positively related to distance from equator and negatively related to settler mortality. In their robustness checks, Rodrik et al include a number of alternative geographical variables such as percent of a land's area in the tropics, access to the sea, number of frost days per month in the winter and the area covered by frost (the latter two measures taken from Masters and McMillan, 2001), and mean temperature. Although the estimates are not reported, the

---

[8] The authors recognize this lack of a statistical relationship for Africa in a footnote.

[9] As we shall see, this latter variable has some similarities to a "Biogeography"-variable constructed by Olsson and Hibbs (2003).

authors claim that most of these measures are significant determinants of institutional quality (Rodrik et al, 2004, footnote 7).

As discussed above, AJR (2001) was primarily concerned with institutional formation and economic development in former colonies. In AJR (2002b), however, attention is now shifted to Europe. What explains the rise of Europe after 1500, or more precisely the rise of Western, Atlantic Europe? AJR (2002b) argue convincingly that the key factor was the emergence of trade with America, India, and East Asia. This new opportunity, available only to the countries with access to the Atlantic, had obvious direct economic effects. AJR's central hypothesis is that Atlantic trade had its most important beneficiary effects through its impact on institutions. The new trade potentially strengthened merchant groups in the bourgeoisie which then opted for strengthening the institutions of private property. The authors provide some econometric evidence in favor of this view. Using an existing index that is supplemented from various sources, they construct a cross-country measure of "Constraint on the executive" for the period 1300-1850. When the average of this index is treated as a dependent variable in an OLS regression, a variable capturing the extent of Atlantic trade has a significant positive effect (AJR, 2002b, Table 9). Further, a simple time series shows that whereas institutional quality was relatively similar up to 1600, the countries involved in Atlantic trade started to diverge after that with the really great divergence happening around 1750 (AJR, 2002b, Figure 8).

But even among the Atlantic traders, there are significant differences. Countries that had good initial institutions, such as Britain and the Netherlands, experienced a greater improvement in their institutions after 1500 than more absolutist countries like Spain and Portugal, in line with the theory of North and Thomas (1973). In any case, it is important to note that the underlying factor behind the rise of Western Europe in AJR's (2002b) story was geographical; access to the sea routes of the Atlantic.[10]

The empirical contributions above essentially show that the variation in institutional quality has its roots in the diverging experiences of countries from 1500 A.D. onwards, which in turn were determined by geographical features such as the prevalence of disease and distance from the harmful tropical zone. Olsson and Hibbs (2003) (as well as a more recent paper Hibbs and Olsson, 2004) trace the origins of the differences in technology and institutions much further back in time. Extending the work of Jared Diamond (1997), they develop two new

---

[10] As will be discussed below, a recent paper by Nunn (2004) uses data on slavery exports between 1400-1913 to show that access to the Atlantic was detrimental to institutional development in several West African nations that were severely affected by the European slave trade.

geography-related measures relevant for explaining the timing of the Neolithic transition to agriculture around the world. The first measure is an index of the quality of biogeography capturing the number of wild plants and animals known to exist in prehistory that were particularly suitable for domestication. The hypothesis is that the greater this number, the earlier the transition to agriculture and the earlier the onset of sustained technological progress in a Malthusian world where greater production capacity is transformed into a greater population, eventually leading up to the industrial revolution when standards of living finally took off. Hence, a favorable biogeography should be positively related to institutional development and income per capita today.

The second variable is a composite index of four factors; distance from equator, the suitability of the climate for annual crop agriculture (based on the Köppen-Geiger scale), size of continent, and orientation of continent along an east-west or north-south axis. Olsson and Hibbs (2003) show that this measure is a good predictor of the biogeography index, as expected. Furthermore, both these underlying geographical conditions and the biogeography variable are strongly related to the GADP measure of institutional quality which was taken from Hall and Jones (1999). The geography variable alone even explains 45% of the variation in the GADP measure. Thus, Olsson and Hibbs' (2003) new measures of geography not only document a causal link from geography to institutions, but also, in line with their main hypothesis, a positive relationship between biogeography and geography on the one hand and income per capita on the other, even after controlling for the quality of institutions. This result distinguishes their article from AJR (2001), Rodrik et al (2004), and Easterly and Levine (2003) where geography only affects economic development via institutions.

4 Theory: From Montesquieu to Acemoglu et al.

A common denominator of the recent empirical studies above is that they all suggest that geographical characteristics are important determinants of the quality of institutions. What is often lacking, however, is a theory of the nature of this causal relationship. Indeed, theories of how climate and the natural environment affect institutions and economic development have long been regarded with suspicion among social scientists. Many of the older works had a strong racist tone that certainly contributed to their present disrepute. Nevertheless, these theories and more recent ones offer comprehensive explanations to how geography and institutions are interrelated. The survey below is structured in accordance with the four geographical subcategories climate, topography, geology, and biogeography.

4.1 Climate and Institutions

Although geography also plays a role in the political theory of Aristotle and Machiavelli, the first systematic framework was presented by Montesquieu in his classic treatise *The Spirit of Laws* (1750).[11] Montesquieu's focus is almost exclusively on climate, or more precisely, on the effects of temperature. His theory is very clear and is outlined in the first sentence of Book XIV:

> "If it be true that the temper of the mind and the passions of the heart are extremely different in different climates, the laws ought to be in relation both to the variety of those passions and to the variety of those tempers." (Montesquieu, 1750, p 246.)

Montesquieu then goes on with an argumentation based on anecdotal evidence that people in colder climates are generally less sensitive, less suspicious, more courageous, more disciplined, and more determined than people in warmer climates. The reason is primarily biological; the blood runs faster through the veins in a colder climate and the heart has more power. People in temperate climates therefore tend to be more vigorous. It also follows that due to these differences in "tempers and passions", societies will adopt different kinds of laws and institutions. For instance, people in southern countries are by nature relatively lazy. Reason will not make such men work so other lazy but more powerful men have to force them. This is one (of several) reasons behind slavery, in Montesquieu's mind. The link between temperature, human biology, human behavior, and various social institutions is therefore clear.

A similar line of reasoning is presented in Ellsworth Huntington's major work in the genre *Civilization and Climate* from 1915. Based on field experiments, survey questionnaires, and the results of earlier similar studies, Huntington attempts to explain scientifically the links between an area's climate and its social institutions such as work norms, respect for law, and stable and honest government. Two aspects of climate are particularly important; temperature and humidity, with the first being the most important. From experiments on working people, Huntington concludes that the ideal climate is one in which mean temperature in winter does not fall below 38° F and does not exceed 65° F. Such temperatures are for instance found in northern California, southern Chile, the London area, and on New Zealand. But temperatures should not be constant throughout the year. At places like Quito, Ecuador, the difference in mean temperature between the warmest and

---

[11] His correct full name is Charles-Louis de Secondat, baron de La Bréde et de Montesquieu.

coldest seasons is only two degrees, and the result of this dreary uniformity in temperature manifests itself (at least among the white population) "...in weaknesses such as drunkenness, immorality, anger, and laziness." (Huntington, 1915, p 136).

This direct effect of climate on people's work effort and productivity is also reflected in the quality of their institutions, which is roughly equivalent to what Huntington refers to as the "status of civilization".[12] Huntington's basic theory appears to be that energetic people, i.e. people living in areas with just the right levels and variation in temperature and humidity, have a greater ability to be honest, to retain self-control, and to take initiatives. Throughout his book, Huntington is careful to point out that climate is just one of several factors that determine how civilized a nation is. Race might be just as important. Nevertheless, the striking (visual) correspondence between the regions of high human energy potential and those with a high level of civilization is interpreted by Huntington as supporting his theory.

In a similar vein, Gilfillan (1920) tries to explain how it could be that early civilizations actually arose in hot climates, despite the disadvantages pointed out by Huntington and others. The foundation of Gilfillan's argument is his construction of a graph showing the "coldward course of progress" from the early centers of Sumer and Egypt in the early third millennium B.C. (with an average temperature of around 74° F), via Rome in antiquity (60° F), to Berlin in early twentieth century (48° F) .[13] Gilfillan's explanation to this "temperate drift" is that simple agriculture most easily emerges in hot climates, but that as civilization and technology progresses, leadership will move northward where the conditions for mental ability and vigor are better. Only during periods of cultural stagnation - as during the Dark Ages after the fall of the Western Roman empire - will civilizational leadership move southward.

Although neither the Huntington/Gilfillan data, nor the inference from that data impresses a modern economist, closely related arguments are presented in David Landes' book *The Wealth and Poverty of Nations* (1998). Landes simply claims that as a general rule, the discomfort of heat exceeds that of cold (Landes, 1998, p 6). He further argues in the spirit of Montesquieu that there is a clear link between hot climates and the use of slavery since white men, unadapted to heat, were unable to work on colonial plantations in the tropics, an

---

[12] The literature on the characteristics and history of civilization includes classical works like those of Alfred Toynbee and Fernand Braudel, as well as Samuel Huntington's (1997) recent book *The Clash of Civilizations*, all nicely surveyed by Fernandez-Armesto (2000).

[13] His prediction for the future is that Scandinavia might have become the center of cilvilization by 2000 A.D.

idea that I will return to below. Whereas Huntington reports results from experiments with workers in order to demonstrate the deleterious effects of heat, Landes cites a Bangladeshi diplomat who claims to feel "reinforced and stimulated by the temperate climate...".

Among the climatic factors, also precipitation is important. One of the key advantages of Europe is its heavy and dependable supply of rain, especially along the Atlantic coast. This characteristic in turn depends on the Gulf stream that brings warm currents as far north as Norway and Ireland. According to Landes, Europe is also less prone to be hit by climatic extremes such as floods, drought, or hurricanes than for instance Asia and North America. Although Landes does not develop an explicit theory of the causal chain from climate to institutions, his verdict is clear: "Life in poor climes, then, is precarious, depressed, brutish." (Landes, 1998, p 14).

4.2 Topography and Institutions

According to several notable scholars, topography - or the general character of the land - is another important determinant of societal development. The most famous and controversial contribution in this area is probably Karl Wittfogel's *Oriental Despotism* from 1957. The main argument in Wittfogel's book is that "riverine civilizations" based on irrigation agriculture gave rise to highly stratified, "hydraulic" societies with significant economies of scale but where private initiatives were nearly non-existent. This pattern of "oriental despotism" then supposedly prevailed throughout most of history in most of Asia.

Wittfogel starts his analysis by noting that unlike most other environmental factors like temperature, soil quality, or the lay of the land, water can be relatively easily controlled and managed by man. The need to manage water is of greatest importance in arid or semi-arid areas where rainfall agriculture is impossible. The presence of great rivers with highly alluvial soils in otherwise relatively arid regions provided the ideal environment for irrigation agriculture. Such environments are found primarily along the Yangtze and Yellow Rivers in China, in the Indus Valley, along the Nile, and on the shores of the Euphrates and Tigris rivers.

The type of hydraulic agriculture practiced in these areas involved the primary tasks of digging, damming, and dredging, as well as supportive activities such as tool making, feeding, and supervision of the workers. Food production was therefore carried out on a scale that required sophisticated organization and a far-reaching division of labor, something that could only be installed and maintained by an elite in control of the mass of workers. Very early in history, these cohorts of forced labor were then used also for the construction of public goods like roads, canals, or defense walls or for erecting monuments glorifying gods or divine leaders. Wittfogel's thesis thus postulates a clear causal relationship between topography (the presence of alluvial, arid river valleys), agricultural technology (hydraulic, irrigation agriculture) and institutions (highly stratified societies with very weak private property rights).

Although this is not developed in Wittfogel (1957), it is implicitly understood that the riverine natural environment described above stands in contrast to conditions in Europe. Eric Jones (1981) and David Landes (1998) complete Wittfogel's comparative analysis by discussing the specific features of European topography. According to Jones (1981), the European continent is naturally fragmented to an extent that most parts of Asia are not. Mountain ranges like the Alps and the Pyrenees, rivers like the Rhine (without vast river plains), the indented coastline, the irregular shape of the continent with peninsulas and large islands in the Mediterranean, and the presence of hardwood forests all meant that no single core civilization on the scale of Sumer, Egypt, or China could develop in Europe. European societies, at least after the fall of the Western Roman empire, rather originated from a number of relatively small core areas, surrounded by water or forest, where no single power was great or strong enough to form a despotic empire like in the Orient. Furthermore, European farmers had access to a steady supply of rain which meant that they were not dependent on a river managing despot (Landes, 1997).

These circumstances were initially a disadvantage for Europe since production per square kilometer was much higher in the fertile river valleys. However, Europe's fragmentation would eventually prove to be advantageous since it fostered competition between the numerous small states. If an entrepreneur with a specific venture in mind was banned from a certain country for religious or conservative reasons, he could always try to convince some other prince in another country of why his project would be a good investment. A similar strategy could supposedly not be employed in the Asiatic empires. An often used example is the sudden decision in 1433 of a Ming emperor in China to abandon the country's very ambitious imperial sea-faring expeditions in the Indian Ocean. Only some decades later, the Genovese Christopher Columbus, on the other hand, could easily convince the Spanish court of financing an expedition to India in an attempt to steal the initiative from the Portuguese.

It is relatively easy to find flaws in the Wittfogel/Jones/Landes-theory. As many scholars have discussed, Wittfogel's identification of a specific Asian type of riverine, despotic empires is not convincing. Throughout its history, the Indian continent has been fragmented in much the same way as Europe and no single empire based on hydraulic agriculture has been established there. Ancient Sumer was divided into several city states in almost the same way as later Greece, but was then repeatedly overrun by foreign invaders such as Assyrians, Babylonians, Persians, Greeks, Romans, Ottomans, British, and, most recently, by Americans. Egypt fits the description of a stable hydraulic society with limited individual freedom, but Egypt is undoubtedly a part of the Mediterranean cultural and natural environment that also shaped the Greeks and the Romans. The Chinese civilization is probably the society that fits best into Wittfogel's schedule.

The fragmented nature of the European continent did not prevent it from being nearly united for several centuries under Roman rule or later during Frankish rule. One must also remember that national competition between Europeans states often took the shape of immensely destructive wars that were detrimental to trade and private property. Still, there appears to be a certain logic in the argument that European topography with its scattered core areas often proved to be relatively favorable for trade, institutional competition, and individual freedom. Most important of all was maybe the presence of the Mediterranean ocean. In his monumental work on the Mediterranean, Fernand Braudel (1972) includes an extensive inquiry into the roles of mountains, plains, seas, coasts and islands for Mediterranean societies. Unlike the works above, Braudel (1972) does not propose a general geography-based theory of social development. He emphasizes that whereas geography was highly heterogeneous, the same basic climate prevailed from Spain in the west to the Levant in the east, a point further developed by Jared Diamond. It is also noteworthy that the Mediterranean constitutes the largest east-west oriented inland ocean in the world.

Yet another critique against the hypothesis above maintains that still by 1500 A.D, Europe was by no means richer or more technologically advanced than China, India, or the Muslim world. According to this explanation, it was another topographical feature that tipped the balance in Europe's favor; access to the Atlantic and to ocean currents that easily took sailing expeditions to America. Variants of this hypothesis are featured in older, Marxist-inspired works, and a relatively recent contribution in this tradition is Mark Blaut's (1993) *The Colonizer's Model of the World*. In brief, the argument here is that among all the prevailing Old World civilizations, the Atlantic countries in Western Europe had by far the easiest access to undeveloped America, which was exceptionally rich in gold and silver. The gold and silver that was pillaged from the American continent then funded the Industrial Revolution, which in turn made Europe race ahead of all the other continents.

However, this somewhat simplistic explanation provides no theory of the links between geography and the development of favorable institutions. In a major work mentioned above, AJR (2002b) give a similar but institutions-related explanation. Like Blaut (1993), they identify Atlantic trade - by which they mean more or less peaceful trade with non-European countries - as the primary factor behind the "rise of Europe". But the causal chain from Atlantic trade to the Industrial Revolution is different. Although the easy pillage of treasures in America played some role for the subsequent development, the lasting contribution of the opening of international trade was that it strengthened the merchant classes or the bourgeoisie. In countries like Great Britain and the Netherlands, the rising political strength of the merchant class gave rise to free trade legislation, a strengthening of property rights, and other capitalist institutions. These institutional changes in turn triggered the Industrial Revolution during the eighteenth century.

This favorable development only arose in states where the crown's powers were already constrained by 1500 A.D. As discussed by North (1990), Britain's history from Magna Carta to the Glorious Revolution in the 1600s was characterized by a gradual increase in Parliament's influence. When the windfall gains of Atlantic trade then materialized, the group that benefitted the most were the private traders and not the crown. In Spain and Portugal, on the other hand, the Crown was the primary organizer and beneficiary of the Atlantic ventures. After some two centuries as a superpower in the world, the failure of Spain to develop capitalist institutions and a constraint on the executive led to economic and political stagnation.

If access to the Atlantic was a blessing for certain Western European countries' institutional development, it seems to have been a curse to most West African nations. In a recent working paper, Nathan Nunn (2004) collects data on slavery exports between 1400 A.D. to 1913 and shows that the current quality of institutions is negatively related to the number of slaves per sq km that were exported from the area by Western traders. Among the worst affected countries were Benin, Ghana, and Senegal, all with an Atlantic coastline (Nunn, 2004, Table 7). The result of this exogenous influence was a degeneration into predatory societies where bandits or warlords roamed the countryside in search of suitable people to enslave. Some scholars argue that certain African countries can still be characterized as warlord societies (Reno, 1998).

4.3 Geology and Institutions

A much discussed empirical regularity that is usually referred to as the "curse of natural resources" shows that there appears to be a negative relationship between natural resource abundance and growth (Sachs and Warner, 1997). The variable that makes up "natural resources" in these empirical investigations contains everything from crops and vegetables to oil, gas, and minerals such as diamonds and iron.

There are two basic groups of explanations for the "curse" in the quickly growing literature. The first explanation focuses on Dutch disease effects, i.e. how a booming natural resource sector might appreciate the country's currency and thereby crowd out exports from the manufacturing sector. If the manufacturing sector is the long-run engine of growth, this crowding-out hurts development.

The second explanation concerns political economy and how natural resource abundance might induce rent seeking behavior (Auty and Gelb, 2001) or even armed conflicts (Collier and Hoeffler, 1998). In particular, extremely valuable minerals with a relatively simple extraction technology like diamonds might easily become the prize in an appropriative struggle between a kleptocratic ruler and a group of predators among the population. The struggle to control diamond deposits has been a key factor behind recent violent conflicts in Sierra Leone, Liberia, Angola, and the Democratic Republic of the Congo (Olsson, 2003). Botswana, however, seems to form a counter example since the huge diamond rents accumulated there since the early 1970s have rather contributed to the creation of a stable and relatively wealthy democracy (AJR, 2003). In any event, geology appears to have an impact on social institutions.

How about seismology then? The relevance of extreme events such as earthquakes and volcanoes for institutions is discussed primarily by Jones (1981) who claims that the economics of disaster is a neglected area of research. (The disaster category also includes hurricanes, floods, drought, epidemics, and warfare which admittedly have nothing to do with geology.) According to Jones (1981, Table 2.2), the Asian population has been disproportionately hit by earthquakes since the 1500s. Europe, on the other hand, has always been relatively calm.[14] Maps of volcanic activity in the world further suggest that Tropical and North-East Asia, the Middle East, Africa's horn, and the Western coasts of North and South America are more prone to outbreaks than Europe. However, Vesuvius' eruption in 79 A.D. that destroyed Pompeii and the gigantic eruption on the Greek island of Thera around 1500 B.C. - which is generally believed to have caused the rapid decline of the Minoan civilization on nearby Crete - demonstrate that Europe was severely affected on occasion.

Jones' (1981) theory of the linkage between geology and institutions is that the greater probability of death from a natural disaster for the

---

[14] More recent estimates support this claim. A calculation based on data from Encyclopaedia Britannica (2003) shows that out of about 530,000 earthquake casualties in the world since 1950, only 8,000 (or 1.5 %) died in Europe (including Turkey).

average man in Asia had its consequences for the institutions of the family. In particular, having many children was a rational, insurance-like response to the greater likelihood of death by disaster. Also the practice of early marriage in Asia might have been a result of this riskier natural environment. Both these institutions were harmful for long-run development. High fertility rates prevented a rise in incomes per capita and crowded out investments in human capital, whereas early marriage supposedly prevented Asian adults from accumulating savings before they started producing children.

4.4 Biogeography and Institutions

One of the most influential books in social science during recent years is probably Jared Diamond's (1997) *Guns, Germs, and Steel: The Fates of Human Societies*. The crucial variable in Diamond's theory is biogeographic potential, i.e. the quantity of wild plants and animals suitable for domestication in Neolithic times. The factors determining this potential were in turn a mixture of climate and topography: A temperate, mediterranean climate with wet winters and dry summers were ideal for annual grasses like wheat and barley. A great continental landmass meant a larger diversity of species whereas an east-west orientation of the continent implied similar day length and roughly similar temperatures which facilitated the spread of agricultural techniques.

Diamond identifies biogeographic potential as the primary factor explaining why certain regions developed agriculture earlier than others. Based on the food surplus from domesticated species, these regions then saw the emergence of sedentary, densely populated societies that gradually developed very complex systems of social organization. Soon regular states appeared with a far-reaching division of labor where the great majority of peasants provided seasonal labor to communal irrigation or the creation of public monuments. A small elite, only engaged in food production as managers, were then free to develop the hallmarks of civilization; writing, science, religion, and a state bureaucracy. In line with Wittfogel (1957) and many other works, Diamond then implicitly assumes a considerable degree of institutional persistence; the head start that was granted the old civilizations explains why their social organization was superior to other regions by 1500 A.D.[15]

---

[15] Diamond's theory actually proposes that the early biogeographic potential gave especially Western Eurasia three proximate advantages apart from institutions; some resistance against epidemic diseases (that killed off most of the American native population), the horse (which proved to be an almost unbeatable weapon), and technology (ocean-going ships, guns, and steel).

Olsson and Hibbs (2003) develop a formal, growth-theoretic model along the lines above. As in Diamond (1997), the key event is the Neolithic agricultural revolution which induced the creation of a non-food sector that specialized in organization and the advancement of technological knowledge. For thousands of years, however, standards of living remained roughly the same all over the world since Malthusian population growth neutralized technological progress. Olsson and Hibbs (2003) then go a step further and argue that the early start in the "development race" meant that some regions would also adopt industrial production earlier than others. Accordingly, the Industrial Revolution first happened in Western Eurasia where the Malthusian link for various reasons soon collapsed and income per capita started its well-documented nearly exponential rise.[16]

The weakest link in the theory of Diamond (1997) and Olsson and Hibbs (2003) is probably their account of history from the rise of early civilizations to around 1500 A.D. A uniquely favorable biogeography implied that the area called the Fertile Crescent in the Near East was the first to develop intensive food production and complex states. These innovations then spread to the rest of Western Eurasia, which in Diamond's (1997) and Olsson and Hibbs' (2003) theory constitutes a single sphere of influence. But how can we explain the very different historical trajectories within Western Eurasia after the diffusion of agriculture? Why did the great colonial expansion start from Spain and Portugal rather than from Egypt, as the pure theory would have suggested? And why was Mesopotamia maybe two hundred years after the peripheral British islands to develop industrial production? Diamond's otherwise eloquent theory has very little to say about this "reversal of fortune" within Western civilization. On the other hand, the main question in *Guns, Germs, and Steel* is why it was that Western Eurasians colonized Americans instead of the contrary.

As discussed above, the Western reversal was specifically addressed by Gilfillan's (1920) theory of a temperate drift throughout history. Using Gilfillan's somewhat dubious empirical observations as an established fact, Lambert (1971) proposes an alternative hypothesis for the falling temperature in the centers of civilization; intense agricultural production meant an increasing population density and the emergence of urban populations. This greatly facilitated the spread of harmful parasites, mainly internal ones like hookworm. Supposedly, the great civilizations of Sumer and Egypt stagnated partly because of this climate-related heath problem, and the center of civilization therefore gradually

---

[16] A more explicit treatment of the collapse of the Malthusian link where geographical factors might affect the timing of the transition, is provided by Galor and Weil (2000).

moved northwards where frosts and lower temperatures gave parasites a harder time.

It was mentioned in a previous section that the biogeography-category used here also includes medical geography, i.e. the geographical distribution of diseases. Like in Lambert (1971), disease plays an important role in AJR (2001). What they are concerned with is the comparative development among countries formerly colonized by Western powers. Institutions are the key variable for understanding current economic levels. The quality of a country's institutions today, as well as the quality hundreds of years ago, depends ultimately on the colonizing country's colonial strategy.

In essence, AJR (2001) argue that colonists settled down themselves and created institutions conducive to economic development where the disease environment - for climatic and topographical reasons - was favorable, for example in New Zealand, Australia, and Northern United States. In regions nearer the equator with lowland tropical rain forests the probability of being killed by malaria or yellow fever was so high for the colonists that permanent settlements were often not a feasible strategy. Since they could not settle, they instead developed extractive institutions, aimed at squeezing the countries as much as possible. An example of this latter colonial strategy was king Leopold's management of his Congo Free State.[17] The link from geography to institutions thus runs from climate and topography via the disease environment to institutions.

However, the very heterogeneous nature of the colonization movement constitutes a problem for AJR (2001). As discussed by Grier (1999) and Olsson (2004), it is very resonable to assume that countries that were colonized early (i.e. the Americas during the sixteenth centuries) should have been affected differently by Western rule than colonies that were set up in the late 'imperialist' wave of colonization after 1880 (i.e. most of Africa). A key difference between the two eras was that by 1880, medical advances in tropical medicine had greatly reduced potential settler mortality, so much in fact that colonial policy in Africa appears to have been relatively unaffected by disease-related considerations (Curtin, 1998). This might further explain why there is no significant relationship between settler mortality (measured between 1817-1848) and the current quality of institutions in Africa when AJR's (2001) sample is disaggregated (Olsson, 2004).

Whereas AJR (2001, 2002a) study the evolution of institutions in former colonies, Sokoloff and Engerman's (2000) biogeographic analysis

---

[17] AJR (2002a) complement this story by arguing that colonists were more likely to set up extractive institutions where there were lots of easily lootable riches and a dense population that could be used as forced labor in mines and on plantations.

deals with the variation in institutional configurations on the American continent. Sokoloff and Engerman also note a reversal in economic development in America; by the late eighteenth century, Caribbean colonies like Haiti, Cuba, and Barbados were richer than the United States and Canada. The reversal then happened which made North America prosperous whereas the Caribbean stagnated.

The fundamental reason for this development, according to Sokoloff and Engerman, can be traced back to geography (i.e. initial factor endowments). The climate and soil of the West Indies were extraordinarily well-suited for large scale plantations where staple crops like sugar were grown. These plantations had substantial economies of scale, and the native population was not numerous enough to cover the plantation-owners' need for labor. The solution was a massive importation of black slaves.[18] The huge inequality between the small elite of wealthy plantation-owners and the working black population that prevailed even after the abolition of slavery, could only be kept in place with very strict institutions that protected the privileges of the rich. In contrast, in the northern parts of America, climate was not favorable for large scale sugar plantations, which implied a smaller importation of black slaves, a greater degree of equality between the mainly white settlers, and the creation of institutions strengthening individual property rights that in the longer run would prove beneficial for economic development.

Sokoloff and Engerman's (2000) line of argument is further developed in a model by Galor et al (2004) who argue that countries that were initially endowed with a great deal of high-quality land also tended to have a great inequality of income and a landed aristocracy that resisted reforms (again the West Indies might serve as an example). In contrast, countries that were not land abundant had a relatively equal income distribution and compensated their land misfortune by an early development of human capital promoting institutions like public education. Hence, whereas geography in the form of land abundance initially made certain regions wealthy, an institutional reversal occurred by the time of industrialization when less land abundant countries surged ahead.

5 A Grand Synthesis?

From all the theory and evidence presented above, is it possible to outline a universal theory of the historical links between geography and institutions that can help to explain the current state of institutions across the world? Such grand attempts should naturally be regarded with caution. But before we can say anything further, it is necessary to

---

[18] The economics of American slavery has been analyzed extensively by Robert Fogel (1989).

analyze the potential building blocks of such a theory. The title of the paper indicates that some theories can be judged as being more plausible than others. Choosing the term "plausible" rather than "probable" or even "validated" reflects my belief that the true historical relationship between geography and institutions can neither be satisfactorily estimated, nor be accepted or rejected with certainty by using the conventional tools of econometrics. What can be discussed is how plausible the various hypotheses are given the present stock of empirical evidence.

I would argue that most of the hypotheses regarding the direct link between climate and institutions seem rather implausible. My reading of modern physiology or psychology does not suggest that a hot climate corrupts the mind, makes people lazy and less "civilized" in the manner proposed by Montesquieu, Huntington, Gilfillan, and Landes. Fig. 2 might of course be interpreted as supporting this "temperature hypothesis" of institutions, but as was discussed in the empirical section, there is convincing evidence that the effects of climate are primarily indirect, working through the geography of plants, animals, and disease vectors.

Wittfogel's theory of a specific Oriental despotism – prevailing throughout history – due to a natural inequality in those early agrarian societies that were dependent on a system of irrigation, does not seem very plausible either, although the argument might have some relevance for China. Jones' (1981) discussion of the importance of disasters for economic institutions is suggestive, but very little evidence is presented supporting his conjecture.

I would argue that if we should attempt to map the cross-continental differences in institutional trajectories back in time, two major events in world history stand out. The first one is the rise of Neolithic agriculture and the second is the wave of colonization starting around 1500 A.D. Both are highly related to physical geography, or more precisely, to what I refer to as biogeography. Agriculture based on domesticated plants and animals first appeared in regions that were well endowed with suitable wild species. Sedentary farming based on irrigation then led to the early civilizations with written language, science, and complex social organization. This development first happened in Eurasia because of a favorable climate and topology, as described by Diamond (1997). Biogeography and, in the background, climate and topography therefore were the ultimate explanations for the higher average level of institutional development in Eurasia by 1500 A.D.[19] The empirical evidence in Olsson and Hibbs (2003) and Hibbs and Olsson (2004) even suggest that the effect of initial biogeography can be registered today.

---

[19] Not all scholars would agree on that last point. Blaut (1993) contends that Europe and Asia were at all ahead of Africa institutionally or economically by 1500.

The second major influence was the European colonization movement, starting in 1492 and ending with the wave of independent states after World War II. The colonists from Europe created good institutions where they could settle down and weak institutions where ruthless extraction was a more viable alternative. A key determining factor, at least for colonies created during the early mercantilist era in the sixteenth and seventeenth centuries, was the disease environment, as argued by AJR (2001). Tropical regions are more prone to host disease vectors harmful to human beings than temperate regions and hence we expect to find more extractive institutions in the old former colonies near the equator, which indeed appears to be the case. Analogously, we would expect good institutions in regions with a climate and disease environment similar to Europe, a prediction that is also supported by the data (see New Zealand, Australia, and the United States in Fig. 2).

The combination of these two universal theories accounts for the very broad pattern of why Eurasia and its offshoots in America, Oceania, and in other continents on average still have better institutions than the rest of the world. It should be repeated that a key assumption if we are to believe this story is institutional persistence, i.e. that a cluster of institutions are not easily changed once they are in place.

Apart from this macro picture, we might add several plausible theories of why institutions differ within continents. Europe's great degree of geographical fragmentation, discussed by Jones (1981) and Landes (1998), has probably both been a blessing and a curse. Although Europe had no early riverine civilizations, the cultural influences from Egypt and Sumer were significant. The many natural core areas in Europe meant a scatter of small societies which sometimes led each other on in peaceful competition but which just as often fought devastating wars. The best asset that Europe had geographically was probably the Mediterranean with its indented coastline, islands, peninsulas, and many natural ports. The Mediterranean basin is unique among the world's temperate regions in terms of climatic, topographical, and biogeographical variation. Its character has probably contributed to an institutional setting characterized by a favorable view on trade and exchange, pluralism, and individual freedom, as discussed by Braudel (1972).

Institutional differences between Central and Northern South America on the one hand, and North America on the other, presumably also depends to a great extent on geography. Geographical factors explain the large-scale slave plantations in the West Indies and forced labor in the mines of Peru, whereas conditions in North America favored small-scale agriculture with an equal population and relatively strong individual property rights (Sokoloff and Engerman, 2000) and early investments in human capital (Galor et al, 2004). Differences within

Africa are harder to explain, but Nunn's (2004) preliminary results suggest that slavery played an important role.

In general, the literature on institutions and economic development is very "eurocentric", comparing all other regions with the situation in the Western world. AJR (2001), for instance, explain in principle all institutional variation within ex-colonies with their colonial experience since 1500 AD. The importance of indigenous African or American institutions are rarely analyzed by economists. The great degree of ethnic fractionalization is generally believed to be a key factor for understanding African conflicts and weak institutions, but a deeper analysis of the links between geography, natural resources, ethnicity, indigenous institutions, and current institutions has so far not been carried out. This might be an area for future work.

6 Concluding Remarks

This article reviews the empirical and theoretical literature on the possible linkages between geography and economic institutions. The motivation for this undertaking is that although a lot of recent empirical research has focused on geography, many of them lack a theory of why institutions should depend on geography at all. Hence, a survey of the older works on geography and social development is presented. Since no certain conclusions can be drawn because of the limited amount of comparable historical statistics, it is argued that biogeographical factors as discussed by Jared Diamond and the effects of colonialism as discussed by Acemoglu, Johnson and Robinson are at least the most plausible candidates for explaining the very broadest pattern of institutional quality in the world today. A departure from the eurocentric paradigm is probably necessary to get a better understanding for why a continent like Africa appears to have persistently weak institutions.

Acknowledgements

I would like to thank Philippe Aghion, Michael Rauscher, two referees, and seminar participants at Göteborg University and the DEGIT VIII conference in Helsinki for their comments on an earlier draft. The research has received generous financial support from the Malmsten Foundation.

References

Acemoglu, D., Johnson, S., and Robinson, J.A. (2001): "The Colonial Origins of Comparative Development: An Empirical Investigation." *American Economic Review* 91: 1369-1401.

Acemoglu, D., Johnson, S., and Robinson, J.A. (2002a): "Reversal of Fortune: Geography and Institutions in the Making of the Modern World Income Distribution." *Quarterly Journal of Economics* 117: 1231-1294.

Acemoglu, D., Johnson, S., and Robinson, J.A. (2002b): *The Rise of Europe: Atlantic Trade, Institutional Change and Economic Growth.* Mimeo.

Acemoglu, D., Johnson, S., and Robinson, J.A. (2003): "An African Success Story: Botswana." in: Rodrik, D. (ed), *In Search of Prosperity: Analytical Narratives on Economic Growth.* Princeton: Princeton University Press.

Alcala, F., and Ciccone, A. (2004): "Trade and Productivity." Forthcoming in *Quarterly Journal of Economics* 119.

Auty, R.M., and Gelb, A.H. (2001): "Political Economy of Resource Abundant States." In *Resource Abundance and Economic Development,* edited by R.M. Auty, pp. 126-146. Oxford: Oxford University Press.

Blaut, M. (1993): *The Colonizer's Model of the World: Geographical Diffusionism and Eurocentric History.* New York: Guildford Press.

Bloom, D.E., and Sachs, J. (1998): "Geography, Demography, and Economic Growth in Africa." *Brookings Papers on Economic Activity* 2: 207-272.

Braudel, F. (1972): *The Mediterranean and the Mediterranean World in the Age of Philip II.* London: Collins.

Collier, P., and Hoeffler, A. (1998): "On the Economic Causes of Civil War." *Oxford Economic Papers* 50: 563-573.

Curtin, P. (1998) *Disease and Empire: The Health of European Troops in the Conquest of Africa.* Cambridge: Cambridge University Press.

Diamond, J. (1997) *Guns, Germs and Steel: The Fates of Human Societies.* London: W W Norton & Company.

Easterly, W., and Levine, R. (2003): "Tropics, Germs, and Crops: How Endowments Influence Economic Development." *Journal of Monetary Economics* 50: 3-39.

Encyclopedia Britannica (2003). "Major historical earthquakes." *Encyclopædia Britannica Online.* http://search.eb.com/eb/article?eu=126170 [Accessed August 29, 2003].

Fernandez-Armesto, F. (2000): *Civilizations.* Oxford: MacMillan.

Fogel, R.W. (1989): *Without Consent or Contract: The Rise and Fall of American Slavery.* New York: Norton.

Frankel, J., and D. Romer (1999) "Does Trade Cause Growth?" *American Economic Review* 89: 379-399.

Gallup, J.L., Sachs, J., and Mellinger, A. (1999): "Geography and Economic Development" *International Regional Science Review* 22(2): 179-232.

Galor, O., Moav, O., and Vollrath, D. (2004): "Land Inequality and the Origin of Divergence and Overtaking in the Growth Process: Theory and Evidence." Brown University.

Galor, O., and Mountford, A. (2003): "Trading Population for Productivity." Brown University.

Galor, O., and Weil, D. (2000): "Population, Technology, and Growth: From Malthusian Stagnation to the Demographic Transition and Beyond." *American Economic Review* 90: 806-828.

Gilfillan, S.C. (1920) "The Coldward Course of Progress." *Political Science Quarterly* 35: 393-410.

Grier, R. (1999) "Colonial Legacies and Economic Growth" *Public Choice* 98: 317-335.

Hall, R., and Jones, C.I. (1999): "Why Do Some Countries Produce So Much More Output Than Others?" *Quarterly Journal of Economics* 114: 83-116.

Hibbs, D.A., and Olsson, O. (2004): "Geography, Biogeography, and Why Some Countries Are Rich and Others Are Poor." *Proceedings of the National Academy of Sciences of the USA* 9, 101: 3715-3720.

Huntington, E. (1915): *Civilization and Climate.* (Reprinted in 2001) Honolulu: University Press of the Pacific.

Huntington, S. (1997): *The Clash of Civilizations and the Remaking of World Order.* London: The Free Press.

Jones, E.L. (1981): *The European Miracle: Environments, Economies and Geopolitics in the History of Europe and Asia.* Cambridge: Cambridge University Press.

Kamarck, A. M. (1976): *The Tropics and Economic Development.* Baltimore: John Hopkins University Press.

Kaufmann, D., Kraay, A., and Zoido-Lobatón, P. (1999): "Aggregating Governance Indicators." *World Bank Research Working Paper* 2195.

Knack, S., and Keefer, P. (1995): "Institutions and Economic Performance: Cross-Country Tests Using Alternative Institutional Measures." *Economics and Politics* 7: 207-225.

Lambert, L.D. (1971): "The Role of Climate in the Economic Development of Nations." *Land Economics* 47: 339-344.

Landes, D. (1997): *The Wealth and Poverty of Nations.* New York: W.W. Norton and Company.

Masters, W., and McMillan, M.S. (2001): "Climate and Scale in Economic Growth." *Journal of Economic Growth* 6(3): 167-186.

McArthur, J.W., and Sachs. J. (2001): "Institutions and Geography: Comment on Acemoglu, Johnson, and Robinson (2000)." *NBER Working Paper* 8114.

Montesquieu, C.L. (1750): *The Spirit of Laws.* (Reprinted in 2001) Kitchener, Ontario: Batoche Books.

North, D., and Thomas, R.P. (1973): *The Rise of the Western World.* Cambridge: Cambridge University Press.

North, D. (1990): *Institutions, Institutional Change and Economic Performance.* Cambridge: Cambridge University Press.

Nunn, N. (2004): *Slavery, Institutional Development, and Long-Run Growth in Africa, 1400-2000.* University of Toronto.

Olsson. O. (2003): "Conflict Diamonds." *Working Papers in Economics* 86. Department of Economics, Göteborg University.

Olsson, O. (2004): "Unbundling Ex-Colonies: A Comment on Acemoglu, Johnson, and Robinson (2001)." Göteborg University.

Olsson, O., and Hibbs, D.A. (2003): "Biogeography and Long-Run Economic Development." forthcoming in *European Economic Review.*

Reno, W. (1998): *Warlord Politics and African States.* London: Lynne Rienner Publishers.

Rodrik, D., Subramanian, A., and F. Trebbi (2004): "Institutions Rule: The Primacy of Institutions Over Geography and Integration in Economic Development." Forthcoming in *Journal of Economic Growth 9.*

Sachs, J. (2001): "Tropical Underdevelopment" *NBER Working Paper* 8119.

Sachs, J. (2003): "Institutions Don't Rule: Direct Effects of Geography on per Capita Income." *NBER Working Paper* 9490.

Sachs, J., and Warner, A. (1995): "Economic Reform and the Process of Global Integration." *Brookings Papers on Economic Activity* 1: 1-118.

Sachs, J., and Warner, A. (1997): *Natural Resource Abundance and Economic Growth.* Mimeo, Harvard University.

Sokoloff, K.L., and Engerman, S.T. (2000): "History Lessons: Institutions, Factor Endowments, and Paths of Development in the New World." *Journal of Economic Perspectives* 14: 217-232.

Wittfogel, K. (1957): *Oriental Despotism: A Comparative Study of Total Power.* New Haven: Yale University Press.

Address of author: – Ola Olsson, Department of Economics, Goteborg University, Box 640, 405 30 Goteborg, Sweden (e-mail: ola.olsson@economics.gu.se)

SpringerJournals

Journal of Economics

Zeitschrift für Nationalökonomie

Managing Editor
Giacomo Corneo, Berlin

Specializing in mathematical economic theory, **Journal of Economics** focuses on microeconomic theory while also publishing papers on macroeconomic topics as well as econometric case studies of general interest.
Regular supplementary volumes are devoted to topics of central importance to both modern theoretical research and present economic reality.

Fields of Interest
Mathematical economic theory of medium and high level difficulty, econometric case studies of general interest.

Subscription Information
2005. Vols. 84-86 (3 issues each), Title No. 712
EUR 1098,– plus carriage charges (excl. Austria)
ISSN 0931-8658, (print), ISSN 1617-7134 (electronic)

View table of contents and abstracts online at:
http://springer.at/jecon

 SpringerWienNewYork

P.O.Box 89, Sachsenplatz 4 – 6, 1201 Vienna, Austria, Fax +43.1.330 24 26, books@springer.at, **springer.at**
P.O. Box 2485, Secaucus, NJ 07096-2485, USA, Fax +1.201.348-4505, orders@springer-ny.com, springeronline.com
EBS, 3–13, Hongo 3-chome, Bunkyo-ku, Tokyo 113, Japan, Fax +81.3.38 18 08 64, orders@svt-ebs.co.jp
Prices are subject to change without notice. All errors and omissions excepted.

SpringerEconomics

Alfred Taudes (ed.)

Adaptive Information Systems and Modelling in Economics and Management Science

2005. Approx. 200 pages.
Hardcover approx. **EUR 47,–**
(Recommended retail price)
Net-price subject to local VAT.
ISBN 3-211-20684-1
Interdisciplinary Studies in Economics and Management,
Volume 5
Due February 2005

Learning and adaption are key features of "real economies". Studying interesting real phenomena like innovation, industry evolution or the role of expectation formulation in financial markets thus necessitates novel methods of data analysis and modelling. This title covers statistical models of heterogeneity, artificial consumer markets, models of adaptive expectation formulation in financial markets and agent-based models of industry evolution, product diversification and energy markets. The joint findings are presented in a manner that is both interesting for readers with a background in economics / management and mathematics and statistics in a way that allows also non-expert readers to grasp the ideas of modern management science. This book thus provides a unique integrated toolbox for building realistic agent-based models of learning and adaption in a variety of settings based on sound data analysis.

Please visit our website: **springer.at**

 Springer Wien New York

P.O. Box 89, Sachsenplatz 4 – 6, 1201 Vienna, Austria, Fax +43.1.330 24 26, books@springer.at, **springer.at**
Haberstraße 7, 69126 Heidelberg, Germany, Fax +49.6221.345-4229, sdc-bookorder@springer-sbm.com, springeronline.com
P.O. Box 2485, Secaucus, NJ 07096-2485, USA, Fax +1.201.348-4505, orders@springer-ny.com, springeronline.com
EBS, 3 – 13, Hongo 3-chome, Bunkyo-ku, Tokyo 113, Japan, Fax +81.3.38 18 08 64, orders@svt-ebs.co.jp
Prices are subject to change without notice. All errors and omissions excepted.

SpringerEconomics

Gunther Maier, Sabine Sedlacek (eds.)

Spillovers and Innovations: Space, Environment, and the Economy

2004. Approx. 200 pages.
Hardcover **EUR 47,–**
(Recommended retail price)
Net-price subject to local VAT.
ISBN 3-211-20683-3
Interdisciplinary Studies in Economics and Management,
Volume 4

Innovation processes and related spillovers are of eminent importance in a modern economy. How do they relate to spatial structures and environmental factors? The papers analyse innovation processes and spillovers in the economy from various angles, focussing mainly on regional and environmental aspects. Among others they touch issues on university spillovers, urban tourism, highway investments, industry clusters, and econometrics. An introductory chapter sets the stage for the following discussion, and a concluding chapter evaluates the achievements. Contributors from Austria, other European countries and from the U.S.A. discuss this question from various angles: among others universities, urban tourism, highway investments, and industry clusters.

The volume demonstrates the relevance of the concept of spillovers, particularly in the context of innovations, and stimulates future work in this area.

Please visit our website: **springer.at**

SpringerWienNewYork

P.O.Box 89, Sachsenplatz 4–6, 1201 Vienna, Austria, Fax +43.1.330 24 26, books@springer.at, **springer.at**
Haberstraße 7, 69126 Heidelberg, Germany, Fax +49.6221.345-4229, sdc-bookorder@springer-sbm.com, springeronline.com
P.O. Box 2485, Secaucus, NJ 07096-2485, USA, Fax +1.201.348-4505, orders@springer-ny.com, springeronline.com
EBS, 3–13, Hongo 3-chome, Bunkyo-ku, Tokyo 113, Japan, Fax +81.3.38 18 08 64, orders@svt-ebs.co.jp
Prices are subject to change without notice. All errors and omissions excepted.

Springer and the Environment

WE AT SPRINGER FIRMLY BELIEVE THAT AN INTER-national science publisher has a special obligation to the environment, and our corporate policies consistently reflect this conviction.

WE ALSO EXPECT OUR BUSINESS PARTNERS – PRINTERS, paper mills, packaging manufacturers, etc. – to commit themselves to using environmentally friendly materials and production processes.

THE PAPER IN THIS BOOK IS MADE FROM NO-CHLORINE pulp and is acid free, in conformance with international standards for paper permanency.